# DICTIONARY OF REAL ESTATE TERMS

Jack P. Friedman, PhD, CPA, SRPA
Laguarta Professor of Real Estate
Department of Finance/Real Estate Research Center
Texas A&M University

Jack C. Harris, PhD
Associate Research Economist
Real Estate Research Center
Texas A&M University

J. Bruce Lindeman, PhD
Professor of Real Estate
University of Arkansas at Little Rock

SECOND EDITION

BARRON'S

New York • London • Sydney • Toronto

# CONTENTS

# PREFACE

The dynamic world of real estate presents a constant challenge to stay up to date. In the past few years, an array of new concepts and terms has become a part of the real estate practitioners' language. New ways of financing property, major changes in tax laws, and new developments in urban growth have contributed to the list. Even before these changes, real estate vocabulary was already extensive and complicated.

This book will help you find your way through modern real estate language. Terms of real estate financing, brokerage law, investment, appraisal, planning, architecture, and structure are presented. Each entry is clearly and concisely defined and presented with a helpful example of its use. Where appropriate, pictorial examples are provided.

Whether you are a first-time home buyer, a real estate investor, or a veteran broker, you will find this a timesaving alphabetical guide to real estate terminology and real estate organizations. When appropriate, related terms are cross-referenced. The appendix includes a list of common abbreviations, a mortgage payment table, a diagram showing the parts of a house, and tables of measure for convenient reference.

A decisive key to effective business communication is a common vocabulary. Business decisions can be disastrous when made on the basis of misunderstood terminology. This book is dedicated to those who realize that a key to success with real estate is maintaining an up-to-date understanding of the field's concepts and language. Users will find that they can easily recover the cost of this book many times if only one wrong decision is avoided or one good decision promoted. In addition, a thorough reading of the book is an investment in self-improvement that may pay off in a richer life experience.

The authors wish to acknowledge the contributions of the following who were instrumental in bringing this volume to fruition. For providing the support, encouragement, and intellectual atmosphere, we are grateful to Dr. H.O. Kunkel, Dean of the Texas A&M College of Agriculture, and Dr. Richard L. Floyd, Director of the Texas Real Estate Research Center. For careful attention to detail in preparing the original manuscript, we are indebted to Mrs. Gretchen Shipman. For meticulously proofreading the manuscript and offering countless points of advice on better presentation of the material, we thank our copy editor, Ms. Lillian Steinfeld. Finally, for coordinating all the necessary details within the publishing process, we are grateful to the staff at Barron's.

*Jack P. Friedman*
*Jack C. Harris*
*J. Bruce Lindeman*

# HOW TO USE THIS BOOK EFFECTIVELY

**Alphabetization:** All words are alphabetized by letter rather than by word. Thus, for the purpose of arrangement, all multiple word terms are treated as if they were one word. For example, the word "ad valorem" follows "adult," rather than preceding as would be the case if "ad" were treated as a separate word. Abbreviations, in the rare instance that they appear as entries, are treated as if they were a word. The term "MAI," which stands for "Member, Appraisal Institute," appears before "maintenance fee." A separate list of abbreviations is included, so as a general rule, abbreviations and acronyms do not appear as entries. In the case of "MAI," the initials are understood by many who are not familiar with the formal name. Thus, MAI becomes the entry.

**Parentheses:** Parentheses are used in two instances. The first application is to indicate an abbreviation commonly applied to the term. For example, "ADJUSTABLE RATE MORTGAGE (ARM)" indicates that the abbreviation "ARM" commonly refers to adjustable rate mortgages. The second application is to indicate the context of the term as defined. For example, "TO RETIRE (A DEBT)" indicates the context under which the word "retire" is defined is when it is applied to retiring a debt. The definition is not appropriate to other legitimate uses of the word retire, such as in the expression "retirement benefits."

**Cross References:** When an entry is used in the definition or example for another entry, the term is printed in **boldface type.** This provides a cross reference in case the term is used in the definition is unclear to the reader. In general, the term is printed in boldface only the first time it appears in the definition. Occasionally, when a term is a closely related concept or provides contrast, it is cross-referenced, even though not used in the definition. In the former case, the term is referenced as follows: "See **cash flow.**" In the latter case, the reference appears as: "Contrast with **net lease.**" When an entry is merely another expression for a term defined elsewhere in the book, a reference rather than a definition is provided; for example, "NOMINAL RATE same as **face rate.**"

**Examples and Addresses:** At least one example is given for each definition in the book. In the case of organizations listed as entries, a current address is supplied in lieu of an example. The examples are intended to illustrate how the term is used in a sentence or to provide a sample of specific things which fall under the purview of the term. For example, under the entry for "closing costs" a list of specific closing cost items is provided. When an entry has more than one definition, an example is provided for each definition. Where applicable, an illustration is provided as an example. e.g., under "cluster housing," an illustration of a sample cluster housing plan is included.

# A

**ABANDONMENT** the voluntary surrender of property, owned or leased, without naming a successor as owner or tenant. The property will generally revert to one holding a prior interest or, in cases where no owner is apparent, to the state. Abandonment does not relieve obligations associated with lease or ownership unless the abandonment is accepted by the entity to which the obligation is owed.
**Example:** Abel owns a dilapidated apartment house with 2 years delinquent property taxes. Rather than pay the back taxes, Abel *abandons* the building by disclaiming ownership.

**ABATEMENT** a reduction in amount or intensity.
**Example:** A manufacturing plant may install equipment for pollution *abatement*.
**Example:** Tenants may ask for an *abatement* in rent over a period when their use of the property has been interrupted or inhibited by actions of the landlord, such as renovation of the structure.

**ABSENTEE OWNER** an owner who does not personally manage or reside at property owned.
**Example:** Abel, living in New York, purchases an apartment building in Houston. Abel is an *absentee owner*.

**ABSORPTION RATE** an estimate of the expected annual sales or new occupancy of a particular type of land use.
**Example:** The demand for new homes in a market area is estimated to be 500 per year. Developer Abel's new subdivision, when completed, is expected to capture 10% of the market. Therefore Abel's subdivision has an expected *absorption rate* of 50 homes per year (10% of 500 = 50).

**ABSTRACT OF TITLE** a historical summary of all of the recorded instruments and proceedings that affect the title to property.
**Example:** A title insurance company will have an attorney prepare an *abstract of title* prior to granting a title insurance policy.
**Example:** An abstract company will compile an *abstract of title* with copies of all recorded instruments affecting title to a specific tract.

**ABUT** adjoining or meeting. See also **adjacent.**
**Example:** The 2 properties shown in Figure 1 *abut* one another. The property on the right also *abuts* the road.

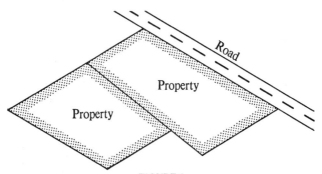

FIGURE 1

**ACCELERATED COST RECOVERY SYSTEM (ACRS)** a method of depreciation introduced by the Economic Recovery Tax Act of 1981 and modified by the Tax Reform Acts of 1984 and 1986. As *ACRS* applies to real estate, depreciable lives for buildings depend on when they are placed in service. See Table 1 for depreciable lives and rates.

**Example:** If an apartment building were purchased in January 1988 for $1,000,000 exclusive of land, $34,800 (3.48%) could be claimed as depreciation in 1988, and $36,400 each year for the following 26 years.

**ACCELERATED DEPRECIATION** depreciation methods, chosen for income tax or accounting purposes, that offer greater deductions in early years. See **accelerated cost recovery system, double declining balance, sum-of-years-digits depreciation.**

**Example:** One method of *accelerated depreciation* is the double declining balance method (DDB). If straight-line deductions equal 5% of depreciable basis, DDB allows a deduction of 10% (200% of 5%), but applied to the undepreciated basis. Thus the deductions decline each year (Figure 2).

**ACCELERATION CLAUSE** a loan provision giving the lender the right to declare the entire amount immediately due and payable upon the violation of a specific loan provision, such as failure to make payments on time.

**Example:** Collins sells her house to Baker, who assumes the existing 8% interest rate mortgage. They do not notify the lender of the sale. Clause 17 in the mortgage states that the full principal *accelerates* unless the lender approves of the sale. Collins must now pay the balance of the principal.

**TABLE 1**

Post-1986 Recovery Percentages for Residential Rental Depreciable Property

| Recovery Year | Month Placed in Service | | | | | | | | | | | |
|---|---|---|---|---|---|---|---|---|---|---|---|---|
| | 1 | 2 | 3 | 4 | 5 | 6 | 7 | 8 | 9 | 10 | 11 | 12 |
| 1 | 3.48 | 3.18 | 2.88 | 2.58 | 2.27 | 1.97 | 1.67 | 1.36 | 1.06 | .76 | .45 | .15 |
| 2–27 | 3.64 | 3.64 | 3.64 | 3.64 | 3.64 | 3.64 | 3.64 | 3.64 | 3.64 | 3.64 | 3.64 | 3.64 |
| 28 | 1.88 | 2.18 | 2.48 | 2.78 | 3.09 | 3.39 | 3.64 | 3.64 | 3.64 | 3.64 | 3.64 | 3.64 |
| 29 | 0 | 0 | 0 | 0 | 0 | 0 | .05 | .36 | .66 | .96 | 1.27 | 1.57 |

Post-1986 Recovery Percentages for Non-residential Depreciable Property

| Recovery Year | Month Placed in Service | | | | | | | | | | | |
|---|---|---|---|---|---|---|---|---|---|---|---|---|
| | 1 | 2 | 3 | 4 | 5 | 6 | 7 | 8 | 9 | 10 | 11 | 12 |
| 1 | 3.04 | 2.78 | 2.51 | 2.25 | 1.98 | 1.72 | 1.46 | 1.19 | .93 | .66 | .40 | .13 |
| 2–31 | 3.17 | 3.17 | 3.17 | 3.17 | 3.17 | 3.17 | 3.17 | 3.17 | 3.17 | 3.17 | 3.17 | 3.17 |
| 32 | 1.86 | 2.12 | 2.39 | 2.65 | 2.92 | 3.17 | 3.17 | 3.17 | 3.17 | 3.17 | 3.17 | 3.17 |
| 33 | 0 | 0 | 0 | 0 | 0 | 0 | .27 | .54 | .80 | 1.07 | 1.33 | 1.60 |

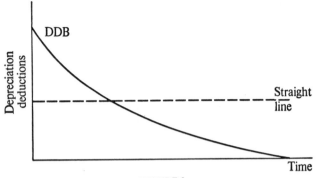

FIGURE 2

**ACCEPTANCE** the act of agreeing to accept an offer.
  **Example:** Abel offers property for sale, Baker makes an offer to buy the property for a specified price. Upon Abel's *acceptance* a sales contract is complete.

**ACCESSION** additions to property as a result of annexing fixtures or alluvial deposits.
  **Example:** The lease on a restaurant expires. The proprietor of the restaurant leaves some counters and bar stools. They become a part of the property by *accession*.
  **Example:** Property bordering on a river is legally enlarged by soil deposited by the river **(alluvium).**

**ACCESS RIGHT** the right of owners to get to and from their property.
  **Example:** If Baker is granted an *access right* to the property in Figure 3, a curb cut may be made onto the highway.

**ACCOMMODATION PARTY** one who has signed an agreement without receiving value for it, for the purpose of lending his or her name so that another person can secure a necessary loan or other arrangement.
  **Example:** The young developer asked an experienced friend to act as an *accommodation party*. The experienced developer signed the loan agreement even though there was no monetary benefit to him.

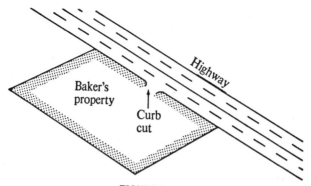

FIGURE 3

**ACCRETION** the addition to land through processes of nature, such as deposits of soil carried by streams. See **alluvium**.
**Example:** Figure 4.

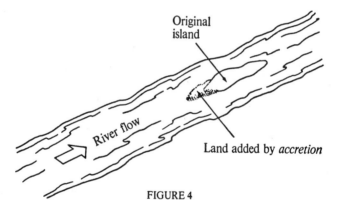

FIGURE 4

**ACCRUAL METHOD** a method of accounting that requires income or expense to be entered when the amount is earned or the obligation is payable. Distinguished from **cash method** in which amounts are posted when paid or received.
**Example:** The home buyer bought and paid for a 3-year hazard insurance policy at closing. On the *accrual method,* only the current year's expense is indicated.
**Example:** Interest on a loan is 3 months delinquent. The expense, though unpaid, appears in the current year's financial statement

under the *accrual method*. Under the cash method it would appear on the financial statements when paid.

**ACCRUED INTEREST** interest that has been earned but not paid.
**Example:** If 6% interest is earned on a $100 deposit, then $6 of interest has *accrued* to the depositer.

**ACKNOWLEDGMENT** a declaration by a person who has signed a document that such signature is a voluntary act, made before a duly authorized person.
**Example:**

I, Albert Abel, hereby deed to Robert Baker, the land that I own in Fair County, further described below.

*Albert Abel*
Albert Abel

*Jack Jones*
Witness

*Sigs R. Real*
Notary Public
Acknowledgment

*George Smith*
Witness

FIGURE 5

**ACCUMULATED DEPRECIATION** in accounting, the amount of **depreciation** expense that has been claimed to date. Same as accrued depreciation. See **adjusted tax basis.**
**Example:** A building was bought for $100,000. The annual **straight-line depreciation** expense is $2,500. The *accumulated depreciation* in 3 years is $7,500.

**ACQUISITION COST** the price and all fees required to obtain a property.
**Example:** Abel purchases a property for $90,000 plus $5,000 in **closing costs** (attorney's fees, loan fees, **appraisal** costs, **title insur-ance,** and loan **discount points**). Abel's *acquisition cost* is $95,000.

**ACQUISITION LOAN** money borrowed for the purpose of purchas-ing a property.

**Example:** The developer negotiated an *acquisition loan* for the purchase of land and a construction loan to improve the land for home sites.

**ACRE** a 2-dimensional measure of land equaling 160 square rods, 10 square chains, 4,840 square yards, or 43,560 square feet.

**Example:** A land survey shows that Abel owns 1.3774 *acres* of land (Figure 6).

200 ft

Abel's land

300 ft

60,000 sq ft = 1.3774 acres

FIGURE 6

**ACTIVE PARTICIPATION** type of investor position which determines how rental income is taxed. Requirements for *active participation* are less stringent than for **material participation.** An investor may have a manager for rental real estate and still be considered an active participant. Indicators of *active participation* in real estate are:
• Approving new tenants
• Deciding on rental terms
• Approving capital or repair expenditures
*Active participation* excludes:
• Owners of a 10% interest or less
• Limited partners
An active participant with adjusted gross income under $100,000 without regard to passive losses, may deduct up to $25,000 of passive losses against other income. This allowance is phased out on a 50% ratio as adjusted gross income increases from $100,000 to $150,000.

**Example:** Anna earns $40,000 from her job as an attorney, and is an active investor in an apartment complex. If the apartments generate a tax loss, she may offset up to $25,000 of her salary with the loss.

**ACTIVE SOLAR HEATING** a system that uses energy from sunlight to heat a structure and/or provide hot water. Contrasted with **passive solar heating** by the use of pumps or fans to move the energy-transporting medium through the system. Installation of active solar heating equipment is eligible for certain income tax credits.

**Example:** A schematic of a typical *active solar heating* system is shown in Figure 7.

FIGURE 7

**ACT OF GOD** an unpreventable destructive occurrence of the natural world.
  **Example A contract** has a provision that allows the buyer to **default** if the property is damaged by an *act of God*.
  Examples of an *act of God* are:
  • earthquake
  • flood
  • hurricane
  • lightning
  • tornado

**ADDENDUM** (plural: ADDENDA) something added, as an attachment to a **contract**.
  **Example:** An *addendum* to the **contract of sale** described the type of **financing** that the buyer must secure to be required to purchase the property.
  Commonly added *addenda* in real estate purchase agreements are for financing terms and property **inspection** requirements.

**ADDITIONAL FIRST-YEAR DEPRECIATION (TAX)** under the 1986 tax act, up to $10,000 of depreciable personal property purchased each year may be expensed, rather than depreciated, provided not more than $200,000 is purchased in a year. The $10,000 is phased out, dollar for dollar, when purchases exceed $200,000 in a year.
**Example:** Barbara is a real estate broker. She bought a $4,000 computer to assist with her business; she may expense the cost in the year purchased, rather than depreciate the equipment.

**ADD-ON INTEREST** interest that is added to the principal of a loan. The amount of interest for all years is computed on the original amount borrowed.
**Example:** Abel borrows $1,000 at 8% *add-on interest* for 4 years. Total interest is $320 (8% of $1,000 for 4 years). Abel will repay the $1,320 total in equal monthly installments.

**ADJACENT** nearby but not necessarily **adjoining.**
**Example:** Lot B is *adjacent* to lot A (Figure 8).

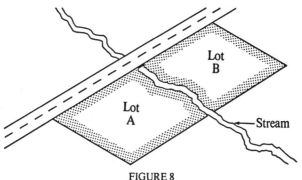

FIGURE 8

**ADJOINING** **contiguous;** attaching; sharing a common border.
**Example:** A warehouse with *adjoining* office space (Figure 9).

**ADJUSTABLE MORTGAGE LOAN (AML)** a mortgage instrument authorized by the Federal Home Loan Bank Board in 1981 for use by all federally chartered savings and loan associations. The *AML* provides to local associations maximum flexibility in selecting the terms under which interest rates and payments may be adjusted

FIGURE 9

over the maturity of the loan. See **adjustable rate mortgage, renegotiated rate mortgage, variable rate mortgage.**
**Example:** Major Savings and Loan offers several types of *adjustable mortgage loans* as described in Table 2.

TABLE 2

| Loan plan | Interest rate adjusted every: | Payments adjusted every: | Index used | Maximum rate change each year |
|---|---|---|---|---|
| 1 | year | year | average mortgage rate | 2% |
| 2 | 6 months | 3 years | 6-month treasury bill rate | none |
| 3 | year | year | average cost of funds | none |
| 4 | 3 years | 3 years | 3-year treasury bond yield | 1% |

**ADJUSTABLE RATE MORTGAGE (ARM)** a mortgage loan that allows the interest rate to be changed at specific intervals over the maturity of the loan.
**Example:** A person obtains an *adjustable rate mortgage* to finance the purchase of a home. After a 2-year period, the lender may adjust the rate of interest on the loan in accordance with an established index.

**ADJUSTED SALES PRICE** 1. In appraisal, the indicated price of a comparable property after adjustments have been made to account for differences between the comparable and the subject property. 2. In income taxation, the selling price of a home less expenses of sale, less fixing-up expenses. When the purchase price of a new principal residence equals or exceeds the *adjusted sales price* of a former residence, any gain on the sale of the former residence will be deferred. See **Section 1034.**
**Example:** The comparable is identical to the subject property except that the comparable has an additional half bath. The sales price of $70,000 is adjusted by subtracting $3,000 for the extra bath. The *adjusted sales price* is $67,000.
**Example:** A principal residence sold for $90,000. Just prior to the sale the seller had a contractor paint at a cost of $3,000; sales commissions and other seller-paid closing costs were $7,000. If the seller acquires another residence for $80,000 or more, there will be no income tax due on the sale of the former home.

**ADJUSTED TAX BASIS** the original cost or other basis of property, reduced by **depreciation** deductions and increased by **capital expenditures.**
**Example:** Collins buys a lot for $10,000. She erects a retail facility for $60,000, then depreciates the improvements for tax purposes at the rate of $4,000 per year. After 3 years her *adjusted tax basis* is $58,000. ($10,000 + $60,000 − 3 × $4,000)

**ADJUSTMENTS (IN APPRAISAL)** dollar value or percentage amounts that, when added to or subtracted from the sales price of a **comparable,** provide an indication of the value of a subject property. *Adjustments* are necessary to compensate for variation in the features of the comparable relative to the subject.
**Example:** An appraisal is to be made of a three-bedroom house. One **comparable** is a similar house with two bedrooms which sold for $50,000. The appraiser makes an adjustment of $1,000 to the comparable to account for the difference of bedrooms. The adjusted sales price of the **comparable** is $51,000.

**ADMINISTRATOR** a person appointed by a court to administer the estate of a deceased person who left no will.
**Example:** The *administrator* of the estate called a meeting of the deceased's relatives for the purpose of dividing the property.

**ADMINISTRATOR'S DEED** a deed conveying the property of one who died without a will **(intestate).**
**Example:** At the hearing called by the administrator, the heir received an *administrator's deed* to her father's home.

**ADULT** one who has attained the age of **majority.**
**Example:** Abel enters into a contract to purchase land. Because he is 17 years of age he, is a **minor** (not an *adult*) and may **void** the contract.

**AD VALOREM** according to value. See **ad valorem tax.**

**AD VALOREM TAX** a tax based on the value of the thing being taxed.
**Example:** If the *ad valorem tax* rate is 1%, the tax would be $1 per $100 of assessed value.

**ADVERSE POSSESSION** a means of acquiring title to real estate where an occupant has been in actual, open, **notorious,** exclusive, and continuous occupancy of property for the period required by state law.
**Example:** Although the elderly Ms. Davis held no official **deed** to the land, she was awarded title by *adverse possession,* since she had lived on the property all her life and the legal owner was unknown.

**AFFIDAVIT** a written statement, sworn to or **affirmed** before an officer who is authorized to administer an oath or affirmation.
**Example:** The *affidavit* affirmed that the landlord was solely entitled to lease out the property.

**AFFIRM** to confirm; to ratify; to verify.
**Example:** At a meeting between the buyer, seller, and broker, the voidable sales contract was *affirmed* by the party who could have voided it. All parties are now bound by the stipulations of the contract.

**"A" FRAME** a post World War II style house with a frame in the shape of one or more "A's."
**Example:** Figure 10.

**AFTER-TAX CASH FLOW** cash flow from income-producing property, less income taxes, if any, attributable to the property's income. If there is a tax loss which can provide a tax saving from the shelter of income earned outside the property, that savings is added to the **cash flow** that is earned by the property.
**Example:** A property generates $1,000 per year of cash flow. In the first year of ownership, depreciation and interest deductions pro-

FIGURE 10

vide a tax loss of $3,000. The loss saves $900 of income taxes that the investor would otherwise pay on salary earned as a teacher. The *after-tax cash flow* is $1,900.

**AGENCY** the legal relationship between a principal and his **agent** arising from a contract in which the principal engages the agent to perform certain acts on the principal's behalf.
**Example:** Under the law of *agency*, agents must be loyal to their employers. Therefore broker Roberts submits to employer Davis all offers on property.

**AGENT** one who undertakes to transact some business or to manage some affair for another, with the authority of the latter.
**Example:** An owner engages a **broker** to act as *agent* in selling real property; the broker in turn engages salespersons to act as *agents* to sell the same property.

**AGREEMENT OF SALE** a written agreement between seller and purchaser in which the purchaser agrees to buy certain real estate and the seller agrees to sell upon terms of the agreement. Also called **offer and acceptance, contract of sale, earnest money** contract.
**Example:** Abel's **broker** prepared an *agreement of sale* to sell a home to Baker. Both principals signed it. It states that the price of $50,000 is to be paid in cash at closing, subject to Baker's ability to arrange a $40,000 loan at a 12% interest rate.

**AIR RIGHTS** the right to use, control, or occupy the space above a designated property. Air rights can be leased, sold, or donated to another party.
**Example:** The Pan Am building in New York City is situated in the *air rights* of Grand Central Station (Figure 11).

FIGURE 11

**ALIENATION** to convey or transfer **title** and **possession** of property. May be voluntary (by the owner) or involuntary (without the owner's consent) such as in **condemnation**.
**Example:** By signing a **deed**, there is an *alienation* of property.

**ALLODIAL SYSTEM** a legal system that allocates full property ownership rights to individuals. The allodial system is the basis for property rights in the United States.
**Example:** Under the *allodial system,* an individual may obtain **fee simple** ownership of a parcel of real estate. This allows the individual to enjoy the full set of rights entailed in property ownership, subject to restriction only by governmental powers of taxation, **police power,** and **eminent domain.**

**ALLUVIUM (or ALLUVION)** soil deposited by **accretion.** Usually considered to belong to the owner of the land to which it is added.
**Example:** Figure 12.

FIGURE 12

**ALTERNATIVE MINIMUM TAX** a type of flat-rate tax that applies to individual taxpayers who have certain types of income. A 21% rate applies to broadly based income. If this tax exceeds the regular income tax, then the *alternative minimum tax* is to be paid instead of the regular income tax. See **tax preference items.**

**ALTERNATIVE MORTGAGE INSTRUMENT (AMI)** any mortgage other than a fixed interest rate, level payment **amortizing** loan.
**Examples:**
Various types of *AMI's:*
• variable rate mortgages
• rollover loans
• graduated payment mortgages
• shared appreciation mortgages
• adjustable rate mortgages
• growing equity mortgages

**AMENITIES** in **appraisal,** the nonmonetary benefits derived from property ownership, such as pride of home ownership.
**Example:** Graham bought a **condominium** overlooking Lake Michigan with a prestige address, thus enhancing the *amenities* of ownership.

**AMERICAN INSTITUTE OF REAL ESTATE APPRAISERS (AIREA)** a professional organization of real estate appraisers affiliated with the **National Association of Realtors®**. AIREA publishes the *Appraisal Journal* and several reference works on appraisal, provides educational services, and confers the professional designations of **MAI** (Member, Appraisal Institute) and RM **(Residential Member).**
**Address:**
American Institute of Real Estate Appraisers
430 North Michigan Avenue
Chicago, Illinois 60611

**AMERICAN LAND TITLE ASSOCIATION (ALTA)** a national association of title companies, abstractors, and attorneys established to promote uniformity and quality in **title abstract** and insurance policies.
**Example:** The title company employed in the purchase of the property is a member of the *American Land Title Association* and, therefore, used standard ALTA forms when underwriting the title policy.

**AMERICAN MANSARD OR SECOND EMPIRE STYLE** a nineteenth century style house whose main and distinguishing characteristic is the roof design. The mansard roof slopes gently back from the wall line and then is topped with an invisible (from the street) section resembling a conventional hip roof. Multiple dormers protrude through the roof.
**Example:** Figure 13.

Massive cornice and supporting brackets

Mansard roof

Decorative iron work

Many dormers

Colored glass windows

French doors

FIGURE 13

**AMERICAN PLANNING ASSOCIATION (APA)** a professional organization of regional and urban planners for the purpose of promoting professional standards, research, and education. APA was formed by the merger of the American Institute of Planners (AIP) and the American Society of Planning Officials (ASPO). APA publishes a monthly magazine, *Planning,* and a quarterly journal, *Journal of the APA.*

**Address:**
American Planning Association
1313 East 60th Street
Chicago, Illinois 60637

**AMERICAN REAL ESTATE AND URBAN ECONOMICS ASSOCI-ATION (AREUEA)** an organization of scholars, researchers, and practitioners concerned with economic analysis of real estate related problems. Publishes the *AREUEA Journal* quarterly.
**Address:**
Jeffrey Fisher
Secretary-Treasurer
College of Business Administration
Indiana University
Bloomington, Indiana 47401

**AMERICAN REAL ESTATE SOCIETY (ARES)** an organization of scholars, researchers and practitioners who are mainly concerned with solving business problems related to real estate.
**Address:**
James L. Kuhle
Secretary/Treasurer
College of Business
California State University
Sacramento, CA 95819

**AMERICAN SOCIETY OF APPRAISERS (ASA)** a professional organization of appraisers (not restricted to real estate). ASA publishes the biannual journal, *Valuation*.
**Address:**
American Society of Appraisers
International Headquarters
Dulles International Airport
P.O. Box 17265
Washington, D.C. 20041

**AMERICAN SOCIETY OF REAL ESTATE COUNSELORS (ASREC)** a professional organization of real estate investment counselors and consultants. Affiliated with the **National Association of Realtors®**. Awards the designation of Counselor of Real Estate (CRE). Publishes the biannual journal, *Real Estate Issues*.
**Address:**
American Society of Real Estate Counselors
430 North Michigan Avenue
Chicago, Illinois 60611

**AMORTIZATION** a gradual paying off of a debt by periodic installments.

**Example:** A $100,000 loan is arranged at a 12% interest rate. The borrower pays $13,500 in the first year. Of the payment, $12,000 is for interest, $1,500 for *amortization*. After the payment, the loan balance is amortized to $98,500.

**AMORTIZATION SCHEDULE** a table that shows the periodic payment, interest and principal requirements, and unpaid loan balance for each period of the life of a loan.
**Example:** An *amortization schedule* for a $1,000 principal, 5-year self-amortizing loan at 10% interest with annual payments is shown in Table 3.

**TABLE 3**

| End of year | Payment required | Interest at 10% of unpaid balance | Principal retirement | Unpaid balance at end of year |
|---|---|---|---|---|
| 1 | $263.80 | $100.00 | $163.80 | $836.20 |
| 2 | 263.80 | 83.62 | 180.18 | 656.02 |
| 3 | 263.80 | 65.60 | 198.20 | 457.82 |
| 4 | 263.80 | 45.78 | 218.02 | 239.80 |
| 5 | 263.78 | 23.98 | 239.80 | 0 |
| Total retired | | | $1000.00 | |

**ANCHOR TENANT** the main tenant in a shopping center.
**Example:** Big Buy Foods is the *anchor tenant* in Figure 14. (Note: Large scale centers may have more than one anchor tenant).

FIGURE 14

**ANNEXATION** the process by which an incorporated city expands its boundaries to include a specified area. The rules of annexation are established by state law and generally require a public ballot within the city and the area to be annexed. Other incorporated areas are generally protected from annexation by an adjacent city.

**Example:** *Annexation* is generally sought by a city to expand its boundaries by taking in an area to which it may already be providing services. Many unincorporated suburban areas, however, resist efforts to annex them into the city because of possibly higher tax rates and loss of local control over schools and other services.

**ANNUAL CAP** a limit on the amount of adjustment in the interest rate on an **adjustable rate mortgage** over a twelve month period. See **cap.**

**Example:** An adjustable rate mortgage has a current interest rate of 8% and an *annual cap* of 2 percentage points. After one year, the highest the interest rate can be is 10% and the lowest it can be is 6%, due to the cap.

**ANNUAL DEBT SERVICE** required annual principal and interest payments for a loan.

**Example:** A loan of $100,000 calls for 300 equal monthly payments to fully **amortize** the principal. Interest is 15% annually. Monthly payments are $1280.83. *Annual debt service* is the sum of 12 monthly payments, or $15,369.96.

**ANNUAL MORTGAGE CONSTANT** the amount of **annual debt service** compared to the principal; also expressed as a dollar amount. The formula is:

$$\text{Annual mortgage constant} = \frac{\text{annual debt service}}{\text{mortgage principal}}$$

**Example:** A loan, at a 15% interest rate, is amortizing over 30 years with monthly payments. The *annual mortgage constant* is 15.1733%. Total principal and interest payments in a year are 15.18 per $100 borrowed. Note: the annual mortgage constant must exceed the interest rate for **amortization** to occur.

**ANNUAL PERCENTAGE RATE** the effective rate of interest for a loan per year, disclosure of which is required by the **Truth-In-Lending** Law. See **yield to maturity.**

**Example:** Abel gets a loan for $50,000 at 10% interest plus **2 discount points,** payable over 30 years. Because of the discount points $49,000 has been effectively borrowed but $50,000 must be repaid with 10% interest on $50,000. Considering the effective amount borrowed, the *annual percentage rate* is 10.25%.

**ANNUITY** a series of equal or nearly equal periodic payments or receipts.

**Example:** The receipt of $100 per year for the next 5 years constitutes a $100 five-year *annuity.*

**ANNUITY DUE** same as **ordinary annuity.**

**ANNUITY IN ADVANCE** a series of equal or nearly equal payments, each payable at the beginning of the period.
**Example:** A landlord leases property for 5 years. The rent, payable at the beginning of each period, constitutes an *annuity in advance* (Figure 15).

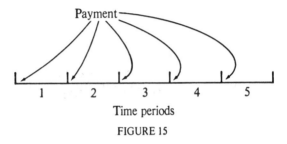

Time periods

FIGURE 15

**ANNUITY IN ARREARS** same as **ordinary annuity.**

**ANNUITY FACTOR** a mathematical figure that shows the present value of an income stream that generates one dollar of income each period for a specified number of periods.
**Example:** Collins is to receive $1,000 each year for 10 years for rental of her land. To value this income, she used an *annuity factor* at a 10% rate that is 6.144. The estimated rent has a present value of $6,144 (6.144 × $1,000).

$$\text{Annuity factor} = \frac{1 - \dfrac{1}{(1 + i)^n}}{i}$$

where $i$ is the periodic interest rate in decimal form and $n$ is the number of periods that the income stream will last.

**ANTITRUST LAWS** federal and state acts to protect trade and commerce from monopolies and restrictions.
**Example:** In the early 1960's several real estate boards required all members to charge the same rate of commission. Some boards were found to be in violation of *antitrust laws.* Now there are no boards that require specific commission rates.

**APARTMENT (BUILDING)** a dwelling unit within a multifamily structure, generally provided as rental housing. An apartment building is a structure with individual apartment units but a common entrance and hallway. See **multifamily housing.**
**Example:** *Apartments* may vary in size from small, 1-room effi-

ciencies to large, multibedroom units. *Apartment buildings* may be as small as a 1-story, 4-unit building to a high-rise building with hundreds of units and retail and office space included.

**APPORTIONMENT** 1. the **prorating** of property expenses, such as taxes and insurance, between buyer and seller.
**Example:** A house is sold on July 1. Property taxes, paid in **arrears,** are due on January 1 of the following year. At closing taxes are *apportioned*, so the seller pays the buyer one half of the estimated taxes as his share of the estimated tax payment due in January.
2. the partitioning of property into individual parcels by tenants in common.
**Example:** A sister and a brother inherit a property and hold it as tenants in common. The brother wishes to sell. The property is *apportioned* into 2 separate parcels to allow for the sale.

**APPRAISAL** an opinion or estimate of the value of a property.
**Examples:** A property owner may have an *appraisal* made of a specific property to:

• determine a reasonable offering price in a sale
• determine the value at death for estate tax purposes
• allocate the purchase price to the land and improvements
• determine the amount of **hazard insurance** to carry

**APPRAISAL APPROACH** one of 3 methods to estimate the value of property: **cost approach, income approach,** and **market comparison approach.**
**Example:** An independent fee appraiser generally uses each of the 3 *appraisal approaches* when preparing an appraisal report.

**APPRAISAL BY SUMMATION** same as **cost approach.**

**APPRAISER** one qualified to estimate the value of real property.
**Example:** One may hire an *appraiser* to render an opinion of a property's market value. In a court of law, an *appraiser* may be called upon for expert testimony.

**APPRECIATION** an increase in the value of property.
**Example:** Abel sold for $100,000 land that he purchased 10 years ago for $60,000. During that time the amount of *appreciation* was $40,000.
*Appreciation* gains from investment property are generally subject to favorable **capital gains** tax rates.

**APPROPRIATION** setting aside land for a public use.
**Example:** Abel plans to develop a subdivision in Pleasantville. In order to obtain permission from the city council, Abel is required

to *appropriate* 2 acres to the city for construction of an elementary school.

**APPURTENANCE** something that is outside the property itself but is considered a part of the property and adds to its greater enjoyment, such as the right to cross another's land (i.e., **easement** or **right-of-way**).
**Example:** *Appurtenances* (Figure 16).

FIGURE 16

**ARBITRAGE** 1. buying in one market, selling simultaneously in another to make a profit.
**Example:** Graham bought gold in London for $500 per ounce; simultaneously she sold it in New York for $502. The *arbitrage* allowed $2 profit per ounce, less transaction costs.
2. buying one type of security and selling an equivalent to make a profit.
**Example:** Baker bought bonds for $5000 that could be converted into 500 shares of stock. Simultaneously, he sold 500 shares of stock at $11 per share. He earned $500 for this *arbitrage,* minus transaction costs.

**ARCHITECTURE** the manner in which a building is constructed, including the layout, **floor plan,** style and appearance, materials used, and the building technology used.
**Example** The *architecture* of the houses in the neighborhood is characteristic of the design common to the 1930's: small rooms, much attention to detail, an elaborate **facade,** high ceilings, and thick walls.

**AREA** a 2-dimensional space defined by boundaries; such as floor area, area of a lot, and market area.
**Example:** A rectangular lot is 50 × 100 feet in dimension. Its *area* is 5,000 square feet or 0.11 acre.

**ARM'S LENGTH TRANSACTION** a transaction among parties, each of whom acts in his or her own best interest.
**Examples:** Transactions between the following parties would, in most cases, *not* be considered arm's length:
• a husband and wife
• a father and son
• a corporation and one of its subsidiaries

**ARREARS** 1. at the end of a term.
**Example:** Interest on mortgage loans is normally paid in *arrears*. This means that interest is paid at the end of a month or other period. Generally, rent and insurance are paid in advance.
2. sometimes used to signify default; overdue in payment.

**ARTESIAN WELL** a deep-drilled shaft that reaches water that rises because of natural underground pressure.
**Example:** Schematic drawing of an *artesian well* (Figure 17).

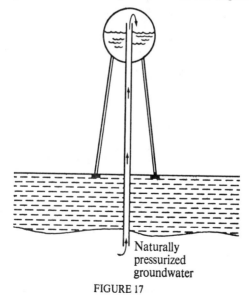

Naturally
pressurized
groundwater

FIGURE 17

**AS IS** without guarantees as to condition, as in a sale.
  **Example:** Baker purchases a building from Abel with the understanding that the building is to be conveyed *as is*. When Baker discovers that the roof leaks, Abel is not legally responsible for repairs.

**ASKED** the amount a property owner sets as a selling price for his property.
  **Example:** Abel has *asked* $75,000 for 20 acres of land, even though its **appraised** value is only $60,000.

**ASKING PRICE** the list price that an owner would like to receive.
  **Example:** Abel advertises a property for sale at a price of $100,000. The advertised price is Abel's *asking price.*

**ASSEMBLAGE** combining of 2 or more parcels of land. See **plottage value.**
  **Example:** Abel buys 2 **adjoining** properties of land for $10,000 each. The large unified tract is worth $25,000. The process is *assemblage.*

**ASSESSED VALUATION** the value established for property tax purposes.
  **Example:** Abel receives a statement indicating that, in the judgment of the local tax **assessor**, Abel's property is worth $40,000. By law, properties in this jurisdiction are assessed at 75% of **market value.** Thus Abel's *assessed valuation* is $30,000 (75% of $40,000) and property taxes will be based on this assessed amount.

**ASSESSMENT** 1. the amount of tax or special payment due to a municipality or association.
  **Example:** Abel owns a parcel of land assessed on the tax roll for $40,000. The tax rate is $1.00 per $100 of value. The tax *assessment* for Abel's land is $400.
  2. an owner's or lessee's proportionate share of a common expense.
  **Example:** Abel rents office space under a **net lease.** Abel pays an *assessment* each month for maintenance of the building lobby and elevators.

**ASSESSMENT RATIO** the ratio of assessed value to **market value.**
  **Example:** A county requires a 40% *assessment ratio* on all property to be taxed. Property with a $10,000 market value is therefore

assessed at $4000 (40% of $10,000), and the **tax rate** is applied to $4000.

**ASSESSMENT ROLL** a public record of the assessed value of property in a taxing jurisdiction.
**Example:** The *assessment roll* of Anytown, USA lists each individual tract of land within its taxing jurisdiction and shows the assessed value of each. The total assessed value of property is $10 million.

**ASSESSOR** an official who determines property tax assessments.
**Example:** Jones inspects Abel's property and estimates its value at $50,000 for property tax purposes. Jones is an *assessor.*

**ASSET** something of value.
**Example:** Land, houses, cars, furniture, cash, bank deposits, and securities owned are *assets.*

**ASSET DEPRECIATION RANGE** generally applies to property purchased before 1981. Limitations on the period over which assets may be depreciated. Generally allows depreciable lives 20% longer or shorter than the guidelines provided by the Internal Revenue Service. Also provides maximum amounts that can be spent annually on assets and still be a deductible repair.
**Example:** Farm buildings purchased before 1981 may be depreciated over 25 years or within a range of 20 to 30 years, according to the *asset depreciation range.* Up to 5% of the cost can be spent annually and be treated as repair, not as a capital improvement.

**ASSIGNEE** the person to whom an agreement or contract is sold or transferred.
**Example:** See **assignor.**

**ASSIGNMENT** the method by which a right or contract is transferred from one person to another.
**Example:** A tenant signs an *assignment* giving another the rights to use the leased space.

**ASSIGNMENT OF LEASE** the transfer of rights to use leased property. The **assignee** acquires the same rights and privileges as the **assignor.** The assignor remains liable unless released by the landlord.
**Example:** Abel signs a 20-year lease for a warehouse. After 5 years, Abel no longer needs the warehouse and *assigns the lease* to Baker.

**ASSIGNOR** a party who assigns or transfers an agreement or contract to another.
**Example:** Davis has an option to buy certain land. She assigns her

rights to Baker, so that Baker now has the same rights. Davis is the *assignor*. Baker is the **assignee**.

**ASSUMABLE LOAN** a mortgage loan which allows a new home purchaser to undertake the obligation of the loan with no change in loan terms. This is generally true of loans without **due-on-sale clauses.** Most FHA and VA mortgages are assumable.

**Example:** Abel sells a home with an *assumable loan* to Baker. Baker takes over the payments of the loan and accepts liability under the mortgage note.

**ASSUMPTION OF MORTGAGE** the purchase of mortgaged property whereby the buyer accepts liability for the debt that continues to exist. The seller remains liable to the lender unless the lender agrees to release him.

**Example:** Abel owes a 30-year mortgage loan of $50,000 against his house. Baker wants to buy the house and keep the same mortgage. Baker pays $20,000 cash for the **equity** and *assumes* the mortgage. Baker becomes liable for the debt, but Abel remains liable also.

**AT-RISK RULES** tax laws that limit the amount of tax losses an investor (particularly a **limited partner**) can claim. *At-risk rules* were extended to real estate by the 1986 tax act, and apply to property placed in service after 1986. This means that losses on real estate investments will be deductible only to the extent of money the equity investor stands to lose.

**Example:** If an investor has $10,000 at risk in a real estate investment that generates $3,333 per year in tax losses, the losses may be used for only three years. Thereafter, the losses may be used only if the investor contributes more money or property (net of withdrawals) or becomes liable to repay borrowed money.

Amounts at-risk include:
• Cash contributed to the activity.
• Borrowed money for which the investor is personally liable.
• Property pledged as security for the real estate activity, provided the property is not used in the activity.

An exception is made for qualified third party non-recourse financing. These loans may be treated as amounts at-risk provided:
• A third-party, unrelated to the investor, provides the loan.
• The third-party lender is neither the seller of the property nor related to the seller.
• The lender is not paid a fee with respect to the equity investor's investment in the property.

Related Parties: Non-recourse loans from related parties qualify as amounts at-risk only if the terms are "commercially reasonable" and on substantially the same terms as loans involving unrelated persons.

**Partnerships.** A partnership's non-recourse financing may increase a general or limited partner's amount at risk provided the financing is qualified non-recourse for both the partner and the partnership. However, the amount treated at risk cannot be more than the total qualified non-recourse financing at the partnership level.

**ATTACHMENT** legal seizure of property to force payment of a debt.
**Example:** The landlord obtained an *attachment* that created a **lien** on the tenant's property to enforce payment of back rent.

**ATTEST** to witness by observation and signature.
**Example:** Many contracts require a third party to *attest* to the signing by the principals.

**ATTORNEY-IN-FACT** one who is authorized to act for another under a **power of attorney,** which may be general or limited in scope.
**Example:** Collins wishes to sell her home but is planning a 6-month vacation in the Middle East. She gives authorization to her friend Baker to sign the **deed** over to a buyer. Baker becomes her *attorney-in-fact* for this situation.

**ATTORNMENT** a tenant's formal agreement to be a tenant of a new landlord.
**Example:** Abel defaulted on the mortgage against his shopping center, so the Happy Life Insurance Company **foreclosed** and became the landlord. Happy Life asked all tenants to sign an *attornment* recognizing the new landlord.

**AUCTION** a way of marketing property to the highest bidder. **Bids** are taken verbally or simultaneously through mail or telegrams, and the property is sold to the highest bidder. Auctioning real estate may require both an auctioneer's license and a real estate license.
**Example:** Land in Iowa, since it is relatively homogeneous, lends itself to *auction* sales where it is sold to the highest verbal bidder.
**Example:** **Fannie Mae** agrees to buy mortgages once a week via an *auction*. Mortgage sellers state the price or yield they want, and Fannie Mae accepts the highest yields offered.

**AVULSION** the sudden removal of land from one parcel to another, when a body of water, such as a river, abruptly changes its channel. Contrast to **accretion.**
**Example:** Because of the change in the river's channel, in Figure 18 parcel A gains use of a portion of the land in the original river

bed through *avulsion*. Similarly, parcel B loses land which is now covered by the river.

FIGURE 18

# B

**BACKFILL** the replacement of excavated earth into a hole or against a structure.
**Example:** Figure 19.

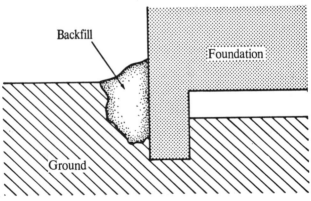

FIGURE 19

**BACKUP CONTRACT** a contract to buy real estate that becomes effective if a prior contract fails to be consummated.
**Example:** Abel contracts with Baker to sell a property contingent on Baker's ability to obtain financing within 30 days. In the meantime, Abel arranges a *backup contract* to sell to Collins, should Baker fail to obtain financing.

**BALANCE SHEET** a financial statement in table form showing **assets**, liabilities, and **equity**, in which assets equal the sum of **liabilities** plus **equity**.
**Example:** Table 4:

**TABLE 4**

**BALANCE SHEET**

| Assets | | Liabilities & Equity | |
|---|---|---|---|
| Cash | $1,000 | Charge account debts | $500 |
| Cars | 5,000 | Auto loan balance | 2,000 |
| Furniture | 5,000 | Home mortgage | 28,500 |
| House | 50,000 | Equity | 40,000 |
| Stocks | 10,000 | | |
| Total assets | $71,000 | Total liabilities & equity | $71,000 |

**BALLOON MORTGAGE** a mortgage with a **balloon payment**.
**Example:** The *balloon mortgage* called for payments of $500 per month for 5 years, followed by a **balloon payment** of $50,000.

**BALLOON PAYMENT** the final payment on a loan, when that payment is greater than the preceding installment payments and pays the loan in full.
**Example:** A debt requires interest-only payments annually for 5 years, at the end of which time the principal balance (a *balloon payment*) is due, as seen in Figure 20.

**BAND OF INVESTMENT** an income property **appraisal** technique where the overall interest rate is derived from weighting **mortgage** and **equity** rates.
**Example:** Table 5.

**BANKRUPTCY** the financial inability to pay one's debts when due. The debtor seeks relief through court action that may work out or erase debts.
**Example:** Carter lost his job but continued to live extravagantly on **credit**. When accounts were overdue, Carter filed a *bankruptcy* petition. The court allowed him to pay creditors 10 cents per dollar of debt, payable over 3 years.

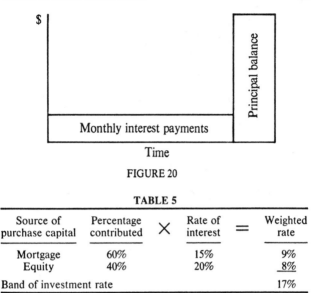

FIGURE 20

**TABLE 5**

| Source of purchase capital | Percentage contributed | × | Rate of interest | = | Weighted rate |
|---|---|---|---|---|---|
| Mortgage | 60% | | 15% | | 9% |
| Equity | 40% | | 20% | | 8% |
| Band of investment rate | | | | | 17% |

**BARGAIN AND SALE DEED** in which the **grantor** implies to have or
have had an interest in the property but offers no warranties of title
to the **grantee.** This type of deed is typically used in many states to
transfer title. Contrast **general warranty deed, quitclaim deed, special warranty deed.**
**Example:** Abel gives Baker a *bargain and sale deed* which
includes no warranty of title but states, "for $10 and other valuable
consideration, the grantor does hereby grant and release to the
grantee, the following property."

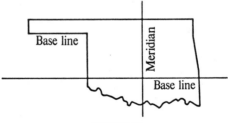

FIGURE 21

**BASE AND MERIDIAN** imaginary lines used by **surveyors** to find and describe the location of land. The base line is east-west; the meridian line is north-south.
**Example:** Principal *base and meridian* lines for Oklahoma (Figure 21).

**BASE LINE** part of the **Rectangular Survey** or **Government Rectangular Survey** method of land description. The *base line* is the major east-west line to which all north-south measurements refer.
**Example:** See **base and meridian.**

**BASE RENT** the minimum rent due under a lease that has a percentage or participation requirement.
**Example:** Spinning Records leases retail space in Majestic Mall. Under the lease Spinning Records must pay a *base rent* of $2,000 per month plus 5% of all sales revenue over $50,000 per month.

**BASIC INDUSTRY MULTIPLIER** in economic base analysis, the ratio of total population in a local area to employment in basic industry. Basic industry is considered to be any concern which attracts income from outside the local area. The job added in basic industry may also contribute to the need for local service jobs (telephone operator, nurse, waitress, etc.); and, if the workers have families, additional new people may be brought to the area.
**Example:** The Maintown economic base has a *basic industry multiplier* of 6. It is estimated that each new job added at Maintown's basic industries will increase the town's population by 6.

**BASIS (TAX)** the point from which gains, losses, and **depreciation** deductions are computed. Generally the cost or purchase price of an asset.
**Example:** Collins purchases land for $10,000 and erects a store for $80,000. Her *tax basis* is $90,000. If she then sells the property for $95,000 she has a $5,000 gain. If she instead depreciates the property, the $80,000 cost basis of improvements are depreciable; the $10,000 *basis* of the land remains because land is not depreciable.

**BASIS POINT** one 100th of 1%.
**Example:** Mortgage loan interest rates are 12.75% this week. They were 12.25% last week. The increase was 50 *basis points* (1275 minus 1225 equals 50).

**BEARER INSTRUMENT** a **security** that does not indicate the owner; payable to whoever presents it.
**Example:** A *bearer instrument* is open to theft because it can be redeemed without proof of legitimate ownership.

**BEDROOM COMMUNITY** a residential community in the **suburbs,** often near an employment center, but itself providing few employment opportunities.
**Example:** *Bedroom communities* frequently offer uncrowded schools, uncongested streets, and less noise and air pollution than the nearby industrial city. However, property tax rates are generally higher than in the city.

**BEFORE-TAX CASH FLOW cash flow** prior to deducting income tax payments or adding income tax benefits. See **cash throw-off.**
**Example:** After deducting **debt service** of $500 from a **net operating income** of $1000, Abel has a *before-tax cash flow* of $500.

**BENCHMARK** a permanently affixed mark that establishes the exact elevation of a place; used by **surveyors** in measuring site elevations, or as a starting point for **surveys.**
**Example:** The U.S. Coast and Geodetic Survey implants brass markers in the sidewalks of downtown areas to serve as *benchmarks*. The benchmark indicates the official elevation above sea level for the spot at which the marker is placed.

**BENEFICIARY** the person who receives or is to receive the benefits resulting from certain acts.
**Example:** Whitman takes out a $10,000 life insurance policy with her husband as the *beneficiary*. Should Whitman die, her husband will receive the benefits from the policy.

**BEQUEATH** to specify by **will** the recipient of personal property. Compare **devise.**
**Example:** In Abel's will he *bequeaths* his automobile and wrist watch to his son.

**BEQUEST** that personal property given by the terms of a **will.**
**Example:** Collins received a set of sterling silverware as a *bequest* from her deceased aunt.

**BETTERMENT** an improvement to real estate.
**Example:** Abel purchases a **site** and constructs a building. The building is considered a *betterment* to the site.

**BIANNUAL** occurring twice a year. Same as **semiannual.** Contrast **biennial.**
**Example:** Under a lease, Abel is required to make *biannual* rent payments, one in January and one in July (Figure 22).

**BID** the amount someone offers to pay.
**Example:** Abel places a property for sale at an **asking price** of $90,000. Baker makes a *bid* of $65,000 for the property, indicating he is willing to pay that amount for the property.

FIGURE 22

**BIENNIAL** occurring every 2 years.

**Example:** Abel arranges to pay premiums on a property insurance policy on a *biennial* basis. If the current premium is paid in 1984, the next premium is due in 1986 (Figure 23).

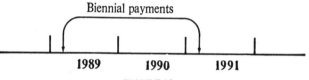

FIGURE 23

**BILATERAL CONTRACT** a contract under which each party promises performance. See **unilateral contract.**

**Example:** A sales contract is a *bilateral contract,* since the seller promises to convey a property and the buyer agrees to pay a specified sum, given certain conditions.

**BI-LEVEL** a house built on 2 levels in which the main entrance is situated above the lower level but below the upper level.

**Example:** Drawing of a *bi-level* house (Figure 24):

FIGURE 24

**BILL OF SALE** a written **instrument** given to pass **title** of personal property from a seller to a buyer. Used when furniture and portable appliances are sold.
**Example:** Figure 25.

```
                    Bill of Sale

    I, Ernest Abel, do hereby sell my dining
    room suite, which I represent to be free
    and clear, to Bill Baker.

                    Signed,

                    Ernest Abel
```

FIGURE 25

**BINDER** an agreement, accompanied by a **deposit,** for the purchase of real estate, to evidence **good faith** on the part of the purchaser.
**Example:** Abel gave Baker a *binder* on the house; Abel then contacted his attorney to prepare the papers for a contract.

**BIWEEKLY LOAN** a mortgage which requires principal and interest payments at two-week intervals. The payment is exactly half of what a monthly payment would be. Over a year's time, the 26 payments are equivalent to 13 monthly payments on a comparable mortgage loan. As a result, the loan will amortize much faster than loans with monthly payments.
**Example:** A 30-year mortgage for $70,000 at 12 percent interest requires monthly payments of $720. A *biweekly loan* for the same amount and interest rate requires a payment of $360 every two weeks. The biweekly mortgage will be fully amortized (paid off) after 19 years.

**BLANKET MORTGAGE** a single **mortgage** that covers more than one parcel of real estate.
**Example:** A developer subdivides a tract of land into lots and obtains a *blanket mortgage* on the whole tract. A **release** provision in the mortgage allows the developer to sell individual lots over time without **retiring** the entire mortgage.

**BLENDED RATE** an **interest rate,** applied to a **refinanced** loan, that is higher than the rate on the old loan but lower than the rate offered on new loans. Generally offered by the lender to induce home buyers to refinance existing, low-interest rate loans as an alternative to assuming the existing loan. Compare **assumption of mortgage.**

**Example:** Jones wishes to sell a home to Brown. Brown can assume the existing loan of $20,000 at an interest rate of 8%. Jones' lender offers the alternative of refinancing the loan for $40,000 at a *blended rate* of 10%. Brown could get a new loan at a rate of 12%.

**BLIGHTED AREA** a section of a city in which a majority of the structures are dilapidated.

**Example: Urban renewal** is planned for several *blighted areas* of the city. Within these areas, houses that do not meet **housing codes** are to be rehabilitated or demolished and new buildings constructed.

**BLIND POOL** an investment program in which monies are invested into an association without investors knowing which properties will be purchased.

**Example:** Each of 100 investors contributes $5,000 into a joint venture. The **syndicator** has not located the property to be purchased, so the investment money is said to be a *blind pool.*

**BLOCKBUSTING** a racially discriminatory and illegal practice of coercing a party to sell a home to someone of a minority race or ethnic background, then using scare tactics to cause others in the neighborhood to sell at depressed prices.

**Examples:** A sales agent arranges a sale in which a minority family enters a previously all-white neighborhood. The agent then engages in *blockbusting* by contacting other owners in the neighborhood and informing them that their property's value will fall if they don't sell right away at a depressed offered price.

**BLUE-SKY LAWS** state laws requiring the offeror of securities to give full disclosure, and register the offering as required by federal and state law.

**Example:** A **syndicator** wishes to sell 10,000 units of a partnership to investors throughout the U.S. He registers the offering with the **Securities and Exchange Commission** and complies with *blue-sky laws* in 50 states. The term comes from fraudulent practices of exaggerated offerings to investors, including part of the blue sky.

**BOARD OF EQUALIZATION** a government entity whose purpose is to assure uniform property tax assessments.

**Example:** A *board of equalization* at the local level may review **assessments** to be certain that the assessment for each parcel is fair; at the state level, the board will assure that each county is assessing property at the mandated proportion of market value.

**BOARD OF REALTORS®** a local group of real estate licensees who are members of the State and **National Association of Realtors®**.
**Example:** The Springfield *Board of Realtors®* has 200 members. They meet monthly to discuss business matters, and form the **multiple listing** service in Springfield.

**BOILER PLATE** standard language found in contracts. Preprinted material.
**Example:** Collins decided to lease her property. At a stationery store she finds a preprinted *boiler plate* form. She fills in rental rates and dates in the blank places, than asks her tenant, Baker, to sign the lease.

**BONA FIDE** in **good faith,** without fraud.
**Example:** To be certain that the signatures to the deed were *bona fide,* the county clerk insisted they be **notarized.**

**BOND** a certificate that serves as evidence of a debt and of the terms under which it is undertaken. See **promissory note.**
**Example:** Abel loans $10,000 to Baker, who gives a **note** or *bond* to evidence the debt (Figure 26).

---

Bill Baker owes Ernest Abel $10,000, payable at maturity in 10 years with interest payable semiannually at 10%.

                              Signed
                              *Bill Baker*
                              Bill Baker
                              August 15, 1989

---

FIGURE 26

**BOOK VALUE** the carrying amount of an **asset,** as shown on the books of a company. Generally the amount paid for an asset, less depreciation.
**Example:** X Corporation purchases a building for $100,000, then **depreciates** it by $10,000 on its financial statements. The *book value* was $100,000 and is now $90,000.

**BOOT** unlike property included to balance the value of like properties exchanged.
**Example:** In an exchange of property under **Section 1031** of the

**Internal Revenue Code,** Collins exchanges her warehouse worth
$100,000 and receives Baker's land worth $125,000. Collins pays
$15,000 cash and a car worth $10,000 to *boot* in order to equalize
the values of properties exchanged. The car and cash are *boot*
(Figure 27).

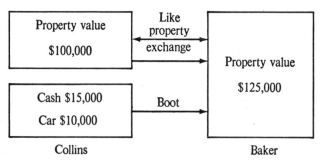

FIGURE 27

**BOTTOMLAND** 1. low land near a river, lake, stream, which is
often flooded, see **flood plain.**
**Example:** Figure 28.

FIGURE 28

2. land in a valley or dale.
**Example:** Figure 29.

FIGURE 29

**BOUNDARY** same as **property line.**

**BREACH OF CONTRACT** a violation of the terms of a legal agreement; **default.** Breach of contract allows the nonbreaching party to rescind the contract, sue for damages, or sue for performance of the contract.
**Example:** Baker contracts with owner Brown to purchase a property. When the closing date arrives, Brown refuses to **convey** title to the property. Brown's action is not supported by any special conditions in the sales contract and therefore constitutes a *breach of contract*. Baker may rescind the contract and recover his **deposit,** may sue Brown for any expenses and damages incurred, or may sue to force Brown to sell.

**BREAK-EVEN POINT** the amount of **rent** or the **occupancy level** needed to pay **operating expenses** and **debt service.** Also called **default** point.

$$\text{Break-even point} = \frac{\text{operating expenses and debt service}}{\text{potential gross income}}$$

**Example:** Annual operating expenses for a 100-unit apartment complex are estimated at $200,000 per year. Debt service requirements are $250,000 per year. Therefore, total cash requirements are $450,000. If all apartments are rented all year, the **gross income** would be $600,000. The *break-even point* is at 75% occupancy. At that level, gross income would exactly equal cash requirements.

**BRIDGE LOAN** mortgage financing between the termination of one loan and the beginning of another loan.
**Example:** Collins, who is a developer, has a construction loan outstanding. She is in the process of negotiating better terms for permanent financing than the commitment previously arranged. She has arranged a *bridge loan* to pay off the construction loan when it is due. When new permanent financing is arranged, that loan will pay off the bridge loan.

**BROKER** a state-licensed **agent** who, for a fee, acts for property owners in real estate transactions, within the scope of state law.
**Example:** A person wishing to sell or lease property often engages a *broker* to arrange the sale or locate tenants. A broker may also be engaged by a prospective buyer or tenant to locate acceptable property.

**BROKERAGE** 1. the business of being a **broker.**
**Example:** One may open a *brokerage* office, upon receiving a broker's license, for the purpose of engaging in brokerage.
2. the **commission** received by a broker for his services.
**Example:** The *brokerage* was $6,000 on the sale of a $100,000 house.

**BROWNSTONE, BRICK ROW HOUSE, OR EASTERN TOWN-
HOUSE** a nineteenth century style house, usually having 4 or 5
stories with a stoop leading up to the first floor. They have common side walls with the house on either side.
**Example:** Figure 30.

FIGURE 30

**BUDGET MORTGAGE** a **mortgage** that requires monthly payments
for taxes and insurance in addition to interest and principal.
**Example:** Abel borrows $50,000 on a *budget mortgage* at 12%
interest. His monthly mortgage payment is $700, which consists of
$514 principal and interest, $150 taxes, and $36 insurance.

**BUFFER ZONE** a transitional area between 2 areas of different pre-
dominant land uses.
**Example:** In Figure 31 a *buffer zone* of **apartments** separates an
area of **single-family** houses from a **commercial property** area:

FIGURE 31

**BUILDER WARRANTY** a guarantee on the quality of construction offered by the developer or building contractor. See **homeowner warranty program.**

**Example:** Abel buys a newly built home. The home carries a *builder warranty* which guarantees that the home is free of structural defects for a period of time.

**BUILDING AND LOAN ASSOCIATIONS** see **savings and loan associations.**

**BUILDING CODES** regulations established by local governments describing the minimum structural requirements for buildings; includes foundation, roofing, plumbing, electrical, and other specifications for safety and sanitation.

**Example:** Abel is developer who wishes to construct houses. He must comply with the standards of the local *building codes* and submit to inspections by a building inspector.

**BUILDING LINE** a line fixed at a certain distance from the front and/or sides of a lot, beyond which the building may not project.

**Example:** Figure 32.

FIGURE 32

**BUILDING LOAN AGREEMENT** an agreement whereby the lender advances money to an owner at specified stages of construction, i.e., upon completion of the foundation, framing, etc. Same as **construction loan** agreement.

**BUILDING OWNERS AND MANAGERS ASSOCIATION (BOMA)** an organization of practitioners who own and manage buildings, notably office space.
**Address:**
1221 Massachusetts Ave., N.W
Washington, D.C. 20005

**BUILDING PERMIT** permission granted by a local government to build a specific structure at a particular site.
**Example:** Abel desires to construct a small office building at the corner of First and Main. A *building permit* must be obtained from the city to allow the construction to proceed legally.

**BUILDING RESIDUAL TECHNIQUE** an **appraisal** technique whereby income to land is subtracted from **net operating income** to result in the building income. Building income is capitalized into building value.
**Example:** Table 6:

TABLE 6

| | |
|---|---|
| Net operating income | $13,000 |
| Less: Land income (Land value $50,000×10% rate of return) | − 5,000 |
| Building income | $8,000 |
| Divided by building rate of return (10%+2% **depreciation**) | ÷ .12 |
| Building value | $66,666 |

**BUNDLE OF RIGHTS THEORY** the theory that ownership of realty implies a group of rights such as occupancy, use and enjoyment, and the right to sell, **bequeath**, give, or **lease** all or part of these rights.

**Example:** Under the *bundle of rights* concept, Abel may sell mineral rights, hunting rights, **easements**, and other partial interest, then give a **life estate** to his wife with the **remainder** to their daughter.

**BUNGALOW** a small, early twentieth century style, 1-story house that usually has an open or enclosed front porch.
**Example:** Figure 33.

Open or enclosed front porch  1 story  Shingle roof

FIGURE 33

**BUSINESS DAY** a standard day for conducting business. Excludes weekends and holidays.
**Example:** On Monday, July 1, Abel agrees to buy real estate. Closing will be 5 *business days* later, which is July 9 (Table 7):

**TABLE 7**

|  |  | Business days |
|---|---|---|
| Tuesday | July 2 | 1 |
| Wednesday | July 3 | 2 |
| Thursday | July 4 | holiday |
| Friday | July 5 | 3 |
| Saturday | July 6 | weekend |
| Sunday | July 7 | weekend |
| Monday | July 8 | 4 |
| Tuesday | July 9 | 5 |

**BUY-BACK AGREEMENT** a provision in a contract under which the seller agrees to repurchase the property at a stated price upon the occurrence of a specified event within a certain period of time.

**Example:** The *buy-back agreement* in the sales contract requires the builder-seller to buy the property back if Collins, the buyer-occupant, is transferred by her company within 6 months.

**BUY DOWN** 1. the action to pay additional **discount points** to a lender in exchange for a reduced rate of interest on a loan. The reduced rate may apply for all or a portion of the loan term. 2. a loan that has been bought down by the seller of the property for the benefit of the buyer.

**Example:** In order to achieve a sale of a property, Jones arranged for a *buy down* loan. If a seller agreed to Jones' price, Jones would *buy down* the interest rate for the first 3 years by paying the lender 5% of the loan amount at closing.

**BUYER'S BROKER** an agent hired by a prospective purchaser to find an acceptable property for purchase. The broker then represents the buyer and negotiates with the seller in the purchaser's best interest.

**Example:** Abel wishes to purchase a small apartment complex. Abel hires Baker, a licensed real estate broker, to find such a property. Baker is acting as a *buyer's broker* and earns a commission from Abel when an acceptable property is found and the owner is willing to sell.

**BUYER'S MARKET** a situation where buyers have a wide choice of properties and may negotiate lower prices. Often caused by overbuilding, local population decreases, or economic slump.

**Example:** Abel can purchase properties below their appraised values because of the existence of a *buyer's market*.

**BUY-SELL AGREEMENT** a pact among partners or stockholders under which some agree to buy the interests of others upon some event.

**Example:** Collins and Baker are partners. In the event Baker dies, Collins has agreed to buy Baker's interest for $25,000. If Collins dies first, Baker will buy her interest for $25,000.

**BYLAWS** a set of regulations by which an organization conducts its activities.

**Example:** An association of **condominium** owners prepares *bylaws* that state the minimum number of owners to conduct a meeting, to decide on policies, to elect officers, and other matters.

# C

**CALIFORNIA BUNGALOW** a 1-story, small, compact, early twentieth century house.
**Example:** Figure 34

Small, compact shape          1 story

FIGURE 34

**CALIFORNIA RANCH** a post-World War II style, 1-story, ground-hugging house with a low, pitched roof.
**Example:** Figure 35.

**CALL PROVISIONS** clauses in a loan that give the lender the right to accelerate the debt upon the occurrence of a specific event or date. See **acceleration clause.**
**Example:** Abel, the **mortgage** lender, notices that Baker, the homeowner, has begun to demolish the property. *Call provisions* in the loan allow Abel to claim that the full debt is now due.

**CANCELLATION CLAUSE** a contract provision that gives the right to terminate obligations upon the occurrence of specified conditions or events.
**Example:** a *cancellation clause* in a **lease** may allow the landlord to break the lease upon the sale of the building.

**CAP** in adjustable rate mortgages, a limit placed on adjustments to protect the borrower from large increases in the interest rate or the payment level. See **annual cap, life-of-loan cap, payment cap.**

**CAPACITY OF PARTIES** one of the requirements for a valid contract. Parties with less than full capacity include **minors,** the mentally insane, and those who are intoxicated.
**Example:** Collins, at age 17, entered into a contract to buy a tract of land. Collins can void that contract because it was entered into without full legal capacity.

1 story | Low-pitched roof | Picture windows | Ground-hugging | Sliding windows

FIGURE 35

**CAPE COD COLONIAL** an early American style 1½ story compact house that is small and symmetrical with a central entrance. The roof is the steep gable type covered with shingles. The authentic types have low central chimneys, but end chimneys are very common in the new versions. Bedrooms are on the first floor. The attic may be finished into additional bedrooms and a bath. A vine covered picket fence is traditional.
**Example:** Figure 36.

Shingles | Gable roof | 1½ stories

Central entrance

FIGURE 36

**CAPITAL ASSET** an asset defined in **Section 1221** of the **Internal Revenue Code** that once received favorable tax treatment upon sale. Excludes **inventory,** property held for resale, property used in a trade or business, copyrights in certain instances, and certain U.S. government obligations. There is no favorable tax treatment for *capital assets* sold after 1987.

**Example:** The dwelling that one owns and lives in, investment land, a limited partnership interest, or securities held for investment are *capital assets*.

**CAPITAL EXPENDITURE** an improvement (as distinguished from a **repair**) that will have a life of more than one year.

**Example:** Collins adds a new 25-room wing to her motel, at a cost of $250,000. The new wing is a *capital expenditure*.

**Example:** Baker, a rancher, has a fence that is in such poor condition it cannot be repaired. He makes a $50,000 *capital expenditure* to replace the fence.

**CAPITAL GAIN** gain on the sale of a **capital asset.** The 1986 tax act provides a maximum tax rate of 28% for *capital gains* in 1987; in 1988 and thereafter, there is no distinction in rates for *capital gains* as compared with **ordinary income.** There are limits on the deduction of **capital losses** against ordinary income.

**Example:** Collins purchases land, for investment purposes, for $10,000. Thirteen months later she sells it for $14,000. She reports the $4,000 profit as a long-term *capital gain* on her income tax return.

**CAPITAL IMPROVEMENT** same as **capital expenditure.**

**CAPITAL RECOVERY** see **recapture rate.**

**CAPITALIZATION** 1. in finance, a process whereby anticipated future income is converted to one lump sum capital value. A **capitalization rate** is divided into the expected periodic income to derive a capital value for the expected income. Sum of **interest rate** and **recapture rate.** See **capitalization rate.**

**Example:** A property is expected to produce an annual income of $10,000. It is judged to have a value of $80,000, which represents *capitalization* of the $10,000 per year income stream. Also, when taxes on the property increased by $500 per year, the property's value was reduced by $6,000 due to the *capitalization* process.

2. in accounting, setting up an **asset** on the financial records, rather than deducting it currently.

**Example:** *Capitalization* is required for an asset that has a 15-year **depreciable life;** the cost will be deducted over that time period, not deducted currently.

**CAPITALIZATION RATE** a rate of return used to derive the capital value of an **income stream.** The formula is

$$\text{Value} = \frac{\text{annual income}}{\text{capitalization rate}}$$

**Example:** The estimated net operating income of an office building is $12,000 per year. An appraiser decides the appropriate *capitalization rate* is 12%, comprised of a 10% return on investment and 2% for **depreciation.** The estimated value of the building is $100,000.

**CAPITALIZE** 1. to estimate the present lump sum value of an **income stream..** See **capitalization rate.**
**Example:** An **income stream** of $1,000 per year expected for 20 years is *capitalized* to result in a value of $8,513, based on a 10% interest rate.
2. to set up the cost of an asset on financial records.
**Example:** Abel acquires a building at a cost of $100,000. Since the cost cannot be deducted in the year paid, the $100,000 is *capitalized* as an asset and **depreciates** over its estimated useful life.

**CAPITAL LOSS** loss from the sale of a **capital asset.**
**Example:** Collins, an investor, purchases land for $10,000. Two years later she sells it for $8,000. The $2,000 difference is a *capital loss,* since the land is a capital asset. Note: There are limitations on the amount of loss that can be used to offset **ordinary income.**

**CAP RATE** same as **capitalization rate.**

**CAPTURE RATE** the sales or leasing rate of a real estate development compared to the sales or leasing rate of all developments in the market area.
**Example:** Two thousand condominium units are built in a rapidly growing metropolitan area, including one project of 500 units built by the Gibraltar Development Company. Sales in the area during July are 200 units, of which half are sold by Gibraltar. Gibraltar's *capture rate* is 50%.

**CARRYING CHARGES** expenses necessary for holding property, such as taxes and interest on idle property or property under construction.
**Example:** The annual *carrying charges* on a $100,000 tract of land are: $2,000 for taxes and $12,000 for interest.

**CARRYOVER BASIS** in a tax-deferred exchange, the **adjusted tax basis** of the property surrendered that is used to determine the tax basis of the property acquired. See **basis (tax)..**
**Example:** Abel exchanges land with Baker in a tax-deferred

exchange. Abel's **adjusted tax basis** in the **land** given up was $10,000. The *carryover basis* will therefore be $10,000 and (in the absence of **boot**) that will be Abel's tax basis in the land acquired from Baker.

**CASH METHOD** a method of accounting based on cash receipts and disbursements. Contrast **accrual method.**
**Example:** Abel, a *cash method* taxpayer, has the carpets in his office building shampooed on December 20 and immediately gets a bill for the service. He pays the bill on January 1 so the tax deduction is taken in the next year.

**CASH FLOW** periodic amounts available to an **equity** investor after deducting all periodic cash payments from rental income. See **before-tax cash flow, cash throw-off, after-tax cash flow.**
**Example:** Table 8.

**TABLE 8**

| | |
|---|---:|
| potential gross income | $10,000 |
| less: vacancy and collection allowance | − 1,000 |
| add: miscellaneous income | + 500 |
| effective gross income | 9,500 |
| less: operating expenses | − 3,000 |
| less: replacement reserve | − 500 |
| net operating income | 6,000 |
| less: interest | − 4,000 |
| less: principal payment | − 500 |
| cash flow | $1,500 |

**CASH THROW-OFF** same as **cash flow.**

**CAVEAT EMPTOR** "let the buyer beware." The buyer must examine the goods or property and buy at his own risk, except for **latent defects.**
**Example:** Often a property is offered "as is," with no expressed or implied guarantee of quality or condition. When entering such transactions, *caveat emptor* is a worthy admonishment.

**CENTRAL BUSINESS DISTRICT (CBD)** the downtown section of a city, generally consisting of retail, office, hotel, entertainment, and governmental land uses with some high **density** housing.
**Example:** Elaine chose to live in the suburb of Great Neck because it is only 30 minutes from the Manhattan CBD.

**CERTIFICATE OF DEPOSIT (CD)** a type of savings account that carries a specified minimum deposit and **term** and generally provides a higher **yield** than passbook-type savings accounts.

**Example:** Carny purchases a 3-year *certificate of deposit* from Local Savings and Loan. Carny must deposit at least $1000 and may not withdraw the money for 3 years without forfeiting a portion of the interest earned. Carny receives a yield of 8% annually.

**CERTIFICATE OF ELIGIBILITY** issued by the Veterans Administration to those who qualify for a **VA loan.**

**Example:** A person honorably discharged after serving a certain number of days on active duty in the armed forces is entitled to a *certificate of eligibility.* It indicates eligibility for a VA mortgage loan.

**CERTIFICATE OF INSURANCE** a document issued by an insurance company to verify the coverage.

**Example:** Under the **net lease,** the tenant had to keep adequate insurance and provide the landlord with a *certificate of insurance* as evidence.

**CERTIFICATE OF NO DEFENSE** same as **estoppel certificate.**

**CERTIFICATE OF OCCUPANCY** a document issued by a local government to a **developer** permitting the structure to be occupied by members of the public. Issuance of the certificate generally indicates that the building is in compliance with public health and **building codes.**

**Example:** Upon obtaining **zoning** and **subdivision** approvals and passing inspection by code enforcement officials, the developer is issued a *certificate of occupancy.*

**CERTIFICATE OF REASONABLE VALUE** a document issued by the Veteran's Administration, based on an approved **appraisal.** Establishes a ceiling on the maximum **VA mortgage loan** principal.

**Example:** A *certificate of reasonable value* (CRV) was received for a home that was under a **contract of sale.** Since the CRV was $1,000 more than the contracted price, the VA lent the full purchase price.

**CERTIFICATE OF TITLE** an opinion rendered by an attorney as to the status of **title** to a property, according to the public records. See **title search.**

**Example:** Abel's attorney issues a *certificate of title* that indicates no public record of claims against Abel's ownership of the property.

**CERTIFIED COMMERCIAL INVESTMENT MEMBER (CCIM)** a designation awarded by the **Realtors National Marketing Institute,** which is affiliated with the **National Association of Realtors®.**

**Address:**
Realtors National Marketing Institute
430 N. Michigan Ave.
Chicago, Illinois 60611

**CERTIFIED HISTORIC STRUCTURE** see **historic structure.**

**CERTIFIED PROPERTY MANAGER (CPM)** a professional designation awarded to real estate managers by the **Institute of Real Estate Management,** an affiliate of the **National Association of Realtors®.**
**Address:**
Institute of Real Estate Management
430 N. Michigan Ave.
Chicago, Illinois 60611.

**CERTIFIED RESIDENTIAL BROKER (CRB)** a designation awarded by the **Realtors National Marketing Institute,** which is affiliated with the **National Association of Realtors®.**
**Example:** Upon completing the necessary requirements, Abel was awarded the title of *Certified Residential Broker.*

**CERTIFIED RESIDENTIAL SPECIALIST (CRS)** a professional designation awarded by the **Realtors National Marketing Institute,** based on education and experience in residential sales. Candidates must hold the **GRI** designation.

**CHAIN** a linear unit of land measurement used in surveying: 66 feet in length. Each chain consists of 100 links.
**Example:** A plot 66 ft square measures 1 chain by 1 chain.

**CHAIN OF TITLE** a history of **conveyances** and **encumbrances** affecting a **title** from the time that the original **patent** was granted, or as far back as records are available. See **abstract of title, certificate of title.**
**Example:** An abstractor can research title to property going back to the date that the property was granted to the United States. This *chain of title* is helpful in preparing an attorney's **opinion of title,** as to whether the owner has a marketable or **insurable interest.** See **marketable title.**

**CHATTEL** personal property. Anything owned and tangible, other than real estate. See **personalty.**
**Example:** Furniture, automobiles, and jewelry are all *chattels.*

**CHATTEL MORTGAGE** a pledge of personal property as **security** for a **debt.**
**Example:** Abel borrows money against his automobile; the lender grants a *chattel mortgage.*

**CLEAR TITLE** a **marketable title;** one free of **clouds** and disputed interests.
**Example:** It is necessary to obtain *clear title* in order to convey a general **warranty deed** in a transaction.

**CLIENT** the one who engages a **broker,** lawyer, accountant, **appraiser,** etc.
**Example:** Unless otherwise specified in the sales contract, the *client* of the broker, most often the seller, pays the **brokerage** commission.

**CLOSING** 1. the act of transferring ownership of a property from seller to buyer in accordance with a sales contract. 2. the time when a closing takes place.
**Example:** Abel agrees to purchase a property from Baker. A *closing* is set up for June 15, at which time Abel and Baker will sign all documents and pay all expenses necessary to transfer ownership and secure financing.

**CLOSING COSTS** various fees and expenses payable by the seller and buyer at the time of a real estate **closing** (also termed transaction costs).
**Examples:** The following are some *closing costs:*
• **brokerage** commissions
• lender **discount points**/other fees
• **title insurance** premium
• deed **recording** fees
• loan **prepayment penalty**
• **inspection** and **appraisal** fees
• attorney's fees

**CLOSING DATE** the date on which the seller delivers the **deed** and the buyer pays for the property.
**Example:** The sales contract generally establishes a *closing date,* at which time the parties will meet and settle all accounts necessary to transfer **title** to the property.

**CLOSING STATEMENT** an accounting of funds from a real estate sale, made to both the seller and the buyer separately. Most states require the **broker** to furnish accurate closing statements to all parties to the transaction.
**Example:** Table 9

**CLOUD ON THE TITLE** an outstanding claim or **encumbrance** that, if valid, would affect or impair the owner's **title.** Compare **clear title.**
**Example:** Abel dies and in his will leaves land to Baker. Abel's widow is contesting the validity of Abel's will. During this period there is a *cloud on* Baker's *title* to the land.

**TABLE 9**

|  | Seller | | Buyer | |
| --- | --- | --- | --- | --- |
|  | Debit | Credit | Debit | Credit |
| Real property |  | $40,000 | $40,000 |  |
| Prepaid taxes |  | 670 | 670 |  |
| Sales commission | $ 2,400 |  |  |  |
| Survey fee |  |  | 75 |  |
| Cash paid by buyer to close |  |  |  | $40,745 |
| Cash received by seller | 38,270 |  |  |  |
| Totals | $40,670 | $40,670 | $40,745 | $40,745 |

**CLUSTER HOUSING** a **subdivision** technique in which detached dwelling units are grouped relatively close together, leaving open spaces as **common areas.**.

**Example:** A *cluster housing* development (Figure 37).

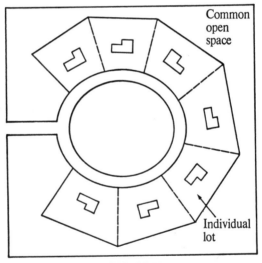

FIGURE 37

**CODE** see **building code, code of ethics, housing code.**

**CODE OF ETHICS** a statement of principles concerning the behavior of those who subscribe to the code.

**Example:** All Realtors® are required to subscribe to a *code of ethics* that defines proper professional behavior and practices that are considered unbecoming a professional real estate **agent.**

**COINSURANCE** a clause in an insurance policy stating the minimum percentage of value to be insured in order to collect the full amount of loss.

**Example:** Abel has a building worth $100,000. He figures that the maximum loss in the event of a disastrous fire will be $60,000, and insures it to $60,000. The policy has an 80% *coinsurance* clause. Since he did not insure it to 80% of its value, he will not receive the full amount of loss. The ratio he will receive is:

$$\frac{\text{amount carried}}{\substack{\text{amount should carry} \\ (\text{property value} \times \text{coinsurance rate})}} = \frac{\$60,000}{\$80,000} \times \text{loss}$$

= maximum recovery, subject to maximum carried

**COLD CANVASS** the process of contacting homeowners in an area in order to solicit **listings.**
**Example:** Abel discovers a growing demand for older homes that are close to the central business district. To increase the number of listings of such homes, Abel *cold canvasses* several older neighborhoods to determine owners' interest in selling.

**COLLAPSIBLE CORPORATION** a term that applies to some corporations that are dissolved within 3 years. The IRS treats gain on the sale or **liquidation** of the corporation as **ordinary income** to the stockholder.
**Example:** Abel forms a corporation and is the sole stockholder. The corporation builds 50 houses and estimates that each is worth $10,000 more than it costs. Abel liquidates the corporation and claims a $500,000 **capital gain** on the corporate stock. The **Internal Revenue Service** claims the gain is ordinary income because of the existence of a *collapsible corporation.*

**COLLATERAL** property pledged as **security** for a **debt.**
**Example:** A borrower who arranges a **mortgage** loan pledges the property as *collateral.*

**COLLATERALIZED MORTGAGE OBLIGATION (CMO)** a security backed by a pool of mortgage loans that may be separated into various classes with varying maturities. Note that **REMICs,** intro-

duced by the Tax Reform Act of 1986, are expected to become the standard vehicle for investing in mortgage instruments.
**Example:** Fidelity Savings and Loan pools $2 million worth of home mortgages to create a *collateralized mortgage obligation.* Investors in the *CMO* receive periodic interest and principal payments as well as return of principal as the loans are repaid.

**COLOR OF TITLE** that which appears to be good title but is not.
**Example:** Abel gives Baker a **deed** to land that he has never actually owned; Baker farms the land under a *color of title.*

**COMMERCIAL BANK** a financial institution authorized to provide a variety of financial services, including consumer and business loans (generally short-term), checking services, credit cards and savings accounts. Certain deposits at most commercial banks are insured by the **Federal Deposit Insurance Corporation.** Commercial banks may be members of the **Federal Reserve System.**
**Example:** Although *commercial banks* do make long-term mortgage loans, they have traditionally concentrated on short-term loans and are good sources for home-improvement loans and second loans secured by home equity.

**COMMERCIAL BROKER** one who **lists** and sells **commercial property,** which may include shopping, office, industrial and apartment projects. Contrast **residential broker.**
**Example:** Collins sells apartment complexes to earn a brokerage fee. She is considered a *commercial broker* despite the fact that apartments are residences.

**COMMERCIAL PROPERTY** property designed for use by retail, wholesale, office, hotel, or service users.
**Example:** An investor is interested in purchasing *commercial property* for investment. A **broker** might show the investor shopping centers, office buildings, hotels and motels, resorts or restaurants.

**COMMINGLE** to mingle or mix, such as the deposit of another's money in a broker's personal account.
**Example:** State law prohibits the *commingling* of **earnest money** deposits with a broker's own money. Most states require a separate account for earnest money held by a **broker.**

**COMMISSION** 1. an amount earned by a real estate broker for his services.
**Example:** Broker Roberts sells a $50,000 home for a client. At a 6% commission rate the client owes the broker a $3,000 *commission.*
2. the official body that enforces real estate license laws. See Figure 38.

**Example:** The State Real Estate *Commission* administers the real estate licensing examination, collects license fees, hears testimony from those who claim misconduct on the part of a licensee, and may punish offenders.

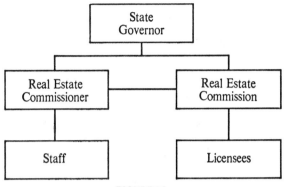

FIGURE 38

**COMMISSIONER** the head administrator of the State **Real Estate Commission.**
**Example:** As *commissioner,* Jones is responsible for maintaining records of licensees and administering examinations (Figure 38).

**COMMISSION SPLIT** the arrangement of sharing commissions earned between a sales agent and sponsoring broker, or between the selling broker and listing broker. See **cooperating broker.**
**Example:** The seller of a $100,000 house paid a $6,000 commission at closing. The *commission split* was 50–50 between the listing and selling broker. Each broker then split the fee received with the sales agent responsible for the sale, in accordance with each firm's *commission split* schedule.

**COMMITMENT** a pledge or promise; a firm agreement.
**Example:** Collins obtains a *commitment* from a **savings and loan association** for a $50,000 loan on a house she wants to buy. She is then assured of the loan so business will proceed to **closing.**

**COMMON AREAS** areas of a property that are used by all owners or tenants.

**Example:** The following are examples of *common areas.*
• the clubhouse and pool of a condominium development
• the hallways and stairs of an apartment building
• the elevators in an office building
• the mall area of a shopping center

**COMMON ELEMENTS** in a **condominium,** those portions of the property not owned individually by unit owners but in which an indivisible interest is held by all unit owners. Generally includes the grounds, parking areas, recreational facilities, and external structure of the building. See **community association.**

**Example:** In a condominium building, each resident unit owner owns the interior space within that unit. The remainder of the building and site are *common elements* enjoyed by each resident according to the condominium bylaws. The common elements are maintained by the owners' association, to which each owner pays a fee.

**COMMON LAW** the body of law that has grown out of legal customs and practices that developed in England. Common law prevails unless superseded by other law.

**Example:** In many disputes between neighboring landowners over damages from the activities of one or the other, the courts apply *common law* to reach a settlement.

**COMMUNITY ASSOCIATION** general name for any organization of property owners to oversee some common interest. In a **condominium** or planned unit development, the association has the responsibility of managing the **common elements** in the project. A **homeowners' association** may be established in a **subdivision** to enforce deed **covenants.**

**Example:** The **Community Associations Institute (CAI)** is a not-for-profit organization to assist in the establishment and operation of *community associations.* Their materials are helpful in setting up the association, maintenance of common elements, enforcing bylaws, and collecting monthly fees.

**COMMUNITY ASSOCIATIONS INSTITUTE (CAI)** a nonprofit educational and research organization concerned with the problems of managing homeowners' associations and other community associations (such as **condominium** owners associations). CAI sponsors educational seminars and publishes various handbooks and brochures.

**Address:**
Community Associations Institute
3000 South Eads St.
Arlington, Va. 22202

**COMMUNITY PROPERTY** property accumulated through joint efforts of husband and wife and owned by them in equal shares. This doctrine of ownership now exists in Arizona, California, Idaho, Louisiana, Nevada, New Mexico, Texas, and Washington State.

**Example:** Mary and Jim are getting divorced. During their marriage she inherited $100,000, which is kept in a separate bank account. All other property was acquired during their marriage. Although she never worked outside the home, half of all property acquired by joint effort during the marriage is hers under the *community property* laws of the state. Her $100,000 is entirely her separate property.

**CO-MORTGAGOR** one who signs a **mortgage** contract with another party or parties and is thereby jointly obligated to repay the loan. Generally a co-mortgagor provides some assistance in meeting the requirements of the loan and receives a share of ownership in the encumbered property.
**Example:** Brown and Jones agree to purchase and share residence in a home. They jointly apply for and receive a mortgage loan to make the purchase and, thereby, become *co-mortgagors*.
**Example:** Sims wishes to assist her son to purchase a home. Sims provides a portion of the **down payment** money and signs the loan contract as a *co-mortgagor*.

**COMPARABLES** properties that are similar to the one being sold or appraised. See **market approach.**
**Example:** A subject property is a detached, 3-bedroom house that is 30 years old and will be bought with an **FHA loan.** *Comparables* would be recently sold houses with similar styling, age, location, and financing. Slight variations in characteristics may be taken into account when making the analysis.

**COMPETENT PARTIES** persons legally capable of entering a **contract.** Must be of legal age, not be insane or a drunkard.
**Example:** If Abel is a **minor** he may generally **void** contracts he entered to buy or sell real estate because the law does not consider him to be a *competent party*.

**COMPLETION BOND** a legal instrument used to guarantee the completion of a development according to specifications. More encompassing than a **performance bond,** which assures that one party will perform under a contract on condition that the other party performs. The completion bond assures production of the development without reference to any contract and without the requirement of payment to the **contractor.**
**Example:** A developer proposes to build a **subdivision** that necessitates a rezoning. The **zoning** commission requires the developer to post a *completion bond* prior to granting a permit for the development.

**COMPONENT DEPRECIATION** dividing real estate improvements into various parts such as the roof, plumbing, electrical system, and shell, then depreciating each component separately for tax purposes. Eliminated by the 1981 Tax Act, for acquisitions after

1980.

**Example:** Abel builds a shopping center. The $1 million total cost was spent on the components with useful lives indicated in Table 10. Abel claims *component depreciation* on each part based on its estimated useful life.

**TABLE 10**

| | | |
|---|---|---|
| roof | $100,000 | 15-year life |
| plumbing | $100,000 | 20-year life |
| electrical | $100,000 | 15-year life |
| heating & A/C | $100,000 | 10-year life |
| paving | $100,000 | 15-year life |
| building foundation and structure | $500,000 | 50-year life |

**COMPOUND INTEREST** interest paid on the original principal and also on the unpaid interest that has accumulated. Contrast with **simple interest.**

**Example:** $100 deposited in a 5% savings account earns $5 interest the first year. Its second-year earnings are 5% of $105, or $5.25. Each year, interest is received on previously earned but undistributed interest, so interest compounds.

**CONCESSIONS** benefits granted by a seller/**lessor** to induce a sale/ **lease.**

**Example:** Abel is leasing out space in an office building. In order to get the Granite Insurance Co. to sign a lease, Abel offers a *concession* in the form of a $2000 remodeling allowance.

**Example:** Baker is converting apartments to **condominium** units. In order to induce tenants to purchase their units, Baker offers a *concession* of a 20% discount on the sales price, available only to tenants.

**CONDEMNATION** 1. taking private property for public use with compensation to the owner under **eminent domain.** Used by governments to acquire land for streets, parks, schools, etc., and by utilities to acquire necessary property. Compare **appropriation.**

**Example:** Abel's home is in the **right-of-way** of the new highway. When Abel refused to sell, the highway department acquired the property through *condemnation*, paying Abel an amount based on a **fair market value** appraisal.

2. declaring a structure unfit for use.

**Example:** The state health department, acting through its *condemnation* powers, prevented use of an old, dilapidated shack because of violations of the **housing code.**

**CONDITION(S)** provision(s) in a contract that some or all terms of the contract will be altered or cease to exist upon a certain event.

See **cancellation clause.**

**Example:** If a house is destroyed by fire before closing, the buyer is not obligated to complete the purchase.

**Example:** If a loan that is described as a *condition* cannot be arranged, the buyer is not required to complete the transaction and may receive a refund of any **earnest money.**

**CONDITIONAL COMMITMENT** an agreement by a lender to provide a loan to a qualified borrower, within a specified time period, but without stating who the borrower will be.

**Example:** The Solid Rock Development Company is completing a project with 200 condominiums. They arrange financing with the Trusty Mortgage Company to provide 90% loan-to-value financing at a 10% interest rate to qualified buyers. Trusty Mortgage issues a *conditional commitment* and will make such loans to qualified buyers.

**CONDITIONAL OFFER** purchase contract tendered to the seller that stipulates one or more requirements to be satisfied before the purchaser is obligated to buy.

**Example:** Baker offers to buy Collins' farm, conditioned on its rezoning for use as a shopping center prior to purchase. If it is not rezoned, Baker can get the earnest money, tendered with the *conditional offer,* refunded.

**CONDITIONAL SALES CONTRACT** a contract for the sale of property stating that the seller retains **title** until the conditions of the contract have been fulfilled.

**Example:** A **contract for deed** or a **land contract** is a *conditional sales contract.* Until the buyer makes full payment, the seller retains title to the property.

**CONDOMINIUM** a system of ownership of individual units in a multiunit structure, combined with joint ownership of commonly used property (sidewalks, hallways, stairs, etc.). See **common elements.**

**Example:** A midrise *condominium* (Figure 39).

**CONDOMINIUM OWNERS ASSOCIATION** an organization of all unit owners in a **condominium** to oversee the **common elements** and enforce the bylaws. See **community association.**

**Example:** When Vivian and Paul Carter purchase a unit in the condominium, they are automatically members of the *owners association.* As such, they are entitled to vote on decisions before the association regarding changes in bylaws, development and repair of common elements, and other matters. They are also required to pay a monthly fee to cover expenses of the association.

FIGURE 39

**CONFORMITY PRINCIPLE** an **appraisal** principle that holds that property tends to reach maximum value when the neighborhood is reasonably homogeneous in social and economic activity.
**Example:** Under the *conformity principle*, a house that cost $300,000 in a neighborhood of $50,000 homes is not worth as much as if it were in a neighborhood of $300,000 homes.

**CONSIDERATION** anything of value given to induce entering into a **contract;** it may be money, personal services, love and affection, etc.
**Example:** Abel ran out of gasoline while driving down the highway. Baker, a passing motorist, gave him a ride to the nearest filling station. Abel promised Baker a $50,000 tract of land for his help, but Baker cannot enforce the promise because of the absence of *consideration*.

**CONSTANT PAYMENT LOAN** a loan on which equal payments are made periodically so as to pay off the debt when the last payment is made. See **level payment mortgage, variable payment plan.**
**Example:** Baker obtains a *constant payment loan* to purchase a home. The loan requires a payment of $450.00 per month (principal and interest) for 30 years. At the end of 30 years, the principal balance will be zero.

**CONSTRUCTION LOAN** one that finances **subdivision** costs and/or improvements to real estate. See **building loan agreements.**
**Example:** Collins plans to develop an office building. She receives a **commitment** for permanent financing and approaches a **commercial bank** for a *construction loan*. The bank agrees to advance money as construction progresses (Figure 40).

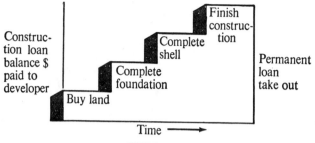

FIGURE 40

**CONSTRUCTIVE NOTICE** the law presumes that everyone has knowledge of a fact when the fact is a matter of public record.
**Example:** Abel buys land from Baker, believing that Baker is the owner. Since Carter's **deed** had been properly recorded, Abel had *constructive notice* of Carter's ownership and cannot claim ownership against Carter.

**CONTIGUOUS** actually touching; contiguous properties have a common boundary.
**Example:** Lots A and B in Figure 41 are *contiguous*. Lot C is **adjacent** to A and B but not *contiguous*.

**CONTINGENCY CLAUSE** see **condition.**

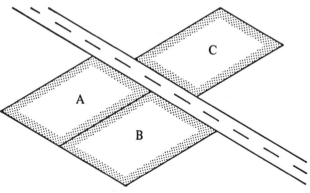

FIGURE 41

**CONTOUR MAP** a map that displays the **topography** of the **site.** A map with contour lines that indicate various elevations

**Example:** A *contour map* of a building **site** (Figure 42).

FIGURE 42

**CONTRACT** an agreement between competent parties to do or not to do certain things for a **consideration.**
**Example:** To have a valid *contract* for the sale of real estate there must be:
1. an **offer**
2. an **acceptance**
3. **competent parties**
4. **consideration**
5. **legal purpose**
6. **written documentation**
7. **description of the property**
8. **signatures by principals** or their **attorney-in-fact**

**CONTRACT FOR DEED** same as **land contract.**

**CONTRACT OF SALE** same as **agreement of sale.**

**CONTRACTOR** one who contracts to supply specific goods or services, generally in connection with development of a property.
**Example:** Abel is developing a residential **subdivision.** In the

course of the project, Abel secures the services of various *contractors,* such as landscapers, carpenters, plumbers, and architects.

**CONTRACT PRICE (TAX)** in an **installment sale,** for tax purposes, generally the selling price less existing mortgages assumed by the buyer. See also **installment sale.**
**Example:** Abel sells land for $100,000 subject to an existing $60,000 first mortgage. Abel receives $5,000 cash in the year of sale and a $35,000 second mortgage from the buyer. The *contract price* is $40,000. Note, if Abel's **adjusted tax basis** in the land exceeds the first mortgage, such excess is a payment in the year and reduces the contract price.

**CONTRACT RATE** same as **face interest rate.**

**CONTRACT RENT** the amount of rent that has been set forth in a contract. Contrast with **economic rent.**
**Example:** Abel signs a lease requiring rent payments of $400 per month. The *contract rent* is $400 per month.

**CONTRIBUTION** a principle of valuation that states that the value of any portion of a property is determined by how it affects the performance of the total property. Therefore, a property is considered a combination of features, each of which adds something to the total value based on its *contribution* to the property's usefulness.
**Example:** The value of an improvement can be appraised based on the principle of *contribution.* If a swimming pool adds $25,000 to the value of a house in a prestigious San Diego neighborhood, then its *contribution* is $25,000 regardless of what it costs to build.

**CONVENTIONAL LOAN** 1. a mortgage loan other than one guaranteed by the Veterans Administration or insured by the **Federal Housing Administration.** See **VA loan, FHA loan.**
**Example:** Abel applies for a *conventional loan* from his **savings and loan association.** If Abel wants to borrow more than 80% of the value of the mortgaged property, he must buy private **mortgage insurance.**
2. A fixed-rate, fixed-term mortgage loan.
**Example: Alternative mortgage instruments,** by commonly used definition, are not *conventional loans.*
**Example:** A *conventional mortage loan* requires a fixed principal and interest payment over its term.

**CONVERSION** 1. changing property to a different use or form of ownership, such as when **apartments** are transformed to **condominiums.**
**Example:** A **condominium** *conversion* allows existing tenants to remain until the expiration of their **lease** and often allows them to

purchase the unit at terms more favorable than those offered to general public.

2. the taking away of property that belongs to another person. See also **involuntary conversion.**

**Example:** An illegal *conversion* of the landlord's property occurred when the tenant removed the landlord's light fixture from the apartment.

3. a change in the ownership form of a **savings and loan association.**

**Example:** Friendly Savings applies to the **Federal Home Loan Bank** Board for *conversion* from a **mutual savings bank** to a stockholder-owned company.

**CONVEY** to **deed** or transfer **title** to another.

    **Example:** At the **closing,** Abel will *convey* the property to Baker.

**CONVEYANCE** the transfer of the **title** of real estate from one to another; the means or medium by which title of real estate is transferred.

    **Example:** A **warranty deed** is most often used as a *conveyance* at the **closing.**

**CO-OP** 1. an arrangement between 2 real estate **agents** that generally results in splitting the **commission** between them.

    **Example:** Abel obtains a **listing** contract on a piece of property. Baker agrees to find a buyer in exchange for a portion of the commission. Abel and Baker have arranged a *co-op* agreement.

2. a type of housing in which each tenant is a shareholder in **a corporation** that owns the building. Also termed **cooperative.**

    **Example:** Upon moving to New York, Abel obtains an apartment in a *co-op.* This requires purchase of shares in the apartment corporation.

**COOPERATING BROKER** one who agrees to share the **commission** with another broker. See **commission split.**

    **Example:** The broker who secured the listing is a *cooperating broker* with the one who brought the purchaser. The brokers agree to a **commission split.**

**COOPERATIVE** a type of corporate ownership of real property whereby stockholders of the corporation are entitled to use a certain dwelling unit or other units of space. Special income tax laws allow the tenant stockholders to deduct interest and property taxes paid by the corporation. See **co-op.**

    **Example:** Apartment buildings in New York City are occasionally converted to *cooperatives.* In simple terms, this requires forming a

**corporation** to own the building and selling shares to those who wish to live in the building.

**CORPORATION** a legal entity properly registered with the secretary of state. Can have **limited liability,** perpetual life, freely transferable shares, and centralized management.
**Example:** Abel wants to start a real estate **brokerage** business with $10,000 of his own money. He asks his attorney to form a *corporation* with Abel as the sole stockholder. The corporation may **bankrupt** but Abel's other assets are not affected.

**CORPOREAL** visible or tangible real or personal property.
**Example:** Buildings, pavement, fences, and the like are *corpo--al.* **Easements** are incorporeal.

**COSIGNER** same as **accommodation party.**

**COST APPROACH** a method of **appraising** property based on the **depreciated** reproduction or replacement cost (new) of improvements, plus the market value of the **site.**
**Example:** Table 11:

**TABLE 11**

| | | |
|---|---:|---:|
| Reproduction cost (new) | | $100,000 |
| Minus: Physical deterioration | $25,000 | |
| Functional obsolescence | $10,000 | |
| Economic obsolescence | $5,000 | |
| Total accrued depreciation | $40,000 | −$40,000 |
| Depreciated value of improvements | | $60,000 |
| Add: Site value | | $20,000 |
| Value indicated by *cost approach* | | $80,000 |

**COST OF LIVING INDEX** an indicator of the current price level for goods and services related to some base year.
**Example:** The Consumer Price Index (CPI), published by the Bureau of Labor Statistics, indicates that the price level for goods and services in 1986 was 330.1 This means that, on average, prices were 230% higher in 1986 than in 1967 (when the CPI was 100). A **lease** made in 1967 with initial annual payments of $1000 and indexed to the CPI, would call for payments of $3,330 in 1986. See **index lease.**

**COTENANCY** any of a number of forms of multiple ownership such as **tenancy in common** and **joint tenancy.**

**Example:** Abel and Baker decide to invest in a parcel of land. Both names are to be on the **deed.** Abel and Baker join together as *cotenants;* each owns one half of the property.

**COUNSELING** the act of advising clients on a variety of real estate investment or development matters.
**Example:** Abel wishes to invest in an office building. Baker offers *counseling* by advising Abel on how to select a property, how to legally structure the investment and how to maximize after-tax returns from the investment.

**COUNSELOR OF REAL ESTATE (CRE)** a member of the **American Society of Real Estate Counselors (ASREC).** Membership is based on experience and professional conduct as a real estate counselor.

**COUNTEROFFER** rejection of an **offer** to buy or sell, with a simultaneous substitute offer.
**Example:** A property is put on the market. An investor offers $75,000 in cash. The owner rejects the offer but submits a *counteroffer* to sell for $80,000. Offers and counteroffers may be negotiated on factors other than price, e.g., **financing** arrangements, **apportionment** of **closing costs,** inclusion of personal property.

**COVENANT NOT TO COMPETE** a clause in an agreement where one party promises not to offer to sell or produce the same goods and services in proximity to the other party.
**Example:** Abel sells his realty firm to Baker. In the sales contract, Abel gives Baker a *covenant not to compete.* This bars Abel from opening a competing realty firm in the same immediate area as Baker.

**COVENANTS** promises written into **deeds** and other instruments agreeing to performance or nonperformance of certain acts, or requiring or preventing certain uses of the property.
**Examples:** Deed *covenants* are often used to:
• maintain a land parcel in a specified use, such as residential
• enforce architectural and design standards
• control the **density** of future development
• prohibit certain practices, such as the sale of liquor

**CREATIVE FINANCING** any **financing** arrangement other than a traditional **mortgage** from a third-party lending institution.
**Example:** *Creative financing* devices include:
• loans from the seller
• **balloon payment** loans
• **wraparound mortgages**
• **assumption of mortgage**

- **sale-leasebacks**
- **land contracts**
- alternative mortgage instruments

**CREDIT** 1. in finance, the availability of money.
  **Example:** When money and *credit* are readily available, it is easier to buy real estate. Credit policy is determined to a large extent by the **Federal Reserve System.**
  2. in accounting, a **liability** or **equity** entered on the right side of the ledger.
  **Example:** In **closing statements,** the *credit* column shows what is due and payable. The buyer is *credited* with amounts paid, the seller is *credited* with the price of the real property and prepaid items.


**CREDITOR** one who is owed money.
  **Examples:** *Creditors* include:
- bond holders
- loan companies
- mortgage lenders


**CREDIT RATING (REPORT)** an evaluation of a person's capacity (or history) of debt repayment. Generally available for individuals from a local retail credit association; for businesses by companies such as Dunn & Bradstreet; and for publicly held bonds by Moody's, Standard & Poors, and Fitch's. Individuals have access to their own files.
  **Example:** Goodmoney Savings Association received and studied the *credit report* on Collins before they issued her a mortgage loan. The report stated credit limits at various stores, current balances, and repayment terms in days. It would have noted **defaults** and slow repayments.


**CUL-DE-SAC** a street with an intersection on one end and a closed turning area on the other. Often valued in the design of residential **subdivisions** for the privacy provided to homes on the street.
  **Example:** A **subdivision** plan showing a *cul-de-sac* (Figure 43).


**CURABLE DEPRECIATION** **depreciation** or deterioration that can be corrected at a cost less than the value that will be added.
  **Example:** An apartment owner estimates that remodeling the dwelling units would allow an increase in rent of $20 per month. The cost of remodeling is $1,500 per unit. The prevailing **gross rent multiplier** in the neighborhood is 100. Thus the value added by remodeling is $100 \times \$20 = \$2,000$ per unit. Thus, the outmoded appearance of the units is a form of *curable depreciation*.

FIGURE 43

**CURRENT YIELD** a measurement of investment returns based on the percentage relationship of annual cash income to the investment cost. The formula is

$$\text{Current yield} = \frac{\text{current income}}{\text{investment cost}}$$

**Example:** Abel purchases a parking lot for $10,000. It provides $5,000 of parking revenues each year. Property taxes and insurance total $3,500, leaving $1,500 of annual before-income-tax **cash flow.** The *current yield* is 15%:

$$\frac{\$1,500}{\$10,000} = 15\%$$

**CURTESY** the right of a husband to all or part of his deceased wife's realty regardless of the provisions of her will. Exists in only a few states.
**Example:** Under the *curtesy* law of some states, a widower may claim a **life estate** to part of the property left by his deceased wife, provided they had a child in their marriage.

**CUSTOM BUILDER** one who builds unique houses; contrast with **tract house.**

**Example:** Abel, a *custom builder*, erects unique homes from plans provided by architects and buyers. Each home is unique, whether built for a specific customer or speculatively.

# D

**DAMAGES** the amount recoverable by a person who has been injured in any manner, including physical harm, property damage, or violated rights, through the act or default of another.
**Example:** Abel forfeited his **earnest money** to the owner of property as *damages* for failing to purchase as agreed.

**DEALER (TAX)** one who buys and sells for his or her own account. The merchandise is **inventory,** consequently any gain on the sale is **ordinary income.**
**Example:** Davis purchases mobile homes from several manufacturers, and sells them to her customers. Davis is a *dealer* and all gains from sales are ordinary income.

**DEBENTURE** an unsecured **note** or **bond.**
**Example:** Abel invests in *debentures* of the XYZ Corporation; Baker invests in a **first mortgage** on a building owned by XYZ Corporation. The XYZ Corporation **bankrupts.** Ultimately Baker receives full payment for the mortgage upon the **foreclosure sale.** Abel is a general creditor and receives only 18 cents per dollar owed to him.

**DEBIT** 1. in a **closing statement** (settlement), an item that is charged to a party. Contrast with **credit.**
**Examples:** The buyer is charged with these typical *debits:*
• purchase price
• taxes prepaid by seller
• deed recording fees
The seller is charged with these typical *debits:*
• cost to **retire** existing mortgage principal.
• **accrued interest** on mortgage being relieved
• **termite inspection** fee
2. in accounting, entries on the left side of the general ledger. Contrast with **credit.**
**Examples:** Debits include:
• acquisition cost of **assets**
• amounts of deductible expenses

**DEBT** an obligation to pay.
**Example:** Abel borrows $1,000 from Baker and thereby incurs a *debt.*

**DEBT COVERAGE RATIO** the relationship between **net operating income** (NOI) and **annual debt service** (ADS). Often used as an **underwriting** criterion for **income property** mortgage loans.
**Example:** Annual debt service for a mortgage loan on a certain office building is $10,000. The property generates $25,000 in annual gross rent, and requires $7,000 for expenses of operation, leaving $18,000 net operating income. The *debt coverage ratio* is 1.80, calculated by the following formula:

$$\frac{\text{NOI}}{\text{ADS}} = \frac{\$18,000}{\$10,000} = 1.8$$

**DEBT SERVICE** see **annual debt service.**

**DECLARATION** 1. formal pleadings by a plaintiff as to the facts and circumstances that gave rise to his cause of action. Also, a statement made out of court.
**Example:** The unhappy land buyer offered a *declaration* explaining the claim that the property was misrepresented.
2. a legal document used to create a **condominium.** Includes a description of the property and the uses to which it is restricted, a description of individual ownership units, **common elements,** and procedures for amending the declaration.
**Example:** A developer constructs apartments and wishes to market them as a condominium. He prepares and records a *declaration*, which describes the division of individual and common ownership, a set of bylaws and a master **deed** for the project.

**DECLARATION OF TRUST** a written statement by a **trustee** to acknowledge that the property is held for the benefit of another.
**Example:** A *declaration of trust* was signed by a **trustee** to state that certain valuable land was being held in **trust** for certain orphaned children.

**DECLINING BALANCE DEPRECIATION** a method of **depreciation,** often used for income tax purposes, whereby a rate is applied to the remaining balance to derive the depreciation deduction. Compare **accelerated depreciation.**
**Example:** Table 12 shows the depreciation schedule for a property with a **tax basis** of $10,000 and **depreciable** life of 5 years, using the 125% *declining balance* method:

**DECREE** an order issued by one in authority; a court order or decision.
**Example:** The court issued a *decree* stating that Abel owed $10,000 to Baker for failing to perform under a **contract.**

**DEDICATION** the gift of land by its owner for a public use and the acceptance of it by a unit of government. See also **appropriation.**

**TABLE 12**

| Year | Remaining balance | Rate* | Annual deduction |
|------|-------------------|-------|------------------|
| 1 | $10,000 | 0.25 | $2,500 |
| 2 | 7,500 | 0.25 | 1,875 |
| 3 | 5,625 | 0.25 | 1,406 |
| 4 | 4,219 | 0.25 | 1,055 |
| 5 | 3,164 | 0.25 | 791 |

*A 5-year life results in 20% per year depreciation using the straight-line method. The 125% declining balance method results in an annual percentage of 25 for an asset with this life (125% of 20% = 25%).

**Example:** A **developer** of a large **subdivision** makes to the local government a *dedication* of the streets, the flood-prone areas and one **acre** of land for a public school. This obligates the government to **maintenance** of these areas and relieves the developer of a property tax liability on the dedicated lands.

**DEED** a written document, properly signed and delivered, that conveys **title** to real property. See **general warranty deed, quitclaim deed, special warranty deed.**
**Example:** In exchange for the agreed upon terms of a **contract**, including the purchase price, at **closing** the seller delivers a *deed* to the buyer.

**DEED IN LIEU OF FORECLOSURE** the act of giving property back to a lender without **foreclosure.**
**Example:** Abel, a builder, has a **construction loan** with a $100,000 balance against the house he is building. He offers the house for sale at $100,000 but no one buys it. He does not have the cash to continue to pay interest on the construction loan, and is in **default.** The lender asks for a *deed in lieu of foreclosure.*

**DEED OF TRUST** an instrument used in many states in lieu of a **mortgage.** Legal title to the property is **vested** in one or more **trustees** to secure the repayment of the loan.
**Example:** Abel borrows $50,000 on his property in Texas from the Good Money Savings Association. He gives a *deed of trust* that is held in the name of I.M. Honest, a trustee. If Abel **defaults** it will not be difficult for Good Money to gain possession.

**DEED RESTRICTION** a clause in a deed that limits the use of land. See **covenants.**
**Example:** A deed might stipulate that alcoholic beverages are not to be sold on the land for 20 years. This is a *deed restriction.*

**DEFAULT** failure to fulfill an obligation or promise, or to perform specified acts.
**Example:** The **contract** required the buyer to close within 3 business days. His failure to appear at **closing** constituted a *default* under the contract.

**DEFEASANCE** a clause in a **mortgage** that gives the borrower the right to redeem the property after **default,** usually by paying the full indebtedness and fees incurred.
**Example:** Graham defaults on the **balloon payment** of the mortgage. Three days later she pays the balance in cash. The *defeasance* clause allows her to redeem the property. It overrides the provision that grants the property to the lender upon default.

**DEFECT IN TITLE** any recorded **instrument** that would prevent a grantor from giving a **clear title.**
**Example:** A **mechanic's lien** that was recorded against the property when it was remodeled was a *defect in title*. The grantor had to clear the **lien** by paying the amount due the electrician who filed the lien.

**DEFENDANT** the party sued in an action at law.
**Example:** Abel brings suit against a former landlord, Baker, for refusing to return a **security deposit.** In the suit, Baker is the *defendant*.

**DEFERRED MAINTENANCE** in appraisal, a type of physical **depreciation** owing to lack of normal upkeep.
**Example:** The appraiser found the following examples of *deferred maintenance* on the subject property:
• broken window glass
• missing roof shingles
• peeling paint
• broken guttering

**DEFERRED PAYMENTS** payments to be made at some future date.
**Example:** On a **graduated payment mortgage** the **principal** payments and some interest payments are *deferred* for the first 3 to 5 years.

**DEFICIENCY JUDGMENT** a court order stating that the borrower stills owes money when the **security** for a loan does not entirely satisfy a defaulted debt.
**Example:** Upon **default** by the **mortgagor,** a lender **forecloses on** the mortgage. The unpaid balance of the loan is $60,000. The property is sold at public **auction** and brings $50,000. The lender then seeks a *deficiency judgment* against the mortgagor to recover the $10,000 shortage.

**DELAYED (TAX-FREE) EXCHANGE** a transaction in which a property is traded for the promise to provide a replacement **like-kind property** in the near future. The Tax Reform Act of 1984 allows investment real estate or real property used in a trade or business to be sold with the tax on the gain deferred, provided replacement property is identified within 45 days and closed within 180 days. Other strict requirements must be observed. See also **tax-free exchange.**

**DELIVERY** transfer of the **possession** of a thing from one person to another.
**Example:** A man dies leaving no will. A search of his possessions uncovers a **deed** giving valuable land to his nephew. Since the deed has not been *delivered,* the court ruled that the land does not belong to the nephew.

**DEMAND LOAN** a loan that may be called by the lender at any time.
**Example:** Abel borrows $10,000 from a bank on a *demand loan* and uses the cash for the downpayment on a parcel of land. The bank may call in the loan and Abel may be forced to sell the property at a distressed price to meet the *demand loan.*

**DEMISED PREMISES** property subject to lease.
**Example:** An apartment is rented under a written lease. In the lease, the apartment is referred to as the *demised premises.*

**DEMOGRAPHIC** pertaining to characteristics of the population, such as race, sex, age, household size, and to population growth and **density.**
**Example:** As a first step in estimating the demand for new housing units, a **developer** commissions a *demographic* study. The study describes the current population density and rate of growth, the age distribution of the population, and average size of households in the local **market area.**

**DEMOLITION** destruction and removal of an existing structure from a **site;** necessary to prepare a site for new construction.
**Example:** A block of old houses in the city is to be converted into a new shopping mall. This conversion will require *demolition* of the houses, site preparation and construction of the mall.

**DENSITY** the intensity of a land use. See also **land use intensity.**
**Example:** A 10-acre **subdivision** contains 30 single-family houses. The *density* is 3 dwelling units per **acre.**

**DENSITY ZONING** laws that restrict **land use intensity.**
**Example:** A **zoning ordinance** states that all zones designated "R-2" may contain no more than 4 **detached housing** units per **acre.** This is an example of *density zoning.*

**DEPLETION** a **tax deduction** to account for reduced **land** value due to removing minerals.
**Example:** The $10,000 tax deduction for *depletion* was allowed because coal was being removed and the land would become virtually worthless when all of the coal was gone.

**DEPOSIT** money paid in **good faith** to assure performance of a contract. Deposits are commonly used with **sales contracts** and **leases.** If the person who put up the deposit fails to perform, the deposit is forfeited, unless conditions in the contract allow a refund. **Brokers** are to put deposits in a separate checking account pending completion of the contract. See **earnest money.**
**Example:** Whitman presented a $1,000 check as an earnest money *deposit* on a home she would buy provided she could get a 10% rate, 30-year loan for 80% of the price. The broker deposited the check in an **escrow account,** and refunded it when Whitman could not arrange said loan.

**DEPOSIT ACCOUNT** an arrangement whereby an individual or organization may place cash under the safekeeping of a financial institution. It is understood that the institution may invest the cash and pay the depositor a specified amount of interest and that the depositor can reclaim the full value of the account according to the agreed upon procedures governing the account.
**Example:** Town Savings maintains several types of *deposit accounts* for the benefit of its depositors. The accounts provide funds which are used to make mortgage loans.

**DEPOSITORY INSTITUTIONS DEREGULATION AND MONETARY CONTROL ACT** federal law that represents significant decontrol of federally regulated banks and savings institutions, including gradual phase out of limits on interest rates paid on passbook accounts. **(Regulation Q).**
**Example:** The *Depository Institutions Deregulation and Monetary Control Act* is a major effort to reform the nation's banking regulations. Among its effects are:
• standardized reserve requirements for banks and **savings and loan associations**
• phase out of deposit interest rate limitations
• authorization for interest-bearing checking accounts
• increased ability for savings and loan associations to make consumer loans
• reduced applicability of state **usury** laws

**DEPRECIABLE BASIS** see basis (tax); see **adjusted tax basis.**

**DEPRECIABLE LIFE** 1. for tax purposes, the number of years over which the cost of an **asset** may be spread. See **accelerated cost recovery.**

**Example:** Abel buys an apartment complex. For tax purposes the building has a 27½-year *depreciable life*.

2. for **appraisal** purposes, the estimated useful life of an asset.

**Example:** Baker buys an apartment complex. An appraiser estimates that the roof will last for 15 years, so it has a 15-year *depreciable life*.

**DEPRECIABLE REAL ESTATE (TAX) realty** that is subject to deductions for **depreciation.** It generally includes property used in a trade or business, or an investment, subject to an allowance for depreciation under **Section 167** of the **Internal Revenue Code.**

**Example:** Abel buys an apartment complex for $1 million. Of the purchase price, $100,000 is the value of the land, the remaining $900,000 is the value of *depreciable real estate*. Abel uses the **straight-line depreciation** method and a 27½-year remaining depreciable life.

**DEPRECIATION (ACCOUNTING)** allocating the cost of an **asset** over its estimated **useful life.**

**Example:** Collins buys a warehouse for $550,000. Of the price, $50,000 is for land, which is not subject to depreciation. Of the remaining $500,000, she claims accounting *depreciation* of $10,000 per year over a 50-year **depreciable life,** despite the fact that the property is expected to increase in value because of the location of the land.

**DEPRECIATION (APPRAISAL)** a charge against the **reproduction cost** (new) of an **asset** for the estimated wear and **obsolescence.** Depreciation may be physical, functional, or economic.

**Example:** The estimated reproduction cost (new) of a theater being appraised is $500,000. **Wear and tear** sustained during its life is estimated at $100,000. Functional obsolescence caused by lack of air-conditioning and high ceilings causes an estimated loss of $100,000. It is in a decaying area of the city estimated at causing $100,000 of economic obsolescence. Total *depreciation* is estimated at $300,000.

**DEPRECIATION RECAPTURE** when real property is sold at a gain and **accelerated depreciation** had been claimed, the owner may be required to pay a tax at ordinary rates to the extent of the excess accelerated depreciation. Excess depreciation on residential real estate after 1980 is recaptured; all depreciation on commercial property after 1980 is recaptured when an accelerated method had been used, under **Section 1250** of the **Internal Revenue Code.** See Figure 44.

**Note:** The importance of *depreciation recapture* for real estate was minimized by the Tax Reform Act of 1986 which mandated straight-line depreciation for buildings bought after 1986, and eliminated favorable tax rates on long-term capital gains after 1987.

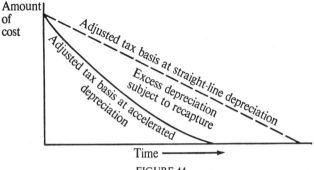

FIGURE 44

**DEPTH TABLES** a set of percentages indicating the proportion of
site value attributable to each additional amount of depth in the lot.
**Example:** A commonly used *depth table* (Figure 45).

FIGURE 45

**DESCRIPTION** formal depiction of the dimensions and location of a
property; generally included in **deeds, leases, sales contracts,** and
**mortgage** contracts for **real property.** See **government rectangular
survey, lot and block, metes and bounds,** for specific methods of
legal description. See also **plat.**
**Example:** A **sales contract** is executed. A portion of the contract
contains a *description* of the property that simply states the street
address of the house. In the deed conveyed at **closing** a more pre-
cise metes and bounds *description* is included based upon a **survey**
of the property.

**DESCRIPTIVE MEMORANDUM** a term used to describe an offering circular of property or securities when a **prospectus** is not
required.

**Example:** A **syndicator** prepared a *descriptive memorandum* about the property after receiving an exemption from registering the offering by the **Securities and Exchange Commission (SEC)**.

**DESCENT** the acquisition of property by an heir when the deceased leaves no will.
**Example:** Abel dies without having prepared a will. His wife and son are awarded **title** to Abel's estate by the courts. They are said to acquire title by *descent*.

**DETACHED HOUSING** **residential** buildings in which each **dwelling** unit is surrounded by freestanding walls and is generally sited on a separate lot. Contrast with **duplex, row house, town house.**
**Example:** Figure 46.

Detached housing                    Townhouses

FIGURE 46

**DEVELOPER** one who transforms **raw land** to **improved** property by use of labor, capital, and **entrepreneur** efforts.
**Example:** Abel buys 25 acres of land for $10,000 per **acre**. After putting in streets and utilities, dividing it into 100 lots, and building homes on each lot, Abel sells the homes. Abel is a *developer*.

**DEVELOPMENT** the process of placing improvements on or to a parcel of land. Such improvements may include drainage, utilities, subdividing, access, buildings and any combination of these elements. Also the project where such improvements are being made.
**Example:** Baker, a developer, acquired a large parcel of land and began the preparation of detailed plans and securing of government permits. Later, the site will be prepared and construction will commence. The *development* will be the first phase of a large multi-use subdivision.

**DEVELOPMENT LOAN** same as **construction loan.**

**DEVISE** a gift of real estate by **will** or last testament. Compare **bequeath.**
**Example:** In his will, Abel *devises* his home to his daughter. He **bequeaths** his automobile to his son.

**DEVISEE** one who inherits real estate through a will.
**Example:** Abel dies. The *devisee* in his will receives his land.

**DIRECTIONAL GROWTH** the location or direction toward which a city is growing.

**Example:** the *directional growth* of Boom Town is toward the northeast (Figure 47).

FIGURE 47

**DIRECT REDUCTION MORTGAGE** a loan that requires both **interest** and **principal** with each payment such that the level payment will be adequate for **amortization** over the loan's term. See **level payment mortgage.**

**Example:** Collins borrows $50,000 at 10% interest over a 30-year term, using a *direct reduction mortgage*. Her monthly principal and interest payment of $438.79 will fully amortize (pay off) the loan over 30 years.

**DISCHARGE IN BANKRUPTCY** the release of a bankrupt party from the obligation to repay **debts** that were, or might have been, proved in a **bankruptcy** proceeding.

**Example:** A real estate resort **developer** filed for bankruptcy. He owned 2,000 unsold vacation lots, and owed $2 million on land acquisition loans. The court granted a *discharge in bankruptcy* for these loans and allowed the creditor to dispose of the lots.

**DISCLAIMER** 1. a statement whereby responsibility is rejected.

**Example:** Abel, a certified public accountant, is asked to write up the **financial statements** of Baker without testing (auditing) the validity of the statements. Abel's report provides a *disclaimer* in which he states that he did not examine the financial statements and does not accept responsibility for their accuracy.

2. Renunciation of ownership of **property.**

**Example:** Because it was no longer profitable, Baker *disclaimed* apartments that had become dilapidated.

**DISCOUNT** the difference between the **face amount** of an obligation and the amount advanced or received.

**Example:** Abel sells land for $100,000 and receives a $60,000 mortgage at 7% interest as part of the payment. Abel then sells the mortgage (the right to collect payments on the mortgage) at a $15,000 *discount,* thereby receiving $45,000.

**DISCOUNT BROKER** a licensed broker who provides brokerage services for a lower commission than that typical in the market. Generally, the services provided are less extensive than those of a full service broker. Many discount brokers charge a flat fee rather than a percentage of the selling price. See **flat fee broker.**
**Example:** Henson, a *discount broker,* offers to list a property for a 3% commission. Henson will refer prospective buyers to the seller and prepare a sales contract. The seller is expected to show the property and negotiate directly with the buyer.

**DISCOUNTED CASH FLOW** a method of investment analysis in which anticipated future cash income from the investment is estimated and converted into a rate of return on initial investment based on the time value of money. In addition, when a required rate of return is specified, a net present value of the investment can be estimated.
**Example:** An asset may be purchased for $1,000. It is expected to generate $100 in income per year for 10 years, after which time it is expected to sell for $1,200. *Discounted cash flow* analysis shows that the internal rate of return on the investment is expected to be 11.2% per year.

**DISCOUNTED LOAN** one that is offered or traded for less than its face value. See **discount, discount points.**
**Example:** When the Deavers sold their house, they accepted a second mortgage as part of the purchase price. The Deavers then sold the loan to an investor for 75% of its face value. The purchaser of this *discounted loan* is entitled to all interest and principal payments stipulated in the mortgage contract.

**DISCOUNT POINTS** amounts paid to the lender (usually by the seller) at the time of origination of a loan, to account for the difference between the market interest rate and the lower face rate of the note (often required when **VA loans** are used).
**Example:** At the time of loan application, conventional mortgages are being made at 15%. The maximum rate on an FHA loan is 14½% with 4 *discount points* added to compensate for the lower face rate of interest. If the loan is for $50,000, the points will require an additional payment of $2,000 at closing. (The 4 points equals 4% of $50,000, which is $2,000.)

**DISCOUNT RATE** 1. a **compound interest** rate used to convert expected future income into a present value. See **capitalization rate, present value of annuity, present value of one.**
**Example:** A *discount rate* of 10% applied to a $100 sum expected to be received in one year results in a present value of $90.90. (The **present value of one** for one year is 0.909.)

2. the rate charged member banks who borrow from the **Federal Reserve System.** Same as **rediscount rate.**
   **Example:** See **rediscount rate.**

**DISCRIMINATION** applying special treatment (generally unfavorable) to an individual solely on the basis of the person's race, religion, or sex.
**Example:** Abel is accused of *discrimination* under the Fair Housing Laws because he refused to rent apartments to nonwhite families.

**DISINTERMEDIATION** situation when deposits are removed from a financial intermediary, such as a **savings and loan association,** and invested in other **assets,** generally for the purpose of obtaining higher yields.
**Example:** Figure 48.

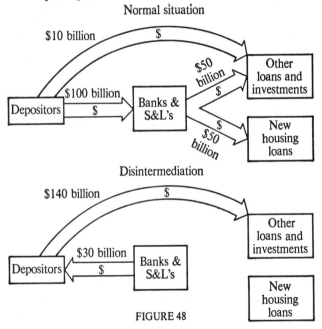

Normal situation

FIGURE 48

**DISPOSSESS PROCEEDINGS** the legal process by a **landlord** to remove a **tenant** and regain possession of property. See **eviction.**
**Example:** After not having received rent for 3 months, the landlord began *dispossess proceedings* to eject the tenant.

**DISTRAINT** the legal right of a **landlord** to seize a tenant's personal property to satisfy payment of back rent.
**Example:** Abel is 6 months in **arrears** on rent. Landlord Baker obtains a court order to seize Abel's furniture to satisfy the rent due. Baker is exercising his right of *distraint*.
See **workout.**
**Example:** An **apartment building** is financed with **mortgages** that require $25,000 in **annual debt service.** Because of high vacancies and rising expenses, **net operating income** drops to $20,000. The owners have ceased making loan payments because their resources are insufficient to pay the **negative cash flow.** The property is considered *distressed property.*

**DISTRESSED PROPERTY** real estate that is under **foreclosure** or impending foreclosure because of insufficient income production.

**DOCUMENTARY EVIDENCE** evidence in the form of written or printed papers.
**Example:** During court proceedings, a **sales contract** was entered in the record as *documentary evidence* of the agreement made between the **plaintiff** and the **defendant.**

**DOMICILE** the state in which one makes his or her principal residence.
**Example:** Mason's job requires her to travel throughout the United States. Although she owns property in several states, Mason's *domicile* is New York, where she has her principal residence. Mason is subject to the laws of New York concerning automobile registration, voting rights, payment of taxes, and other matters.

**DOMINANT TENEMENT** land that benefits from an **easement** on another property. The other property, which usually is **adjacent,** is the **servient tenant.**
**Example:** In Figure 49 the owner of Parcel A has a right-of-way easement to the road by going across Parcel B.

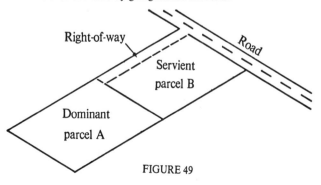

FIGURE 49

**DONEE** a recipient; as of a gift.
  **Example:** Collins was the *donee* of an **estate;** she takes the **property** as a gift.

**DONOR** one who gives.
  **Example:** Whitman was the *donor* of land that she gave to charity; she had owned the land in **fee simple.**

**DORMER** 1. a window projecting through a sloping roof (single dormer); 2. the roofed structure containing such a window (shed dormer).
  **Example:** Figure 50.

Shed dormer
Single dormer

FIGURE 50

**DOUBLE DECLINING BALANCE** a method of **depreciation** for tax purposes whereby twice the **straight-line rate** is applied to the remaining depreciable balance of an asset. See **declining balance depreciation.**
  **Example:** Table 14 is a depreciation schedule for a property with depreciable basis of $10,000 and **depreciable life** of 5 years, using the **double declining balance** method.

**TABLE 14**

| Year | Remaining balance | Rate* | Annual deduction |
|------|-------------------|-------|------------------|
| 1 | $10,000 | .40 | $4,000 |
| 2 | 6,000 | .40 | 2,400 |
| 3 | 3,600 | .40 | 1,440 |
| 4 | 2,160 | .40 | 864 |
| 5 | 1,296 | .40 | 518 |

*.40 = twice the straight-line rate of 20% per year for a 5-year life asset.

**DOUBLE TAXATION** taxation of the same income at 2 levels.
  **Example:** A corporation earns $25,000 of **net income.** The corporation pays a $5,000 corporate income tax, then distributes $20,000 in dividends to its shareholders, who pay an $8,000 tax on this

dividend income. The corporation's earnings are subject to *double taxation.*

**DOWER** under **common law,** the legal right of a wife or child to part of a deceased husband's or father's property. See **curtesy.**
**Example:** In some states a widow can enforce *dower* rights to claim part of her deceased husband's **estate,** regardless of provisions in his will.

**DOWN PAYMENT** the amount one pays for property in addition to the **debt** incurred.
**Example:** Abel buys a house for $50,000. He arranges a $30,000 **first mortgage** and a $5,000 **second mortgage.** The *down payment* he needs is $15,000, which he pays in cash at **closing.**

**DOWNZONING** the act of **rezoning** a tract of land for a less intensive use than the existing use or permitted use.
**Example:** Arlington had a booming single-family residential market, but was not attracting industry. The owner of a large tract of land zoned for industrial use asked for a *downzoning* to **single-family housing** use to develop the land immediately.

**DRAGNET CLAUSE** a provision in a **mortgage** that pledges several properties as **collateral.** A **default** on one mortgage constitutes a default on the one with the *dragnet.*
**Example:** A real estate investor was in financial straits. She failed to pay a certain **mortgage.** The holder of the mortgage on a different property, which was not in **default,** enforced the *dragnet* clause in its mortgage by **foreclosing.**

**DRAW** a periodic advance of funds from a construction lender to a **developer. Construction loans** generally provide for a schedule of draws, either at regular intervals during construction or pending construction of specific segments of the structures.
**Example:** A developer arranges a construction loan of $500,000. The funds are to be advanced in a series of *draws* as follows:
• $50,000 upon completion of final plans and **specifications**
• $200,000 upon completion of the foundation
• $150,000 upon completion of the frame, external surfaces, and roof
• $100,000 upon internal finishing

**DRY MORTGAGE** same as **nonrecourse** mortgage.

**DUE-ON-SALE CLAUSE** a provision in a **mortgage** that states the loan is due upon the sale of the property.
**Example:** Collins owes on a $30,000 mortgage loan against her house at an 8% interest rate. She wants to sell the house to a buyer who will assume the mortgage. The lender says that the $30,000

loan is *due upon the sale* of the house so it cannot be assumed by the buyer. The lender adds that he will **waive** the due-on-sale provision if the interest rate is escalated to 16%.

**DUAL CONTRACT** the illegal or unethical practice of providing 2 different **contracts** for the same transaction.
**Example:** Abel wants to purchase a home from a builder for $50,000 but has no cash for the **down payment.** The builder suggests that they prepare a fictitious contract for $60,000 and try to borrow 90% of $60,000. The bank's attorney discusses the *dual contract* and explains that they could be guilty of attempted **fraud.**

**DUMMY** an individual or **entity** that stands in the place of the **principal** to a transaction.
**Example:** Abel wants to borrow from a bank $100,000 to build houses to sell. Abel requests his attorney to establish a *dummy* **corporation** with $500 of **equity.** The dummy borrows the $100,000 from the bank and, in turn, lends it to Abel as a **nonrecourse** loan.

**DUPLEX** 1. two dwelling units under one roof.
**Example:** General floor plan for a *duplex* (Figure 51).
2. an apartment having rooms on two floors.
**Example:** An artist in a Manhattan *duplex* apartment enjoyed the sunlight that came in from the upper floor to his studio below.

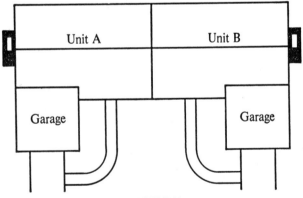

FIGURE 51

**DURESS** compulsion to do something because of a threat.
**Example:** Abel tells Baker that unless Baker will sell his property to Abel for $1,000, Abel will physically harm Baker. Baker signs

the **contract** under *duress,* but can later **void** it by showing he acted under duress.

**DUTCH COLONIAL** an early American style, moderate sized, 2 to 2½ story house with a gambrel roof and eaves that flare outward.
**Example:** Figure 52.

FIGURE 52

**DWELLING** a place of residence.
**Examples:** The following are *dwellings:*
- apartment
- hotel
- mobile home
- nursing home
- single-family house

# E

**EARNEST MONEY** a **deposit** made by a purchaser of real estate to evidence **good faith.**
**Example:** It is customary for the buyer to give the seller *earnest money* at the time a **sales contract** is signed. The earnest money generally is credited to the **down payment** at **closing.** Until closing a

**broker** must hold earnest money in a separate account. See also **commingle.**

**EASEMENT** the right, privilege, or interest that one party has in the land of another.
**Example:** The right of public utility companies to lay their lines across others' property is a utility *easement*.

**EASEMENT BY NECESSITY** the right of an owner to cross over another's property for a special necessary purpose.
**Example:** Figure 53.

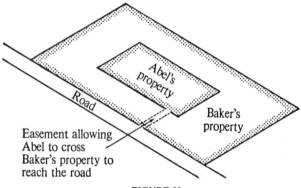

FIGURE 53

**EASEMENT BY PRESCRIPTION** continued use of another's property for a special purpose can ripen into a permanent use if conditions are met.
**Example:** Although Abel can reach the highway by another path, for the last 10 years, Abel has been traveling across Baker's property to reach the highway. Since Abel has been doing this for the length of time required by state law, Abel can continue to do so despite Baker's protests, because Abel has achieved an *easement by prescription* (Figure 54).

**EASTLAKE HOUSE** a nineteenth century style house with three-dimensional ornamentation made with a chisel, gouge, and lathe rather than the scroll saw. Many of the parts of the ornamentation resemble furniture legs and knobs. This distinctive type of ornamentation is the major characteristic of this style and separates the Eastlake style house from the Queen Anne or Carpenter Gothic style.
**Example:** Figure 55.

FIGURE 54

FIGURE 55

**ECONOMIC BASE** industry within a geographic **market area** that provides employment opportunities that are essential to support the community.

**Example:** Steel is the *economic base* for Pittsburgh. For each steelworker added to the economic base there is another job added in service employment (physician, lawyer, switchboard operator, barber). Each new job brings 2 people to the community (spouse, children, nonworking parents, etc.).

**ECONOMIC DEPRECIATION** loss of value from all causes outside the property itself. See **depreciation (appraisal).**
**Example:** An expensive private home may drop in value when an industrial plant is built nearby. This is a form of *economic depreciation* that must be considered in the appraisal of the property.

**ECONOMIC LIFE** that remaining period for which real estate **improvements** are expected to generate more income than **operating expenses** cost. See **useful life.**
**Example:** Figure 56.

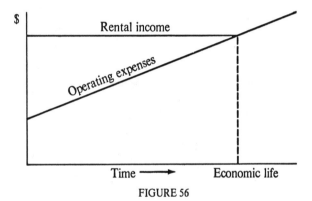

FIGURE 56

**ECONOMIC OBSOLESCENCE** Same as **economic depreciation.**

**ECONOMIC RENT** 1. in economics, the cost commanded by a factor that is unique or inelastic in supply.
**Example:** The portion of rental income attributable to the land is often considered *economic rent*, since the land will exist no matter what the rental rate. In this context, *economic rent* carries a connotation of being "unearned" by its owner.
2. in appraisal, the **market rent.** Contrast with **contract rent.**
**Example:** Big Buy Foods is using a store for $1,000 per month rent. If the landlord could rent the store on a new **lease** now, it would command $4,000 per month. The $1,000 is the **contract rent** and the $4,000 is the *economic rent*.

**EFFECTIVE AGE** the age of a property based on the amount of **wear and tear** it has sustained.

**Example:** Collins' house was built twelve years ago. Because she keeps it in excellent condition it shows only as much wear as a typical 5-year-old house. Collins' house therefore has an *effective age* of 5 years.

**EFFECTIVE RATE** the true rate of return considering all relevant **financing** expenses. See **annual percentage rate.**

**Example:** Abel borrows $10,000 on a one-year bank loan. He pays **2 discount points** and a 10% **face interest rate.** He repays the loan at the end of the year, with interest. Since he really received only $9,800 at the start of the loan and repaid $11,000, the *effective rate* was greater than 10%. It was approximately 12.25%.

**EGRESS** access from a land parcel to a public road or other means of exit.

**Example:** Figure 57.

A lot with *egress*          A lot without *egress*

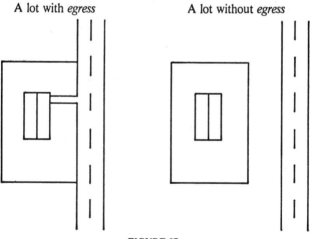

FIGURE 57

**EJECTMENT** action to regain possession of **real property,** when there is no **lease.**

**Example:** The holder of a **conditional sales contract,** through an action in *ejectment,* regains possession when the buyer **defaults.**

**ELIZABETHAN OR HALF TIMBER STYLE** an English style, 2- or 2½-story house, often with part of the second story overhanging

the first. It has less stone work and is less fortlike than the Tudor.
Stone and stucco walls with half timbers are most common.
**Example:** Figure 58.

Second
floor
overhangs
first floor

2 or 2½ stories

Complicated high-
peaked roof

Small
leaded
casement
windows

Half timbers

Nogging

Massive
sculptured
chimney

FIGURE 58

**EMBLEMENT** a growing crop. Annual crops are generally considered **personal property.**
**Example:** Abel, a **tenant,** planted corn on Baker's, land. Three
days prior to harvesting, Baker informs Abel that the **land lease**
has expired. Abel has the right to *emblements* and so can harvest
the corn.

**EMINENT DOMAIN** the right of the government or a public utility
to acquire property for necessary public use by **condemnation**; the
owner must be fairly compensated.
**Example:** Ready Watts Electric Company is granted the power of
*eminent domain* by the state government. This allows the company to acquire private property for specified purposes through the
process of condemnation.

**EMPTY NESTERS** a couple whose children have established separate households; important segment of the housing market, since
empty nesters often seek to reduce the amount of housing space

they occupy. Thus empty nesters are one source of demand for smaller housing units.

**Example:** The Etons have raised 2 children who are now grown and have families of their own. As *empty nesters,* the Etons no longer have need for the big 4-bedroom home they occupy. They purchase a 2-bedroom **town house,** which provides all the space they require.

**ENCROACHMENT** a building, a part of a building, or an obstruction that physically intrudes upon, overlaps, or **trespasses** upon the property of another.

**Example:** A part of the building on lot A is an *encroachment* on lot B. This situation probably occurred because of a faulty **survey** of lot A (Figure 59).

FIGURE 59

**ENCUMBRANCE** any right to or interest in land that affects its value. Includes outstanding **mortgage** loans, unpaid taxes, **easements, deed restrictions.**

**Example:** *Encumbrances* on Blackacres include 3 mortgages, 4 **leases,** a **mechanic's lien,** and a deed restriction preventing the sale of alcoholic beverages on the land.

**END LOAN** same as **permanent mortgage.**

**ENDORSEMENT** 1. the act of signing one's name, as the payee, on the back of a check or **note,** with or without further qualification; the signature itself.

**Example:** Figure 60.

2. offering support or credibility to a statement.

**Example:** The American Association of Homebuilders *endorses* the use of brick as a construction material.

| Pay $1000 to Mary Johns on August 20, 1989 *John Jones* | Mary Johns — Endorsement |
|---|---|
| Front | Back |

FIGURE 60

**ENERGY EFFICIENT** as applied to buildings, generally indicating the existence of extra insulation, weatherproofing, and/or special features and equipment designed to reduce the cost of energy for heating, cooling and hot water.
**Example:** An *energy efficient* home might have an extra layer of insulation in the attic and walls, relatively air tight exterior, a heat pump and a solar hot water heater. An *energy efficient* furnace might be designed to burn fuel more completely and capture more of the heat generated.

**ENERGY TAX CREDITS** a reduction in income tax, generally based on the cost of installing insulation and other energy-saving devices.
**Note:** At the federal level, *energy tax credits* generally expired before 1987 and were not renewed by the 1986 tax act.

**ENTITY** the legal form under which property is owned. See also **corporation, limited partnership, partnership.**
**Examples:** The benefits and risks of owning real property may vary depending on the *entity* that is formed. Among the options are:
• corporation
• individual ownership (see **tenancy** entries)
• **joint venture**
• **limited partnership**
• **partnership**
• **real estate investment trust**

**ENTREPRENEUR** an individual who generates business activity. A businessman or businesswoman. Often associated with one who takes business risks.
**Example:** Business owned by *entrepreneurs* include:
• auto dealerships
• restaurants
• retail stores
• wholesale distributing companies

**ENVIRONMENTAL IMPACT STATEMENT (EIS)** an analysis of the expected effects of a development or action on the surrounding natural and fabricated environment. Such statements are required for many federally supported developments under the National Environmental Policy Act of 1969.

**Example:** Abel seeks to develop a large **subdivision** and obtain **FHA-** insured financing for lot purchasers. Abel must prepare an *environmental impact statement* detailing the effects the development will have on the natural and fabricated environment.

**ENVIRONMENTAL PROTECTION AGENCY (EPA)** an agency of the U.S. government established to enforce federal pollution abatement laws and to implement various pollution prevention programs.

**Example:** The *Environmental Protection Agency* requires **permits** for the siting of manufacturing facilities that may introduce pollution into the air or public waters. The *EPA* also provides grants to local governments to assist in construction of sewage treatment plants.

**EQUAL CREDIT OPPORTUNITY ACT** a federal law, enacted in 1974, to discourage discrimination by lenders on the basis of sex or marital status. Amended in 1976 to prohibit discrimination on the basis of age, race, color, religion, national origin, or receipt of public assistance.

**Example:** Collins, a divorced woman, is denied a **mortgage** loan by a local **savings and loan association.** She feels she would have obtained the loan if she were a man. She sues the savings and loan under the *Equal Credit Opportunity Act.* Her steady, permanent part-time earnings are to be considered in granting the loan.

**EQUALIZATION BOARD** a government agency that determines the fairness of taxes levied against properties.

**Example:** Abel feels the **market value** estimate of his property made by the tax **assessor** is too high. Appeals to the assessor do not result in satisfying Abel's complaint. Abel may take his case to the *Equalization Board* in the hope of reducing the amount of his **assessment.**

**EQUITABLE CONVERSION** a legal doctrine in some states in which, under a **contract of sale,** buyers and sellers are treated as though the **closing** had taken place in that the seller in possession has an obligation to take care of the property. See **equitable title.** Note: A contract of sale may specify which party incurs risk of loss until closing.

**Example:** Though the legal **title** has not passed, the law holds that there has been an *equitable conversion* that effectively **vests** the property in the buyer.

**EQUITABLE TITLE** the interest held by one who has agreed to purchase but has not yet closed the transaction.

**Example:** Collins has agreed in writing to buy Baker's house, with **closing** to be arranged in 2 weeks. In the interim valuable minerals are found on the property. Since Collins has *equitable title,* the minerals belong to her. Similarly, if the property were **condemned** for public use, the value gain or loss would be hers.

**EQUITY** the interest or value that the owner has in real estate over and above the **liens** against it.

**Example:** A property has a **market value** of $100,000. The owner currently owes $60,000 in **mortgage** loans that are against the property. The owner's *equity* is $40,000. See Table 15

**TABLE 15**

| | |
|---|---|
| Market value | $100,000 |
| Liens | −60,000 |
| Equity | $ 40,000 |

**EQUITY KICKER** see **kicker.**

**EQUITY OF REDEMPTION** the right of an owner to recover property that has been **foreclosed.**

**Example:** Abel's property has been foreclosed because he has not met his **mortgage** obligation. If he raises enough money within the period of time set by state laws, he may reclaim the property by paying the **principal, interest,** and legal expenses, under *equity of redemption* laws.

**EROSION** the gradual wearing away of land through processes of nature, as by streams and winds.

**Examples:**
• Deep gullies cut into unvegetated earth, caused by rainwater *erosion*
• The Grand Canyon formed by *erosion* from the Colorado River
• The Sphinx in Egypt, disfigured by wind *erosion*

**ESCALATOR CLAUSE** a provision in a **lease** that requires the **tenant** to pay more rent based on an increase in costs. Same as **stop clause.**

**Example:** A lease requires the tenant to pay increases in real estate taxes over the amount in the base year. Taxes were $1000 for the base year; and were $1,250 the following year. The tenant's rent is *escalated* by $250.

**ESCHEAT** the **reversion** of property to the state in the event that the owner dies without leaving a will and has no legal heirs.

**Example:** Abel dies without a will. No heirs are found. His property *escheats* to the state.

**ESCROW** an agreement between 2 or more parties providing that certain instruments or property be placed with a third party for safekeeping, pending the fulfillment or performance of a specified act or condition.

**Example:** The **deed** to the property and the **earnest money** were both placed in *escrow* pending fulfillment of other conditions to the **contract.**

**ESCROW ACCOUNT** same as **trust account.**

**ESCROW AGENT** any person engaged in the business of receiving **escrows** for deposit or delivery.

**Example:** The **title** company is serving as the *escrow agent.* It holds the **earnest money** and **deed,** pending fulfillment of other conditions to the **contract** (Figure 61).

FIGURE 61

**ESTATE** the degree, nature, and extent of interest that a person has in **real property.**

**Example:** The highest form of an *estate* is **fee simple,** under which the owner can use the property at will and dispose of it without restriction.

**ESTATE AT SUFFERANCE** the wrongful occupancy of property by a tenant after the **lease** has expired. See **dispossess proceedings.**

**Example:** Abel's lease expired and he remained on the property. He has an *estate at sufferance* and may be ejected at the landlord's whim.

**ESTATE AT WILL** the occupation of real estate by a tenant for an indefinite period, terminable by one or both parties at will.

**Example:** Under an *estate at will,* the landlord may evict the tenant at any time, and the tenant may vacate at any time. The tenant may have certain rights, however, such as ownership of **emblements** (crops as a result of annual cultivation).

**ESTATE FOR LIFE** an interest in property that terminates upon the death of a specified person. See **life estate.**

**Example:** Abel deeded his wife an *estate for her life.* When she dies the property will go to Abel's son. She may use the property and may not commit **waste,** but normal **wear and tear** is acceptable.

**ESTATE FOR YEARS** an interest in land allowing possession for a specified and limited time.
**Example:** The **tenant** under a 5-year **lease** holds an *estate for years*.

**ESTATE IN REVERSION** an **estate** left by the **grantor** for himself or herself, to begin after the termination of some particular estate granted by him or her.
**Example:** All landlords have an *estate in reversion* which becomes theirs to possess when the **lease** expires.

**ESTATE IN SEVERALTY** see **tenancy in severalty.**

**ESTATE TAX** a tax based on the value of property left by the deceased. Since 1987, the estate and gift tax laws exempt approximately $600,000 of property.
**Example:** Abel dies, leaving $800,000 worth of **assets.** The estate of Abel will pay an *estate tax*. Abel's heirs may also be liable for an **inheritance tax** under their state law.

**ESTOPPEL** a doctrine of law that stops one from later denying facts which that person once acknowledged were true and others accepted on **good faith.**
**Example:** Abel signs a certificate acknowledging that he owes $10,000 on a **mortgage** as of a certain date. Later he contends that he owed only $5,000. Abel is prevented from asserting this new contention under *estoppel.*

**ESTOPPEL CERTIFICATE** a document by which the **mortgagor** (borrower) certifies that the mortgage debt is a **lien** for the amount stated. The debtor is thereafter prevented from claiming that the balance due differs from the amount stated.
**Example:** The Good Money Savings Association asks Abel to sign an *estoppel certificate*, which he does. Good Money Savings then sells the mortgage to Baker, who buys with confidence. Abel is later estopped (prevented) from denying that he owed the money.

**ESTOVERS** the legally supported right to take necessities from property. Contrast with **waste.**
**Example:** Mason has a **life estate** on property. She needs to cut timber for firewood to heat the residence. The **remainderman,** Baker, complains that Mason is damaging the property. The law supports Mason's use of the *estovers* as she has been doing.

**ET AL.** abbreviation of the Latin *et alii,* "and others."
**Example:** Property owned by John Jones and several others may be referenced as "John Jones, *et al.*"

**ET CON** legal term signifying "and husband." See **et ux.**

**Example:** Hereby signed and delivered by Ellen Smith *et con.*

**ET UX** abbreviation of the Latin *et uxor,* which means "and wife."
**Example:** A house is sold by Bill Baker *et ux.* Baker and his wife both must sign the **deed.**

**EVICTION** a legal proceeding by a **lessor** (landlord) to recover possession of property.
**Example:** When the **tenant** fails to comply with the **lease** agreement (skipping rent payments, unauthorized use of the property, etc.), the landlord may seek *eviction* of the tenant. If successful, this action will terminate the rights of the tenant to use the property.

**EVICTION, ACTUAL** exists where one is removed from the property, either by force or by process of law.
**Example:** An apartment tenant may be subject to *actual eviction,* in which case, a notice will be served requiring the tenant to vacate the apartment within a specified time interval.

**EVICTION, CONSTRUCTIVE** exists when, through the fault of the landlord, physical conditions of the property render it unfit for the purpose for which it was leased.
**Example:** A landlord may allow the physical condition of an apartment building to deteriorate to the point that the premises are no longer safe for occupancy. A tenant may be able to terminate the **lease,** order *constructive eviction,* and end **liability** for future rent payments.

**EVICTION, PARTIAL** exists where the possessor of the property, such as a tenant, is deprived of a portion thereof.
**Example:** A law firm leases a floor of an office building. The **landlord** wishes to make substantial modifications to one side of the building. Because of the disruption caused by the work, the tenant and landlord agree to a *partial eviction* from the property affected by construction. The tenant's rent is reduced accordingly.

**EVIDENCE OF TITLE** documents, such as **deeds,** that demonstrate ownership.
**Example:** The property owner kept the **deed** in a bank vault because it is important *evidence of title.*

**EXCHANGE** under **Section 1031** of the **Internal Revenue Code, like-kind property** used in a trade or business or held as an investment can be exchanged tax-free. See also **boot, realized gain, recognized gain, delayed (tax-free) exchange.**
**Example:** Collins *exchanges* her farm worth $100,000, but subject to a $20,000 **mortgage,** for Baker's apartments worth $80,000.

**EXCLUSIVE AGENCY LISTING** employment **contract** giving only one **broker,** for a specified time, the right to sell the property and also allowing the owner alone to sell the property without paying a **commission.**
**Example:** Graham gives Quick Sale Realty an *exclusive agency listing* on her house. If an agent of Quick Sale or any other **brokerage** firm sells the house during the time of the listing, Quick Sale is entitled to a commission. If Graham sells the house herself, no commission is earned.

**EXCLUSIVE RIGHT TO SELL LISTING** employment **contract** giving the **broker** the right to collect **commission** if the property is sold by anyone, including the owner, during the term of the agreement. See also **multiple listing service.**
**Example:** Abel give Quick Sale Realty an *exclusive right to sell listing* on his house. If the house is sold during the time of the listing, Quick Sale is entitled to a commission.

**EXCULPATORY CLAUSE** a provision in a **mortgage** allowing the borrower to surrender the property to the lender without personal **liability** for the loan.
**Example:** Abel buys land for $100,000, paying $40,000 cash and gives a $60,000 mortgage to the seller with an *exculpatory clause.* The **market value** of the land drops suddenly to $55,000. Abel abandons the mortgaged property, losing the $40,000 investment but keeping everything else he owns.

**EXECUTE** to sign a **contract;** sometimes, to perform a contract fully.
**Example:** Generally when a buyer and seller sign a **sales contract,** they *execute* the contract.

**EXECUTED CONTRACT** a **contract** whose terms have been completely fulfilled.
**Example:** At the **closing,** all parties signed the contract, which made it an *executed contract.*

**EXECUTOR** a person named in a **will** to carry out its provisions for the disposition of the estate.
**Example:** Abel specifies in his will that his attorney shall serve as its *executor.* The attorney, at the appropriate time, assures that Abel's property is distributed according to the will.

**EXECUTORY CONTRACT** a **contract** under which one or more parties has not yet performed.
**Example:** Abel orally has agreed to buy Baker's land, and Baker's attorney has drafted a contract. At this stage it is *executory* because neither Abel nor Baker has signed it.

**EXECUTRIX** a woman who performs the duties of an **executor.**

**Example:** Abel appoints his wife as *executrix* for his estate. She will not need a real estate **license** to sell the property he leaves.

**EXEMPTION** an amount provided by law that reduces taxable income or taxable value.

**Example:** Personal exemptions, generally based on the number of people in a household, reduce taxable income.

**Example: Homestead exemptions,** offered in many jurisdictions, reduce the value of real estate that would otherwise be subject to **ad valorem tax.**

**EXPOSURE (MARKET)** the advertising, whether free or paid, of property that is for sale.

**Example:** Real estate agents provide market *exposure* through such devices as:
• classified ads in local papers
• for sale signs on the premises
• inclusion in **multiple listing service**
• displays in their office

**EXTENDED COVERAGE** insurance that covers specific incidences normally excluded from standard insurance policies.

**Example:** A homeowner who lives **adjacent** to a golf course discovers that the standard homeowners' insurance policy does not cover damage due to errant golf balls. An *extended coverage* policy may be obtained, however, to cover such damage.

**EXTENSION** an agreement between 2 parties to extend the time period specified in a **contract.**

**Example:** When a tenant is unable to **vacate** the property at the termination of the **lease,** an *extension* may be granted by the **landlord.**

**Example:** When a seller fails to clear the **title** in time for a **closing,** an *extension* of the closing date may be granted.

---

# F

---

**FACADE** the outside front wall of a building.

**Example:** *Facade* materials for a building include:
• aluminum
• brick
• glass
• masonry
• wood

**FACE AMOUNT** same as **face value.**

**FACE INTEREST RATE** the percentage interest that is shown on the loan document. Compare with **annual percentage rate, effective rate.**
**Example:** A mortgage has an 8% *face interest rate,* $10,000 **face value,** and 30-year **amortization** term. If market interest rates are 12%, the **market value** of the loan is $7,200.

**FACE VALUE** the dollar amount, shown by words and/or numbers, on a document. Compare with **market value;** see **amortization.**
**Example:** A mortgage has a *face value* of $10,000, **amortization** term of 30 years, and 8% **face interest rate.** It will be amortized in 13 years to $8,000 by annual payments.

**FAIR CREDIT REPORTING ACT** a federal law that allows individuals to examine and correct information used by **credit** reporting services.
**Example:** Abel wishes to purchase property from Baker under an **installment land contract.** Baker refuses to make the contract because of Abel's poor **credit rating.** Under the *Fair Credit Reporting Act,* Abel may demand disclosure of Baker's source of information and then take steps to correct any misinformation in the report.

**FAIR MARKET RENT** the amount that a property would command if it were now available for **lease.** Contrast with **contract rent.** See **economic rent, rent control, Section 8 housing.**
**Example:** The *fair market rent* for an apartment is estimated at $400 per month. Under **Section 8,** the **tenant** is required to pay 20% of income toward rent; the **landlord** would receive a payment from the government to make up the difference.

**FAIR MARKET VALUE** a term, generally used in **property tax** and **condemnation** legislation, meaning the **market value** of a property.
**Example:** Property taxes generally are assessed at some ratio of *fair market value.*
**Example:** When property is condemned for public use, the owner is entitled to be compensated at *fair market value.*

**FALSE ADVERTISING** describing property in a misleading fashion.
**Example:** Examples of false advertising might include:
• representing a property as not being in a **floodplain** when, in fact, it is
• stating, without **caveat,** that a property will appreciate in value
• denying structural flaws that are known to exist

**FANNIE MAE** nickname for **Federal National Mortgage Association.**

**FARMER'S HOME ADMINISTRATION (FmHA)** an agency, within the U.S. Department of Agriculture, that administers assistance programs for purchasers of homes and farms in small towns and rural areas.

**Example:** Abel wishes to develop housing for the elderly in a rural area. He may apply to the *Farmer's Home Administration* for a special 40-year **mortgage** loan.

**FEASIBILITY STUDY** a determination of the likelihood that a proposed development will fulfill the objectives of a particular investor.

**Example:** A *feasibility study* of a proposed **subdivision** should:
• estimate the demand for housing units in the area
• estimate the **absorption rate** for the project
• discuss legal and other considerations
• forecast **cash flows**
• approximate investment returns likely to be produced

**FEDERAL** an early American style of house that is box-shaped and has a flat roof.

**Example:** Figure 62.

FIGURE 62

**FEDERAL DEPOSIT INSURANCE CORPORATION (FDIC)** a public corporation, established in 1933; insures up to $100,000 for each depositor in most **commercial banks.** Has own reserves and can borrow from the U.S. Treasury.

**Example:** The First National Bank has a **liquidity** difficulty and cannot pay depositors who want to withdraw their money. The *FDIC* pays each depositor the full **prinicpal** amount, up to $100,000.

**FEDERAL FAIR HOUSING LAW** a federal law that forbids **discrimination** on the basis of race, color, sex, religion, or national origin in the selling or renting of homes and apartments. See **steering.**

**Example: Broker** Abel is contacted by a black couple wishing to purchase a home. Although homes are currently for sale in several all-white neighborhoods, Abel maintains there are no houses available in these areas. Abel may be prosecuted under the *Federal Fair Housing Law.*

**FEDERAL HOME LOAN BANK SYSTEM** a federally created banking system primarily intended to assure **liquidity** to member **savings and loan associations.**

**Example:** *Federal Home Loan Bank System* (Figure 63).

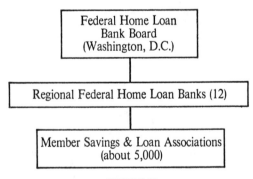

FIGURE 63

**FEDERAL HOME LOAN MORTGAGE CORPORATION (FHLMC)** an organization that purchases **mortgage** loans, mostly from **savings and loan associations.**

**Example:** ABC Savings and Loan Association sells mortgage loans to the *Federal Home Loan Mortgage Corporation* to gain funds for originating new mortgage loans.

**FEDERAL HOUSING ADMINISTRATION (FHA)** an agency, within the U.S. Department of Housing and Urban Development, that administers many loan programs, loan **guarantee** programs, and **loan insurance** programs designed to make more housing available.

**Example:** Abel wishes to purchase a home but lacks funds for a large **down payment.** Through a program provided by the *Federal Housing Administration,* Abel may obtain a loan for up to 97% of the purchase price.

**FEDERAL NATIONAL MORTGAGE ASSOCIATION (FNMA)** a corporation that specializes in buying mortgage loans, mostly from **mortgage bankers.** It adds **liquidity** to the mortgage market. Nicknamed **Fannie Mae,** FNMA is owned by its stockholders, who elect 10 to its Board of Directors. The U.S. president appoints the other 5 directors.

**Example:** A mortgage banker originates conventional and **FHA loans** and periodically sells them to the *Federal National Mortgage Association.*

**FEDERAL RESERVE SYSTEM** the central federal banking system that regulates and provides services to member **commercial banks.** Also has the responsibility for conducting federal monetary policy.

**Example:** The system consists of the Federal Reserve Board and a series of regional Federal Reserve Banks.

**FEDERAL SAVINGS & LOAN ASSOCIATION** a member of the **Federal Home Loan Bank System** and the **Federal Savings and Loan Insurance Corporation.**

**Example:** City Federal Savings and Loan is a *federal savings and loan association.* Its activities are regulated by the Federal Home Loan Bank Board. Home Savings is a state chartered savings and loan association regulated by state government.

**FEDERAL SAVINGS AND LOAN INSURANCE CORPORATION (FSLIC)** an agency of the federal government that insures depositors in **savings and loan associations** against loss of **principal.** Most deposits, including passbooks and saving certificates, are insured up to a maximum amount per account.

**Address:** Federal Savings and Loan Insurance Corporation
1700 G Street, N.W.
Washington, D.C. 20552

**Example:** Graham may deposit savings in a **savings and loan association** without fear of losing her money, since her deposit, up to $100,000, is insured by the *Federal Savings and Loan Insurance Corporation.*

**FEDERAL TRADE COMMISSION (FTC)** a federal agency, headquarters in Washington, D.C., that regulates advertising and other promotion and sales practices of firms engaged in interstate commerce. The FTC does *not* regulate interstate land sales (HUD), anticompetitive activities (JUSTICE), or sale of securities (SEC).

**Example:** Abel, a builder, was found guilty of false television advertising by the *FTC*.

**FEE SIMPLE or FEE ABSOLUTE or FEE SIMPLE ABSOLUTE** absolute ownership of **real property**; owner is entitled to the entire property with unconditional power of disposition during the owner's life, and upon his death the property descends to the owner's designated heirs.

**Example:** The only power that can require Abel to sell his land is **eminent domain**; he owns the property in *fee simple,* so there is no other interest.

**FEE SIMPLE DEFEASIBLE** a type of property ownership in which the grant of **title** or duration of ownership is dependent on a specified condition.

**Example:** A *fee simple defeasible* may be granted on the condition that the property be used for an orphanage home (termed "fee simple subject to a condition subsequent").

**Example:** A *fee simple defeasible* may be granted as long as the property is held as a wildlife refuge (termed "fee simple determinable").

**FHA MORTGAGE LOAN** a **mortgage** loan insured by the FHA. See **Federal Housing Administration.**

**Example:** Abel wishes to purchase a home but has insufficient cash to make a large down payment. By obtaining an *FHA mortgage loan,* Abel may borrow more than the customary 80% of value, with the FHA insuring the loan amount.

**FHLB** Federal Home Loan Bank; a federally chartered bank that supplies **credit** to member banks. See **Federal Home Loan Bank System.**

**FIDELITY BOND** an assurance, generally purchased by an employer, to cover employees who are entrusted with valuable property or funds.

**Example:** A landlord employs a resident manager who, among other duties, collects the **rent.** To safeguard these funds during the collection process, the landlord purchases a *fidelity bond* on the resident manager.

**FIDUCIARY** one who acts, in a financial role, in the best interests of others.

**Example:**
• a **broker** is a *fiduciary* for the seller
• a banker is a *fiduciary* for the bank's depositors

- an attorney may be a *fiduciary* for the client
- a **trustee** is a *fiduciary* for the **beneficiaries**

**FILTERING DOWN** the process whereby, over time, a housing unit or neighborhood is occupied by progressively lower-income residents.
**Example:** Many older residences near the downtown of big cities were once occupied by the upper classes, but have *filtered down* to the relatively poor. At some point in the filtering process, many large houses may be converted into rented **multifamily housing.**

**FINANCE CHARGE** interest or certain other fees charged to a **credit** customer.
**Example:** A customer makes purchases of $400 on credit. Payment is made one month later. Based on an annual percentage rate of interest of 18%, a *finance charge* of $6.00 ($\frac{18}{12} \times \$400$) is added to the bill.

**FINANCIAL INTERMEDIARY** a firm, such as a bank or savings and loan association, which performs the function of collecting deposits from individuals and investing them in loans and other securities. Also includes credit unions and mutual savings banks. See **disintermediation.**
**Example:** First National Bank serves as a *financial intermediary* by taking in deposits and placing them in mortgage loans and various securities. In doing so, the bank links individual investors with demanders of credit and the financial markets.

**FINANCIAL LEVERAGE** the use of borrowed money to complete an investment purchase.
**Example:** The effects of *financial leverage* on return on **equity** are shown in Table 16.

(Note: If **debt service** required is high compared to income, effect of leverage may be to *reduce* return to equity.)

**TABLE 16**

| No Leverage | | Leverage with 50% Debt | |
|---|---|---|---|
| Cost | $100,000 | Cost | $100,000 |
| Debt | 0 | Debt | $50,000 |
| Equity | $100,000 | Equity | $50,000 |
| Income | $20,000 | Income | $20,000 |
| Debt service | 0 | Debt service | −7,500 |
| Cash to equity | $20,000 | Cash to equity | $12,500 |
| Return on equity | $\frac{20,000}{100,000} = 0.20$ | Return on equity | $\frac{12,500}{50,000} = 0.25$ |

**FINANCIAL MANAGEMENT RATE OF RETURN (FMRR)** a method of measuring investment performance that is a variation on the **internal rate of return** method. The user specifies 2 after-tax reinvestment rates:

$i_L$: a safe, liquid rate, obtainable for liquid deposits.

$i_R$: a run-of-the-mill rate, which can be earned from typical investments over a long term.

**Negative cash flows** are generally **discounted** to a present value at the $i_L$ rate, inflows are compounded to the investment resale date at $i_R$. The FMRR is the rate that equates the present value of negative cash flows to the future value of inflows.

**Example:** An investment requires a $10,000 negative cash flow for the first 3 years, then offers $8,500 of cash inflows for years 4-10. If $i_L$ is 5%, the negative cash flows have a present value of $27,232. If $i_R$ is 10%, the cash inflows will become $80,641. The *FMRR* is 11.47% because that is the rate at which $27,232 would grow to $80,641 in 10 years with **compound interest.**

**FINANCIAL STATEMENT** one that shows income and expense for an accounting period, or **assets, liabilities** and **equity** as of a point in time.

**Example:** Table 17.

**Table 17**

| Income statement | | Balance sheet | |
|---|---|---|---|
| | | Assets | Liabilities & equity |
| Rental income | $5,000 | | |
| Interest expense | −2,000 | | |
| Depreciation | −1,000 | Buildings $40,000 | Mortgage $30,000 |
| Real estate taxes | − 500 | Land     10,000 | Equity     20,000 |
| Net income | $1,500 | Total    $50,000 | Total    $50,000 |

**FINANCING** borrowing money to buy property. See **creative financing.**

**Example:** The following are examples of *financing:*
- obtaining a **mortgage** loan on a purchase
- **assumptions of a mortgage** from a seller
- arranging for the seller to take a loan as part of the purchase price
- arranging an **installment sale**

**FINDER'S FEE** money paid to someone other than a **broker** who locates suitable property or a purchaser. Prohibited or limited in most states.

**Example:** Broker Abel has a **listing** on a particular property. Baker knows several people interested in such property. Abel arranges with Baker to provide a *finder's fee* should one of the **prospects** identified by Baker purchase the property.

**FINISH OUT ALLOWANCE** a provision in a lease for an office or retail space that provides a certain sum or amount per square foot to the **tenant** to customize the space provided.

**Example:** A retail tenant leases space for 5 years at a $10 per square foot annual rental rate. The **lessor** provides four concrete walls and a concrete floor, and will pay the tenant a *finish out allowance* of up to $4 per square foot for costs to customize the space.

**FIREPROOF** having all exposed surfaces constructed of noncombustible materials or protected by such materials.

**Example:** The exterior surface of the building was composed of brick, aluminum siding, and asbestos shingles, thereby making the exterior *fireproof*.

**FIRE-RESISTIVE** able to withstand exposure to flame of a specified intensity or for a specified time. Compare **fireproof**.

**Example:** The interior walls in the house were made of *fire-resistive* material. The walls were designed to resist igniting at temperatures below 1,000 degrees if not exposed for more than one hour.

**FIRST MORTGAGE** a **mortgage** that has priority as a **lien** over all other mortgages. In cases of **foreclosure** the first mortgage will be satisfied before other mortgages. See **junior mortgage, second mortgage**.

**Example:** A property costing $100,000 is financed with a *first mortgage* of $75,000, a second mortgage of $15,000, and $10,000 in cash. If the borrower **defaults** and the property is sold upon foreclosure for $80,000, the holder of the *first mortgage* will receive the full amount of the unpaid **principal** plus legal expenses. The second mortgage holder will receive any excess after the first mortgage has been satisfied.

**FIRST REFUSAL RIGHT** same as **right of first refusal**.

**FIRST-YEAR DEPRECIATION** same as **additional first-year depreciation**.

**FISCAL YEAR** a continuous 12-month time interval used for financial reporting; the period starts on any date after January 1 and ends one year later.

**Example:** For agencies of the federal government, *fiscal year* 1988 refers to the time between October 1, 1987 and September 30, 1988.

**FIXED PAYMENT MORTGAGE** a loan secured by real property which features a periodic payment of interest and principal which is constant over the term of the loan. All *fixed payment mortgages* are **fixed rate mortgages**, but some fixed rate mortgages may have variable payments, such as a **graduated payment mortgage**.

**Example:** A *fixed payment mortgage* calls for 360 monthly payments of interest and principal of $1,000. Added to that amount is a payment to an escrow account for taxes and insurance which may change from year to year.

**FIXED RATE MORTGAGE** a loan secured by real property featuring an interest rate that is constant for the term of the loan. Contrast **adjustable rate mortgage.**
**Example:** A *fixed rate mortgage* is originated with an interest rate of 10% for a term of 30 years. The rate will remain at 10% until the loan is retired or the **due-on-sale clause** is exercised at resale of the property.

**FIXING-UP EXPENSES (TAX)** expenses incurred for the purpose of physically preparing a personal residence for sale. Qualified fixing-up expenses may be deducted from the sales price to determine the price that must be spent in the purchase of another residence to defer **capital gains** taxes on the sale of the old one.
**Example:** Abel spends $500 for painting and repairs on a home prior to sale. The house sells for $75,500 and costs $7,000 in transaction costs. The adjusted sales price is calculated in Table 18.

**TABLE 18**

|  |  |
|---|---|
| Sale price | $75,500 |
| *Fixing-up expenses* | − 500 |
| Selling expenses | − 7,000 |
| Adjusted sales price | $68,000 |

Abel must spend at least $68,000 on a new residence to avoid **capital gains** on the sale.

**FIXTURES** **improvements** or **personal property** attached to the land so as to become part of the real estate. Tests to determine whether an item is a fixture include:
• intent of the parties (was it intended to remain?)
• method of annexation (how is it affixed?)
• relation of the parties (was it expected to be part of a tenant's business?)
• adaptation of the article (is it essential to the building?)
**Example:** Abel sells his house. The contract of sale includes all of the real estate. Baker, the buyer, believes that the ceiling fan in the dining room is a *fixture*, but Abel claims it as **personal property.**

**FLAT** 1. an apartment, generally on one level.
**Example:** A 2-room *flat* is an apartment having 2 rooms.
2. a **level payment mortgage** or **lease** requirement.
**Example:** A **flat lease** is one that requires level payments each month or other specified period.

**FLAT FEE BROKER** a licensed broker who charges a fixed fee for the provision of brokerage services instead of a commission based on a percentage of the sales price of the property. See **discount broker.**

**Example:** Kramden, a *flat fee broker,* charges $5,000 to arrange the sale of a home, no matter what price is agreed upon by the buyer and seller. If a sale is not consummated within the term of the listing contract, no fee is paid.

**FLAT LEASE** a rental agreement that requires periodic level rent payments.

**Example:** Pattern of payments for a one-year *flat lease* with monthly payments (Figure 64).

Flat lease payments

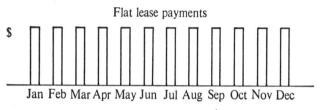

FIGURE 64

**FLEXIBLE PAYMENT MORTGAGE (FPM)** a home-purchase loan plan that allows the borrower to pay interest-only for the first several years of the term. FPM's were authorized by the **Federal Home Loan Bank** Board in 1974 with 2 restrictions:
1. monthly payments must be sufficient to cover **interest** on the **principal**
2. after 5 years, payments must be sufficient to amortize the principal over the remaining term

**Example:** A young couple purchases a home with a *flexible payment mortgage.* The principal is $50,000, interest rate at 14%, and term of 30 years. For the first 5 years, the monthly payments are $583.33. For years 6 through 30, payments will be $601.88. If they had obtained a **level payment mortgage,** monthly payments would have been $592.44 over the entire loan. See the mortgage tables in the Appendix.

**FLOAT** 1. the interval of time after a deposit or withdrawal is made and before the transaction is credited or deducted.

**Example:** Abel writes a check to pay a **debt** to Baker. Baker deposits the check in a bank other than the one used by Abel. Abel's bank may have a *float* of 2 or 3 days before Baker's bank collects the money.
2. the difference between a **variable interest rate** and the **index** to which it is pegged.

**Example:** A bank makes construction loans at 3% over the **prime rate.** The 3% is the *float.*
3. to incur a debt.
**Example:** To fund a project, Atlas Company may *float* a loan or *float* a **bond** issue.

**FLOOD INSURANCE** an insurance policy that covers property damage due to natural flooding. Flood insurance is offered by private insurers but is subsidized by the federal government.
**Example:** Abel owns a home within an area defined as a 100-year **floodplain.** If the local community is participating in a special federal program, Abel may purchase *flood insurance* to cover damage from periodic flooding.

**FLOODPLAIN** a level land area subject to periodic flooding from a **contiguous** body of water. Floodplains are delineated by the expected frequency of flooding. For example, an annual floodplain is expected to flood once each year.
**Example:** Figure 65.

FIGURE 65

**FLOOR-AREA RATIO** the arithmetic relationship of the total square feet of a building to the square footage of the land area.

**FLOOR LOAN** the minimum that a lender is willing to advance. See also **gap loan.**
**Example:** Abel, a lender, agrees to a $700,000 floor on a $1,000,000 permanent loan. When construction is complete, the borrower will receive a $700,000 *floor loan;* when the property is 80% occupied the full $1,000,000 will be loaned.

**FLOOR PLAN** the arrangement of rooms in a building, or a one-plane diagram of that arrangement.
**Example:** The home is difficult to sell due to its awkward *floor plan.* One must pass through a bedroom to enter the master bed-

Formula: floor-area ratio = $\dfrac{\text{building area}}{\text{land area}}$

The floor-area ratio is 0.25 $\left(\dfrac{50' \times 50'}{100' \times 100'}\right)$

**Example:** Figure 66.

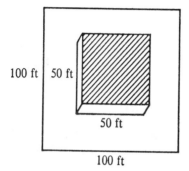

100 ft | 50 ft

50 ft

100 ft

FIGURE 66

room. There is no direct access from the garage to the kitchen and the living room is too small.

**FNMA Federal National Mortgage Association,** which buys and sells existing residential mortgages; nicknamed **Fannie Mae.**

**FORCE MAJEURE** an unavoidable cause of delay or of failure to perform a **contract** obligation in time.
**Example:** A *force majeure* clause is often inserted in a construction contract to protect the **contractor** from delays due to weather, labor disputes, and other unavoidable incidents.

**FORECLOSURE** a termination of all rights of a **mortgagor** or the **grantee** in the property covered by the **mortgage.** Statutory foreclosure is effected without recourse to courts, but must conform to laws (statutes). Strict foreclosure forever bars **equity of redemption.** See **default.**
**Example:** The lender *forecloses* to gain possession of mortgaged land after the borrower missed 3 payments.

**FORFEITURE** loss of money or anything else of value because of failure to perform under **contract.**
**Example:** Because Baker, the prospective purchaser, failed to keep up payments under the **land contract,** he *forfeited* all his rights to the property.

**FRAME HOUSE** a house constructed with a wooden frame over which is placed some form of siding or **veneer.**
**Example:** A *frame house* (Figure 67).

| Wood siding | Wooden frame | Brick veneer |

FIGURE 67

**FRANCHISE** an arrangement between a franchisor and franchisee through which the franchisee uses the company name of the franchisor and is provided specified business services in exchange for a franchise fee. The fee is usually an initial purchase requirement plus an ongoing percentage of gross sales of the business.
**Example:** In real estate brokerage, locally owned firms may operate as *franchises* of such national companies as Century 21, Gallery of Homes and Red Carpet. The franchisor advertises the name and logo of the company, offers training for salespersons, and offers or provides other services to the franchisee.

**FRAUD** the intentional use of deception to cause another person to suffer loss.
**Example:** Abel purchases property from Baker. Abel later discovers that Baker did not hold **title** to the property and had no right to sell. Baker was guilty of *fraud* and is liable for damages suffered by Abel in the purchase of the property.

**FREDDIE MAC** nickname for **Federal Home Loan Mortgage Corporation.**

**FREE AND CLEAR TITLE title** to a property without **encumbrances.** Generally used to refer to a property free of **mortgage**

debt. See **clear title, marketable title.**

**Example:** *Free and clear title* is generally desired by the purchaser of a property. This requires clearing any **clouds on the title** and satisfying any **liens** that may exist.

**FREEHOLD** an interest in **real estate** without a predetermined time span.

**Example:** A **fee simple** or a **life estate** is considered a *freehold* estate because there is not a specified time limit. A **lease** is less than freehold because it has a specified termination date.

**FRENCH PROVINCIAL** a French style formal, 1½- to 2½-story house that is perfectly balanced with a high steep hip roof and curved-headed upper windows that break through the cornice.

**Example:** Figure 68.

1½ to 2½ stories   Perfectly balanced

Curve-headed upper windows that break through cornice

Brick

Formal looking high steep hip roof

Some have 2 symmetrical 1-story wings

French windows and shutters

FIGURE 68

**FRONTAGE** the linear distance of a piece of land along a lake, river, street, or highway.
**Example:** Road *frontage* (Figure 69).

FIGURE 69

**Example:** Lake *frontage* (Figure 70).

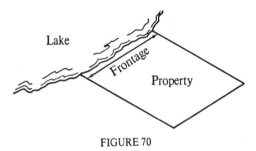

FIGURE 70

**FRONT FOOT** a standard measurement of land, applied at the **frontage** of its street line. Used for lots of generally uniform depth in downtown arces.
**Example:** The lot in Figure 71 sold for $30,000, or $300 per *front foot*.

**FRONT MONEY** cash necessary to start a development project.
**Example:** *Front money* is generally required for purchasing a **site**, preparing plans and studies, obtaining **permits**, and obtaining loan **commitments**.

FIGURE 71

**FSBO** for sale by owner. A term referring to properties on the market that are not listed with a real estate broker. Pronounced "fizz-bo."
*Example:* The Mathers are attempting to find a buyer for their home by placing an ad in the paper and putting up a sign in the yard. Such activities indicate the existence of a *FSBO*.

**FULL DISCLOSURE** a requirement to reveal all information pertinent to a transaction.
*Example:* Under *full disclosure*, a **broker** is required to give the buyer all known facts about the physical, financial, and economic condition of the subject property.

**FULLY INDEXED RATE** in conjunction with **adjustable rate mortgages,** the interest rate indicated by the sum of the current value of the **index** and **margin** applied to the loan. This rate is the interest rate which is used to calculate monthly payments in the absence of constraints imposed by the **initial rate** or **caps.** See **teaser rate, adjustable rate mortgage.**
*Example:* An adjustable rate mortgage is indexed to the one-year treasury bill rate. The current value of the index is 6%. A margin of 2.5 percentage points is applied to the loan. The *fully indexed rate* is 8.5%. However, the loan has an initial rate of 7.5% which determines the interest rate for the first year. When the rate is adjusted, the *fully indexed rate* rises to 10%. A cap of 2 percentage points limits the adjustment in the rate to only 9.5%. If there had been no cap, the interest rate would have risen to 10%.

**FUNCTIONAL DEPRECIATION** loss of value from all causes within the property, except those due to physical deterioration. See **obsolescence.**
*Example:* A poor **floor plan** or outdated plumbing fixtures are types of *functional depreciation.*

**FUNCTIONAL MODERN OR CONTEMPORARY HOUSE** a post
World War II style house with an exterior style that is an integral
part of the overall design. Its function is to enclose some living
areas with modern materials while integrating the indoor and out-
door space into one unit.
**Example:** Figure 72.

Extensive
use of glass

Modern building
materials

No ornamentation

FIGURE 72

**FUNCTIONAL OBSOLESCENCE** same as **functional depreciation.**

**FUTURE INTEREST** a property right or estate that may not be
enjoyed until some time in the future.
**Example:** When a **life estate** is created, the **remainder** is a *future
interest.*
**Example:** The lender's right to a portion of net **appreciation,** under
a **shared appreciation mortgage,** is a *future interest.*

---

# G

---

**GABLE ROOF** one with a triangle, with the ridge forming an angle
at the top and each eave forming an angle at the bottom.
**Example:** Figure 73.

**GAIN** an increase in money or **property** value. See **capital gain, realized gain, recognized gain.**
**Example:** Abel sells for $10,000 land that he bought for $4,000. He
recognizes a $6,000 gain excluding property and income taxes.

Gable

FIGURE 73

**GAMBREL ROOF** one having two slopes on two sides with a steeper lower slope than the upper, flatter sections.
**Example:** Figure 74.

Gambrel

FIGURE 74

**GAP LOAN** one that fills the difference between the **floor loan** and the full amount of the **permanent loan.**
**Example:** A **developer** arranges a permanent **mortgage** that will fund $1,000,000 when the apartments she is building are 80% occupied. From completion of construction until 80% occupancy is reached, the mortgage is only $700,000. The developer arranges a *gap loan* of $300,000 for the **rent-up period.**

**GARDEN APARTMENTS** a housing complex whereby some or all **tenants** have access to a lawn area.
**Example:** Abel is now enjoying a steak that he grilled outside his *garden apartment* (Figure 75).

**GENERAL CONTRACTOR** one who constructs a building or other **improvement** for the owner or **developer.** May retain a construction labor force or use **subcontractors.** See **contractor.**
**Example:** Collins, a landowner, has architectural plans and **specifications** for an office building. She enters into a **contract** with Baker, a *general contractor,* to build the structure. Baker hires

subcontractors who put up the foundation, walls, roof, electrical and plumbing systems, etc.

**GENERAL LIEN** a **lien** that includes all of the property owned by the debtor, rather than a specific property.
**Example:** Abel failed to pay 3 months of rent and moved out. Baker, the **landlord,** obtained a *general lien* against Abel by going to secure a **judgment** against Abel. If Abel doesn't pay the back rent, Baker will apply for a specific lien against Abel's furniture and then have it sold.

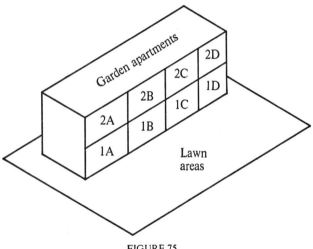

FIGURE 75

**GENERAL PARTNER** in a **partnership**, a partner whose **liability** is not limited. All partners in an ordinary partnership are general partners. A **limited partnership** must have at least one general partner.
**Example:** The *general partner* in a limited partnership is the **syndicator** who arranges the purchase, seeks investors, and assumes all liabilities of the partnership.

**GENERAL WARRANTY DEED** a **deed** in which the **grantor** agrees to protect the **grantee** against any other claim to **title** of the property and provides other promises. See **warranty deed.**
**Example:** Abel received a *general warranty deed* for land he bought from Baker. Five years later a defect is found. Mrs. Cabel, whose deceased husband sold the land to Baker, actually owns

one half of the property. Abel can claim restitution from Baker for the half because the deed warranties against all defects.

**GENTRIFICATION** the displacement of lower-income residents by higher-income residents in a neighborhood. Generally occurs when an older neighborhood is rehabilitated or revitalized.
**Example:** In the past, many large older homes in Inman Park, Atlanta, had been converted to boarding houses. Recently, middle-income families have been buying these houses and converting them back into **single-family homes.** The lower-income residents are often forced to move to surrounding areas and are replaced by the middle-income renovators. As this process is repeated, *gentrification* of the neighborhood occurs.

**GEORGIAN** a large, English style, formal 2- or 3-story rectangular house that is characterized by its classic lines and ornamentation.
**Example:** Figure 76.

Cornice with dentils

Gable or hip roof

2 or 3 stories

2 large chimneys high above each end

Palladian style window

Slate or copper roof

Balustrade

Double-hung windows

Glass lights

Quoins

Brick

FIGURE 76

**GIFT DEED a deed** for which **consideration** is love and affection, and no material consideration is involved.

**Example:** Abel, who is on the brink of **bankruptcy, executes** a *gift deed* to his wife. Since there is no consideration and the apparent reason for the transfer was to remove the property from the reach of Abel's creditors, the deed might not be valid. In other situations the gift deed would be upheld.

**GIFT TAX** federal tax upon a monetary gift to a relative or friend. Generally, each person may give up to $10,000 per year to each **donee** without imposition of a federal gift tax. On higher gifts, there may be a gift tax, or the gift may affect the **donor's estate tax.**
**Example:** Mr. and Mrs. Abel together give $20,000 this year to each of 3 sons ($60,000 total). There will be no *gift tax* imposed.

**GI LOAN** same as **VA loan.**

**GINNIE MAE** nickname for **Government National Mortgage Association.**

**GINNIE MAE PASS THROUGH** a **pass-through certificate** secured by a pool of mortgage loans insured by the Government National Mortgage Association, an arm of the federal government.
*Ginnie Mae pass throughs* often provide high yields with security to investors, although the returns may be affected by the pattern of loan repayments on the mortgages in the pool.

**GOOD FAITH** an act done honestly.
**Example:** Abel pays $1,000 to Baker as a *good faith* **deposit** on land Baker offers for sale. Baker doesn't own the land and doesn't plan to buy it, so his acceptance of the deposit was not in *good faith.*

**GOODWILL** a business **asset** of **intangible value** created by customer and supplier relations.
**Example:** Diversified Enterprises, Inc. bought Acme Hardware Co. They paid a total of $200,000, which included $100,000 for the **property**, $50,000 for **inventory**, and $50,000 for *goodwill.*

**GOVERNMENT NATIONAL MORTGAGE ASSOCIATION (GNMA)** a government organization to assist in housing finance. There are 2 main programs:
1. to **guarantee** payments to investors in mortgage-backed securities
2. to absorb the **write-down** of low-interest rate loans that are used to finance **low-income housing**
   See **secondary mortgage market.**
**Example:** Good Money Mortgage Bankers, who have originated $3,000,000 of **FHA** and **VA mortgages**, have issued **participation**

**mortgage** certificates, backed by the mortgages, to investors. *GNMA* guarantees the participation certificates (Figure 77).

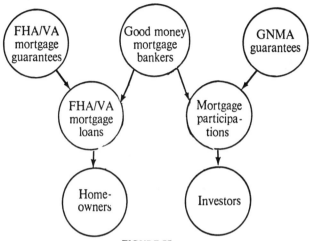

FIGURE 77

**GOVERNMENT RECTANGULAR SURVEY** a rectangular system of land **survey** that divides a district into 24-square mile **quadrangles** from the **meridian** (north-south line) and the **base line** (east-west line); the tracts are divided into 6-mile-square parts called *townships*, which are in turn divided into 36 tracts, each 1 mile square, called **sections**.

**Example:** *Government Rectangular Survey* System (Figure 78).

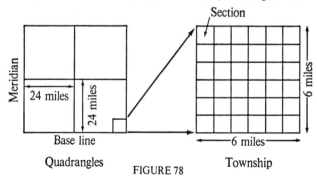

FIGURE 78

**GRACE PERIOD** the period during which one party may fail to perform without being considered in **default**.

**Example:** Rent is due on the first of each month, but the tenant requested and received a 10-day *grace period* from the landlord. If rent is paid on or before the 10th, the tenant is not in default.

**GRADE** 1. ground level at the foundation.
**Example:** Part A of the building in Figure 79 is above *grade;* Part B is below *grade.*

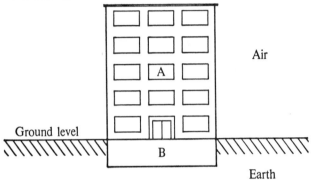

FIGURE 79

2. to prepare a smooth surface on a site.

**Example:** Machinery was brought to the **site** to *grade* the **land** in preparation for the foundation.

**GRADED LEASE** same as **graduated lease.**

**GRADIENT** the slope, or rate of increase or decrease in the elevation of a surface; usually expressed as a percentage:

$$\text{Gradient} = \frac{\text{vertical rise or fall}}{\text{horizontal distance}}$$

**Example:** The lot in Figure 80 has a 10% *gradient:*

$$\frac{10'}{100'} = 0.10$$

FIGURE 80

**GRADUATED LEASE** a lease that provides for graduated changes, at stated intervals, in the amount of rent.

**Example:** A 5-year *graduated lease* calls for annual rent increases of 5%. The yearly payments are shown in Figure 81.

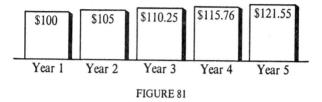

FIGURE 81

**GRADUATED PAYMENT MORTGAGE (GPM)** a mortgage requiring lower payments in early years than in later years. Payments increase in steps each year until the installments are sufficient to amortize the loan.

**Example:** A *GPM* may be made in which monthly payments rise by a set percentage after each year for the first 4 years. The payments would look like Figure 82.

FIGURE 82

**GRADUATE REALTORS® INSTITUTE (GRI)** an educational program sponsored by the **National Association of Realtors®** or State Boards.

**Example:** Broker Abel attends 3 approved courses offered by the California Association of Realtors®, and he passes the examinations. His new business cards read: Broker Albert Abel, *GRI*.

**GRANDFATHER CLAUSE** when a law is changed or a new law is passed, those whose specific activity was legal under the previous

law are often allowed to continue, by virtue of this provision.
**Example:** All real estate **brokers** are allowed to continue to practice as brokers after licensure requirements increase. The new law affects only new **licensees**; old licensees are *grandfathered.*

**GRANT** a technical term used in deeds of **conveyance** of property to indicate a transfer.
**Example:** In a **deed**, Abel *grants* his land to his daughter in **fee simple.**

**GRANTEE** the party to whom the **title** to **real property** is conveyed; the buyer.
**Example:** Edith Andrew Abel is the *grantee* under a **deed** from her father, Albert Abel.

**GRANTOR** anyone who gives a **deed.**
   **Examples:** *Grantors* include:
   • an individual (former) owner
   • a bankruptcy **trustee**
   • a **guardian** for an **incompetent**

**G.R.I.** graduate of the Realtors® Institute, which is affiliated with the **National Association of Realtors®. See Graduate Realtors Institute.**

**GROSS AREA** the total floor area of a building, usually measured from its outside walls.
**Example:** The *gross area* of a 2-story office building (Figure 83) that completely covers a 100′ X 100′ tract of land is 20,000 square feet (10,000 square feet for each story). Exterior walls, interior hallways, stairwells, and utility rooms absorb 4,000 square feet, so the **net leasable area** is 16,000 square feet.

**GROSS INCOME** total income from property before any expenses are deducted.
**Example:** A building with 10,000 net rentable square feet of floor space rents for an average of $10 per square foot. **Concessions** in the lobby produce an additional $20,000 in annual income. An average 5% **vacancy rate** is maintained. Two measures of *gross income* are shown in Table 19.

Table 19

| | | |
|---|---|---|
| Total rent income | $100,000 | (10,000 × $10) |
| Concession income | 20,000 | |
| Potential gross income | $120,000 | |
| Vacancy loss | − 5,000 | (.05 × $100,000) |
| Effective gross income | $115,000 | |

FIGURE 83

**GROSS INCOME MULTIPLIER (GIM)** same as **gross rent multiplier.**

**GROSS LEASE** a lease of property whereby the landlord (**lessor**) is responsible for paying all property expenses, such as taxes, insurance, utilities, and repairs.
**Example:** In a certain apartment complex the **landlord** pays for all utilities and taxes. The lease is a *gross lease*, since the landlord receives rent as a gross figure and must pay **operating expenses.**

**GROSS PROFIT RATIO** in an **installment sale,** the relationship between the gross profit (gain) and the **contract price.** The resulting fraction is applied to periodic receipts from the buyer to determine the taxable gain from each receipt.
**Example:** Land, held as a **capital asset** by Collins, is sold for $10,000. Collins tax basis was $4,000, so the resulting gain was $6,000. The *gross profit ratio* is 60% ($6,000 divided by $10,000 equals 60%). Collins accepted a $1,000 cash **downpayment** with the $9,000 balance of the price to be paid over 3 years. Of each amount paid toward the principal, 60% is gain to be taxed and the balance is a nontaxable return of capital. See **contract price.**

**GROSS RENT MULTIPLIER (GRM)** the sales price divided by the **contract** rental rate.
**Example:** The sales price is $40,000; the gross monthly **contract rent** is $400; the *GRM* = $40,000 ÷ $400 = 100. GRM may also be expressed as the number of years of rent equaling the purchase price ($40,000 ÷ $4,800 annual rent = a *GRM* of 8.333).

**GROUND LEASE** one that rents the land only.
**Example:** The landowner, Abel, gives a 50-year *ground lease* to Baker. Baker must pay $5,000 per year rent. At the end of the 50-year period, Abel owns the land **free and clear** and whatever **improvements** that Baker left on the property.

**GROUND RENT** the rent earned by leased land.
**Example:** The Good Title Company owns an office building situated on a **site** owned by the Widget Makers Retirement Fund. The site is leased to Good Title on a long-term basis and requires the payment of *ground rent* to the Widget Makers Retirement Fund on a semiannual basis.

**GROWING EQUITY MORTGAGE (GEM)** a **mortgage** loan in which the payment is increased by a specific amount each year, with the additional payment amount applied to **principal** retirement. As a result of the added principal retirement, the **maturity** of the loan is significantly shorter than a comparable **level payment mortgage.**
**Example:** Long purchased her home with a *growing equity mortgage.* Long's monthly payments will increase by 5% each year, with the increased amount applied to principal. Long will **retire** the loan in about half the time required to retire a comparable loan with fixed payments.

**(TO) GUARANTEE (A LOAN)** to agree to **indemnify** the holder of a loan all or a portion of the unpaid **principal** balance in case of **default** by the borrower. See also **VA mortgage loan.**
**Example:** Abel takes out a **VA mortgage loan** to purchase a home. The Veterans Administration *guarantees* the loan. In case foreclosure is threatened because Abel fails to make the payments, the VA will reimburse the lender for losses up to the amount guaranteed.

**GUARANTY** an assurance provided by one party that another party will perform under a contract.
**Example:** Fred Garrison is an experienced developer. His daughter, Ruth, decides to branch out and start her own company. The construction lender requires a *guaranty* from Fred Garrison before granting Ruth Garrison a loan for her first project.

**GUARDIAN** one appointed by a court to administer the personal affairs or property of an individual who is not capable of such duties.
**Example:** The *guardian* of an orphan **minor** signs a **deed** to sell property inherited by the minor, to pay the minor's educational expenses.

**GUIDELINE LIVES** **depreciable lives,** for buildings and equipment,

that are used in trade or business. Generally applied to **assets** bought before 1981; the **accelerated cost recovery system** applies to depreciable assets bought since then.
**Example:** *Guideline lives* for certain assets:
- apartments—40 years
- dwellings—45 years
- hotels—40 years
- warehouses—60 years

---

# H

---

**HABENDUM CLAUSE** the "to have and to hold" clause that defines or limits the quantity of the **estate** granted in the **deed**.
**Example:** The *habendum clause* "to have and to hold for one's lifetime" creates a **life estate**.

**HALF BATH** a room in a residence which contains a toilet and wash basin but no bathing facilities, such as a bathtub or shower stall. A three-quarter bath contains a shower but no bathtub.
**Example:** The two story home has two full baths upstairs and a *half bath* downstairs.

**HANDYMAN'S SPECIAL** in real estate classified advertising, generally refers to a house that requires extensive repair and remodeling, selling at a relatively low price.
**Example:** The Williams' looked at a *handyman's special* that needed new carpeting and repainting. They bought it for $50,000, spent $12,000 (not counting the value of their own labor) to repair it, then resold it for $75,000, providing them with a $13,000 profit.

**HANGOUT** the remaining balance of a loan when the **term** of the loan is beyond the term of a **lease**.
**Example:** A lender offers a 30-year loan on property that is leased to Big Buy Foods for the next 25 years. In 25 years the loan balance will be $100,000, which is the *hangout*. The lender estimates that the land value in 25 years will greatly exceed $100,000, so concern for the hangout is minimized.

**HAZARD INSURANCE** a form of insurance that protects against certain risks, such as from fires or storms.
**Example:** **Mortgage** lenders frequently require that owners maintain *hazard insurance*, at least to the extent of the mortgage debt.

**HEARING** a formal procedure, with issues of fact or law to be tried, in which parties have a right to be heard. Similar to a trial and may result in a final order.

**Example:** State **real estate commissions** hold *hearings* to investigate complaints filed against licensed salespersons.

**HECTARE** a metric land measurement equal to about 2.471 **acres** or about 107,637 square feet.

**Example:** Abel sold 6 *hectares* of land in Puerto Rico for $20,000.

**HEIR** one who inherits **property**.

**Example:** A person can decide on *heirs* by leaving a **valid** will. If one dies **intestate**, state laws determine who the heirs are.

**HEIRS AND ASSIGNS** a term often found in **deeds** and **wills** to grant a **fee simple** estate.

**Example:** Abel wills property to "Baker, *heirs and assigns*." Upon inheriting the property, Baker can sell it or will it to **heirs**.

**HEREDITAMENTS** any property, whether real or personal, tangible or intangible, that may be inherited.

**Example:** Buildings, lands, and **leaseholds** are examples of *hereditaments*.

**HIGHEST AND BEST USE** an **appraisal** term meaning the legally and physically possible use that, at the time of appraisal, is most likely to produce the greatest net return to the land and/or buildings over a given period.

**Example:** A vacant lot in the city is valued at $10,000 if developed for a **single-family house**, $20,000 as an **apartment building**, $25,000 as a retail store, and $30,000 as a small chemical processing plant. Because of **restrictions** on water supply and disposal, the chemical plant is not physically or legally possible. **Zoning** laws prohibit commercial development. Therefore, the *highest and best use* of the lot is for an apartment building.

**HIGH RISE** generally a building that exceeds 6 stories in height and is equipped with elevators.

**Example:** A *high-rise* building is constructed to include retail space on the first floor, 8 floors of office space, 10 floors of **condominium** units, and a club/restaurant on the 20th floor.

**HIGH VICTORIAN ITALIANATE** a nineteenth century style house with three different kinds of window arches, the primary distinguishing characteristic of this style. The arches are straight-sided, flat-topped and rectangular.

**Example:** Figure 84.

Flat-topped arch   Large brackets

Straight-sided arch   Entrance way with columns supporting entablature   Hip roof

Rectangular arch   Three different types of arches

Symmetrical bays

FIGURE 84

**HIP ROOF** one formed by four walls sloped in different directions with the two longer sides forming a ridge at the top.
**Example:** Figure 85.

Hip

FIGURE 85

**HISTORIC DISTRICT** a designated area where the buildings are considered to have some significant historic character. Such designation makes the area eligible for certain federal assistance programs and protects the area from clearance in conjunction with federally sponsored programs.

**Example:** Older areas, such as the French Quarter in New Orleans, enjoy protection by being designated as *historic districts*.

**HISTORIC STRUCTURE** a building that is officially recognized for its historic significance has special status under the 1976 Tax Reform Act, which encourages **rehabilitation** and discourages **demolition** or substantial alteration of the structure. In 1981 a special tax law allowed a 25% **tax credit** for rehabilitation of **certified historic structures**, reduce to 20% in 1986.
**Example:** Because the old office building was designated a certified *historic structure*, its owner decided to restore the building to take advantage of allowable tax deductions.

**HOLDBACK** money not paid until certain events have occurred, such as a **floor loan** of a **loan commitment** or **retainage** on a construction contract.

**Example:** On a $1,000,000 loan the lender has a $300,000 *holdback* until the property is 80% rented.
**Example:** The developer has a 10% *holdback* from subcontractors until the building **inspection** is complete.

**HOLDER IN DUE COURSE** one who acquires a **bearer instrument** in **good faith** and is eligible to keep it even though it may have been stolen.
**EXAMPLE:** Abel receives from Baker a $100 bill in payment of rent on his apartment. Police inform Abel that the bill was stolen by Baker from Cobb. Since the bill is bearer paper and Abel accepted it without knowing about the theft, he became a *holder in due course* and is allowed to keep it.

**HOLD HARMLESS CLAUSE** in a **contract**, a clause whereby one party agrees to protect another party from claims.
**Example:** Big Buy Foods is leasing property from its landlord, Lucky Lessors. A customer is injured by a falling light fixture, and she sues both Big Buy Foods and Lucky Lessors. In the **lease**, Big Buy Foods agreed to a *hold harmless clause* whereby they **indemnified** Lucky Lessors against such events.

**HOLDING COMPANY** one that owns or controls another company(ies).
**Example:** Banks and public utilities are often owned or controlled by a *holding company*. Sometimes this arrangement allows more latitude for business practices than the operating company can achieve alone.

**HOLDING COSTS** same as **carrying costs**.

**HOLDING PERIOD** the time span of ownership, often for investment real estate.

**Example:** Some investors prefer short *holding periods* (under 5 years) in an attempt to retain high levels of financial **leverage**. Others hold property longer to reduce frequent **transaction costs** and avoid **depreciation recapture**.

**HOLDOVER TENANT** a **tenant** who remains in possession of leased property after the expiration of the lease **term**. See **tenancy at sufferance.**
**Example:** Abel leases an apartment for one year. At the end of the year, Abel is still in the process of finding a new home. As a *holdover tenant*, Abel may be evicted or allowed to remain on a month-to-month basis by continuing to pay rent, at the landlord's discretion.

**HOME INSPECTOR** a professional who evaluates the structural and mechanical condition of a home prior to its being sold. Some states require home inspectors to be bonded or licensed.
**Example:** Before closing on their new home, the Felixes hired a *home inspector* to check the condition of the structure. The inspector discovered an unsafe furnace burner and a leaking faucet. The seller agreed to have the problems repaired before the closing.

**HOME LOAN** see **mortgage.**

**HOMEOWNER'S ASSOCIATION** an organization of the homeowners in a particular **subdivision**, planned unit development, or **condominium**; generally for the purpose of enforcing **deed** restrictions or managing the **common elements** of the development. See **community association.**
**Example:** All unit owners of the Lakefront Condominiums are members of the Lakefront *Homeowners' Association*. The Association maintains the pool, grounds, and building structure, and regulates use of common elements. They assess each owner a $75 monthly fee.

**HOMEOWNERSHIP** the state of living in a structure that one owns. Contrasted with being a renter or **tenant** in one's home.
**Example:** *Homeownership* is a goal of many families. It provides security from the decisions of landlords, pride of ownership, and investment advantages in exchange for undertaking the responsibilities of a property owner.

**HOMEOWNER'S POLICY** an insurance policy designed especially for homeowners. Usually protects the owner from losses caused by most common disasters, theft, and **liability**. Coverage and costs vary widely.
**Example:** Whitman acquired a *homeowner's policy* for an annual premium of $500. It insures her home from fire losses (up to $100,000), theft (of household goods, excluding jewelry, paintings,

stamp collections, silverware), and gives up to $300,000 of **liability** protection.

**HOMEOWNERS' WARRANTY PROGRAM (HOW)** a private insurance program that protects purchasers of newly constructed homes, when the builder participates in the program, against structural and mechanical faults.
**Example:** Abel purchases a new home. The builder participates in the HOW program and provides Abel with a *homeowner's warranty* to cover any faults or oversights in the construction.

**HOMEOWNER WARRANTY INSURANCE** same as **homeowner warranty program.**

**HOMESTEAD** status provided to a homeowner's principal residence by some state statutes; protects home against **judgments** up to specified amounts.
**Example:** *Homestead* laws in Texas prevent a lender, other than the **mortgage** lender, from forcing the sale of one's principal residence to satisfy a **debt.**

**HOMESTEAD EXEMPTION** in some jurisdictions, a reduction in the **assessed value** allowed for one's principal residence.
**Example:** The *homestead exemption* in Georgia enables a homeowner, upon application, to get $5,000 subtracted from the assessor's **appraisal** of the home. This reduces the property tax burden.

**HOMOGENEOUS** uniform, of like characteristics or quality. Opposite of heterogeneous. The values of an area tend to be maximized when properties are *homogeneous,* because low valued or unusual properties are likely to reduce the value of other nearby properties of higher cost.
**Example:** The houses in the neighborhood were *homogeneous,* all single-family, one-story buildings with brick exteriors. They were readily marketable with asking and selling prices in a tight range.

**HORIZONTAL PROPERTY LAWS** state statutes that enable **condominium** ownership of property. Whereas property laws generally recognize **ownership rights** to all space from the center of the earth to some distance in the air, condominium laws allow individual ownership to be split on a horizontal plane that generally limits the unit owner's interest to the inside dimensions of the unit. See **common elements.**
**Example:** Before passage of *horizontal property laws,* all owners in a condominium were obligated under each individual mortgage loan in the complex. If one owner **defaulted,** the lender could **foreclose** on the entire condominium. Now, to secure a loan, each owner pledges only his or her limited interest in the condominium.

**HOUSING AND URBAN DEVELOPMENT (HUD) DEPARTMENT**
a U.S. government agency established to implement certain federal housing and community development programs.
**Example:** Mason desires to develop a housing project for low-income families. She applies to the *Department of Housing and Urban Development* for a special low-interest loan for the development.

**HOUSING CODE** a local government **ordinance** that sets minimum standards of safety and sanitation for existing residential buildings. Contrast to **building codes,** which pertain to new construction.
**Example:** Because of violations of the *housing code*, including a badly leaking roof and rat infestation, the old apartment building was condemned.

**HOUSING STARTS** an estimate of the number of dwelling units on which construction has begun during a stated period.
**Example:** During the last month, *housing starts* were 20% lower than the same month a year ago, reflecting a lower demand for new houses caused by high **mortgage** rates.

**HUNDRED PERCENT LOCATION** see **one-hundred percent location.**

**HYPOTHECATE** to pledge a thing as **security** without having to give up possession of it.
**Example:** Through use of a **mortgage** or **deed of trust,** the buyer *hypothecates* a newly acquired home to the lender or **trustee.** The buyer uses and controls the property.

# I

**IMPLIED CONTRACT** created by actions but not necessarily written or spoken. See also **Statute of frauds.**
**Example:** Abel posts a for-sale sign on his property that says, "See Your Broker." Davis submits an offer through her **broker** and buys the property. Abel refuses to pay the broker, who then goes to court contending that the sign created an *implied contract*.

**IMPLIED EASEMENT** See **easement by prescription.**

**IMPLIED WARRANTY** one that is not written but exists under the law. Contrasted with "expressed."
**Example:** Under the law in several states there is an *implied warranty* **of habitability** for apartments leased to tenants. This means

that the tenant has the right to a dwelling that is fit for living, i.e., there are no **building code** violations.

**IMPROVED LAND** land that has some improvements. Land that has been partially or fully developed for use.
**Examples:** Any of the following activities on a piece of **raw land** will result in *improved land*:
• landscaping and grading
• installation of utilities
• construction of roads, curbs, and/or gutters
• contruction of buildings

**IMPROVEMENTS** those additions to **raw land**, such as buildings, streets, sewers, etc., tending to increase value.
**Example:** A hypothetical example of how *improvement* costs may affect property and land values is shown in Table 20.

**TABLE 20**

| Improvement | Cost of improvement | Total property value | Value of land |
|---|---|---|---|
| None | $ 0 | $ 500 | $ 500 |
| Curbs, drainage, & utilities | 3,000 | 5,000 | 2,000 |
| House | 70,000 | 85,000 | 15,000 |
| Apartment building | 250,000 | 290,000 | 40,000 |

**IMPOUND ACCOUNT** a fund set aside for future needs. See **reserve fund**, **escrow account**.
**Example:** Each month a homeowner deposits $\frac{1}{12}$ of the estimated annual **property tax** and insurance premium requirements into an *impound account*, so that the balance will be sufficient to pay amounts when they come due.

**IMPUTED INTEREST** implied interest. In a **mortgage** that states an insufficient interest rate, the law will impute that the rate is higher, and the **principal** is less.
**Example:** Abel sells property to Baker. Baker gives Abel a portion of the price in cash and Abel takes a **note** for the remainder. Since the gain on the sale is taxable at **capital gains** rates and the interest paid on the note is taxed as **ordinary income**, it is in Abel's favor to set a higher price in exchange for charging a low rate of interest on

the note. If this is done, the **Internal Revenue Service** will consider a portion of the principal paid on the note as *imputed interest* and tax that portion as ordinary income.

**INCHOATE** unfinished, begun but not completed. In real estate, this can apply to **dower** or **curtesy** rights prior to the death of a spouse.
**Example:** Collins dies, leaving dower rights *inchoate*. Her children by a former marriage sue her widower to recover her share of property he sold.

**INCOME** the money or other benefit coming from the use of property, skill, or business.
**Examples:** In real estate, *income* may be produced by:
• rents
• fees
• royalties
• sales of crops, timber, or livestock
• revenues derived from business activities on the property

**INCOME APPROACH** a method appraising real estate based on the property's anticipated future income. The formula for appraisal by the income approach is

$$\frac{\text{Expected annual income}}{\text{Capitalization rate}} = \text{Market value}$$

See **capitalization** and **gross rent multiplier**.
**Example:** A property is expected to produce a **net operating income** of $100,000 yearly. Recent sales data indicate that the **capitalization rate** for **comparable** properties is 10%. By the *income approach*, the property has a market value of

$$\frac{\$100,000}{.10} = \$1,000,000$$

**INCOME PROPERTY** real estate that generates rental income.
**Examples:** The following are types of *income property:*
• apartment buildings
• shopping centers
• office buildings
• industrial properties and warehouses
• resort and recreational properties
• hotels, motels, and restaurants
The following are generally not considered *income property:*
• personal residences
• undeveloped land (rental income is minimal)
• schools, churches, parks

**INCOME STREAM** a regular flow of money generated by a business or investment.

**Example:** A **net lease** that pays $1,000 per month **rent** for 10 years provides an *income stream*.

**INCOMPETENT** one not legally capable of completing a **contract**. Includes the mentally ill, **minors**, and others considered incapable.
**Example:** Abel, a moron, inherited $100,000, and wants to buy a tract of land. He enters into a contract, but his legal guardian **voids** it because the land is worth under $5,000. It is voidable because Abel is *incompetent*.

**INCORPORATE** 1. to form a **corporation** under regulations provided by the Secretary of State.
**Example:** Abel intends to enter the real estate **brokerage** business and wishes to protect his personal **assets**. He retains a lawyer whom he pays a $1,000 fee to *incorporate* the business. Abel is the sole stockholder and chairman of the board of directors. Abel's personal assets are protected because **liability** is limited to the assets owned by the corporation.
2. to provide a geographic area the legal status of a political subdivision of the state.
**Example:** A large **subdivision** outside a large city petitions the state legislature to *incorporate* as an independent city. The residents of the incorporated area may elect representatives and tax themselves to provide services.

**INCORPOREAL PROPERTY** legal interests in real property that do not entail the right of possession. See **easement, license.**

**INCURABLE DEPRECIATION** a defect that cannot be cured or that is not financially practical to cure; a defect in the "bone structure" of a building. Compare **curable depreciation.**
**Example:** It is estimated that if a specific house had a more convenient **floor plan**, it would sell for an additional $5,000. The cost of rearranging the partitions to improve the plan is $10,000. The poor floor plan is *incurable depreciation*.

**INDEMNIFY** 1. to protect another person against loss or damage.
**Example:** FHA mortgage loans *indemnify* the lender against the risk of a buyer's **default.**
2. to compensate a party for loss or damage.
**Example:** Upon **foreclosure**, the FHA *indemnified* the lender for losses on the defaulted loan.

**INDENTURE** a written agreement made between 2 or more persons having different interests.
**Example:** The *indenture* **trustee** enforces the agreement made between the **bond** issuer (borrower) and the lender.

**INDEPENDENT CONTRACTOR** a **contractor** who is self-

employed.
**Example:** Collins, a real estate salesperson, is an *independent contractor* engaged by **broker** Baker. She has not received any income in the last 3 months but is unable to collect unemployment insurance because she is an *independent contractor*. Last year she paid a self-employment tax instead of social security.

**INDEX** 1. a statistic that indicates some current economic or financial condition. Indexes are often used to make adjustments in wage rates, rental rates, loan interest rates, and pension benefits set by long-term contracts.
**Example:** Office building rental rates are sometimes adjusted in relation to the consumer price *index*.
2. to adjust contract terms according to an index. See **indexed loan.**
**Example:** Mortgage interest rates on **adjustable rate mortgages** are often *indexed* to the average mortgage rate for all lenders or the average cost of funds for all lenders.

**INDEXED LOAN** a long-term loan in which the **term,** payment, **interest rate.** or **principal** amount may be adjusted periodically according to a specific **index.** The index and the manner of adjustment are generally stated in the loan contract.
**Example:** An **adjustable rate mortgage** is an *indexed loan.* At specific intervals the **face interest rate** on the loan may be changed according to variations in the specified **index.**

**INDEX LEASE** a rental agreement that requires changes in rent based on a published record of cost changes. See **cost of living index.**
**Example:** A landlord makes an *index lease* with initial rent at $10,000 per year, adjusted annually by the Consumer Price Index (CPI). If the CPI is 100 at the time of the lease and increases to 110 in the second year, the rent for the second year will be 10,000 × 1.10 = $11,000.

**INDUSTRIAL PARK** an area designed and **zoned** for manufacturing and associated activities.
**Example:** Figure 86.

**INDUSTRIAL PROPERTY** property used for industrial purposes, such as factories.
**Examples:** Types of *industrial property:*
• factory-office multiuse property
• factory-warehouse multiuse property
• heavy manufacturing buildings
• industrial parks
• light manufacturing buildings
• research and development parks

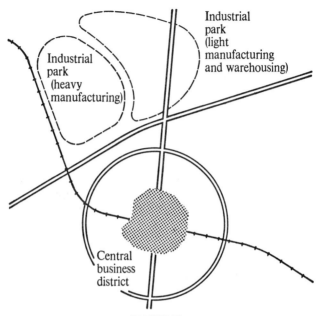

FIGURE 86

**INFORMATION REPORTING** reports provided to the Internal Revenue Service (IRS), such as commissions earned by real estate sales agents and real estate transactions of home sellers, reported by the broker.

**Example:** In January, Baker files a form 1099 with the IRS for real estate transactions she brokered during the past year. Such *information reporting* is required by the Tax Reform Act of 1986.

**INHERITANCE TAX** a tax, based on property **value**, imposed in some states on those who acquire property from a decedent. Compare **estate tax**.

**Example:** An estate tax is based on the value of all property left by the decedent, whereas an *inheritance tax* is based on the amount that an **heir** receives.

**INJUNCTION** an order issued under the seal of a court to restrain one or more parties to a legal proceeding, from performing an act deemed inequitable to another party or parties in the proceeding.

**Example:** Abel begins serving alcoholic drinks on property he bought from Baker. Baker claims that a **deed restriction** prevents consumption of such beverages on the property, and sues Abel. Since the trial is set several months ahead, Baker requests an *injunction* to prevent the sale of drinks until the trial.

**INNER CITY** generally the older and more urbanized area of a large city surrounding the **central business district.** The term often refers to densely populated blighted **areas** characterized by low-income residents and a high proportion of minority racial and ethnic groups.
**Examples:**
• Many *inner city* neighborhoods have been **rehabilitated** by **urban renewal** projects.
• Violence is a problem in some *inner city* schools.
• The mayor promises a construction program to rehabilitate the *inner city*.

**IN REM** Latin: "against the thing." A proceeding against the property directly, as distinguished from a proceeding against a person (used in taking land for nonpayment of taxes, etc.)
**Example:** Baker cannot collect on his past due loan from Abel. Baker, through court action, secures a **judgment** *in rem* against a building lot owned by Abel, which causes a lien against the lot.

**INSIDE LOT** in a **subdivision,** a lot surrounded on each side by other lots, as opposed to a corner lot, which has road frontage on at least 2 sides.
**Example:** An *inside lot* **adjoining** a corner lot (Figure 87).

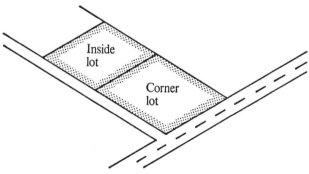

FIGURE 87

**INSPECTION** a physical scrutinizing review of property or of documents.
**Example:** *Inspections* may be required for the following purposes:

- compliance with **building codes**
- sale requirements as to property conditions, such as wood-destroying insects or structural soundness
- legal review of documents such as **leases** and **mortgages** to determine whether they are as purported

**INSTALLMENTS** parts of the same **debt**, payable at successive periods as agreed; payments made to reduce a **mortgage**.
**Example:** Abel purchases a property with a **land contract.** The contract calls for a payment of $30,000 at **closing,** with 10 annual *installments* of $15,000 each.

**INSTALLMENT CONTRACT** same as **land contract.**

**INSTALLMENT SALE** when a seller accepts a **mortgage** for part of the sale, the tax on the gain is paid as the mortgage **principal** is collected. See also **contract price, gross profit ratio, imputed interest.**
**Example:** Collins sells for $10,000 her land that she bought 3 years ago for $4,000. Her gain is $6,000. She received 10% ($1,000) as a cash **down payment** and a 90% ($9,000) **purchase money mortgage.** She will report 10% of the gain in the year of sale and the balance as she collects the principal of the purchase money mortgage. To do so, on her tax return she reports the sale as an installment sale. See Table 21.

**TABLE 21**

|  | Year of sale | Year 1 | Year 2 | Year 3 |
|---|---|---|---|---|
| Principal paid | $1000 | $3000 | $3000 | $3000 |
| Taxable gain | 600 | 1800 | 1800 | 1800 |
| Interest income | 0 | 900 | 600 | 300 |

**INSTITUTE OF REAL ESTATE MANAGEMENT (IREM)** a professional organization of property managers. Affiliated with the **National Association of Realtors®.** Publishes the *Journal of Property Management.*
**Address:**
Institute of Real Estate Management
430 North Michigan Avenue
Chicago, Illinois 60611

**INSTITUTIONAL LENDER** financial intermediaries who invest in loans and other securities on behalf of their depositors or customers; lending and investment activities are regulated by laws to limit risk.
**Example:** *Institutional lenders* are a prime source of real estate

loans. Many organizations, such as **savings and loan associations** and **commerical banks**, originate loans directly; others, such as insurance companies, lend through **mortgage brokers**.

**INSTRUMENT** a written legal document, created to establish the rights and liabilities of the parties to it.
**Examples:** The following are examples of instruments:
• **deed**
• mortgage
• land contract
• lease
• assignment

**INSURABLE INTEREST** an **interest** in a person or property that would cause one a loss if that person or property were injured. Must be present to collect from an insurance policy.
**Example:** The Good Money Savings Association lent $50,000 on Abel's house. Yesterday it was destroyed by fire. Good Money can collect on its insurance policy, because they were insured and had an *insurable interest*. Five Star Savings also had an insurance policy on the home but had no **lien**, so they couldn't collect.

**INSURABLE TITLE** a **title** that can be insured by a **title insurance** company.
**Example:** In some **contracts** for the sale of **real estate** the buyer must receive *insurable title* or he is not obligated to purchase the property.

**INSURANCE COVERAGE** total amount and type of insurance carried.
**Example:** The owner maintained $100,000 of hazard *insurance coverage* on the property, and $300,000 of **liability** *insurance coverage*. The **hazard insurance** coverage was adequate to meet the 80% **coinsurance** requirement in the policy.

**INSURANCE (MORTGAGE)** a service, generally purchased by a borrower, that will **indemnify** the lender in case of **foreclosure** of the loan. Indemnification is generally limited to losses suffered by the lender in the foreclosure process. See **FHA mortgage loan, private mortgage insurance**.
**Example:** Abel took out a **home loan** covered by *mortgage insurance*. After one year, Abel **defaulted** on the loan and the lender foreclosed. Abel owed $50,000, but the foreclosure sale produced only $40,000 in proceeds. The insurance company paid the lender the difference of $10,000.

**INTANGIBLE VALUE** value that cannot be seen or touched.
**Example:** The **goodwill** of an established business is an *intangible value*.

**INTEREST** 1. cost of the use of money.

**Example:** Lenders require payment of *interest* at a specified rate, to compensate for risk, deferment of benefits, inflation, and administrative burdens.

2. the type and extent of ownership.

**Example:** One may hold either a partial or **fee simple** *interest* in a property. That *interest* entitles one to specific ownership rights.

## INTEREST DEDUCTIONS (UNDER THE 1986 TAX ACT)

*Investment Interest.* Investment interest deductions are limited to net investment income, which includes interest, dividends, long-term capital gains and income or loss from working interests in oil and gas interests. However, net investment income includes neither rental or other passive activity income or loss, nor interest paid to buy an ownership in a passive activity. The $10,000 allowance for investment interest expense above investment income allowed before the 1986 tax act is subject to a 4-year phase out, allowing 65% in 1987, then 40%, 20%, and 10%, for each subsequent year.

*Construction Interest.* Interest incurred during the construction and development of most real estate (but not a personal residence) must be capitalized, and deducted over its depreciable life beginning when the property is ready to be placed in service or sold.

*Business Interest.* Interest incurred in an active trade or business in which the investor materially participates is not investment interest, and is fully deductible.

*Housing Interest.* Interest on up to 2 personal residences is allowed as an itemized deduction, provided the mortgages did not exceed the value of the residences and were borrowed before August 17, 1986. However, deductible interest on mortgages borrowed after that is limited to the sum of the home cost, improvements, medical and educational expenses; provided the total debt does not exceed the market value of the residence.

Points paid on a mortgage to acquire a principal residence may be deductible if they are customary in the geographic area; points paid for other purposes such as refinancing are amortized rather than deducted currently.

*Consumer Interest.* Interest on credit cards and auto loans will not be deductible by 1990. The deduction is being phased out over 4 years, allowing 65% in 1987, then 40%, 2% and 10%.

**INTEREST-ONLY LOAN** a loan in which interest is payable at regular intervals until loan **maturity**, when the full loan balance is due. Does not require **amortization**. Contrast **self-amortizing mortgage**.

**Example: Land** was bought with a 5-year *interest-only loan* of $100,000 at 12%. The **interest** of $12,000 was paid annually for 4 years. The $100,000 **principal**, together with the last $12,000 interest payment, was due at the end of the fifth year.

**INTEREST RATE** 1. the percentage of a sum of money charged for its use.
2. the **rate of return** on an investment.
**Example:** A $50,000 mortgage loan is made at 12% interest and 4 **discount points**. The contract *interest rate* is 12% and determines the monthly payment amount. The **effective rate** of interest, which incorporates the effects of the discount points, is 12.55% and is the rate of return to the lender if the loan runs to maturity.

**INTERIM FINANCING** a loan, including a **construction loan**, used when the property owner is unable or unwilling to arrange permanent financing. Generally arranged for less than 3 years, used to gain time for financial or market conditions to improve.
**Example:** Monroe developed an office building but, in the expectation of falling **interest rates**, does not wish to use permanent financing at this time. He arranges a 2-year *interim* loan, during which time he seeks favorable permanent financing.

**INTERNAL RATE OF RETURN (IRR)** the true annual rate of earnings on an investment. Equates the value of cash returns with cash invested. Considers the application of **compound interest** factors. Requires a trial-and-error method for solution. The formula is

$$\sum_{t=1}^{n} \frac{\text{periodic } cash\, flow}{(1+i)^t} = \text{investment amount}$$

where $i$ = internal rate of return
$t$ = each time interval
$n$ = total time intervals
$\Sigma$ = summation

**Example:** Abel sells for $20,000 land that he bought 4 years earlier for $10,000. There were no **carrying charges** or **transaction costs**. The *internal rate of return* was about 19%. That is the annual rate at which compound interest must be paid for $10,000 to become $20,000 in 4 years.
**Example:** Baker received $3,000 per year for 5 years on a $10,000 investment. The *internal rate of return* was about 15%.

**INTERNAL REVENUE CODE** the law, passed by Congress, that specifies how and what income is to be taxed, and what may be deducted from taxable income.
**Example:** Court cases, regulations, revenue rules, and revenue procedures attempt to properly interpret the *Internal Revenue Code*.

**INTERNAL REVENUE SERVICE (IRS)** an agency of the federal government that is responsible for the administration and collection of federal income taxes. The IRS prints and distributes tax forms and audits tax returns.

**Addresses:**
  **Regional Offices**

- Andover, MA 05501
- Atlanta, GA 31101
- Austin, TX 73301
- Cincinnati, OH 45999
- Fresno, CA 93888
- Holtsville, NY 00501
- Kansas City, MO 64999
- Memphis, TN 37501
- Ogden, UT 84201
- Philadelphia, PA 19255

**INTERNATIONAL ARCHITECTURE** an early twentieth century style house whose design is very simple with no ornamentation. The windows appear to be continuous rather than appearing to be holes in the walls.
**Example:** Figure 88.

FIGURE 88

**INTERNATIONAL ASSOCIATION OF ASSESSING OFFICERS (IAAO)** a professional organization of property tax assessors. Awards the designation of Certified Assessment Evaluator (CAE). Publishes the quarterly *Assessors Journal*.
**Address:**
International Association of Assessing Officers
1313 East 60th Street
Chicago, Illinois 60637

**INTERNATIONAL RIGHT OF WAY ASSOCIATION (IR/WA)** an

individual membership association (no corporate membership) that offers courses covering various phases of right-of-way work. Educational curriculum includes law, engineering, appraisal. Offers a designation, SR/WA, and a bimonthly magazine.
**Address:**
International Right of Way Association
6133 Bristol Parkway, Suite 270
Culver City, California 90230

**INTERSTATE LAND SALES ACT** a federal law, administered by the Department of Housing and Urban Development (HUD), which requires certain disclosures and advertising procedures when selling land to purchasers in other states.
**Example:** Rollins, a developer, has a 200-acre subdivision in Florida and wishes to market lots nationally. Under the *Interstate Land Sales Act,* she must register with the Office of Interstate Land Sales Registration (OILSR, a division of HUD), and make certain disclosures in the prospectus sent to prospective purchasers.

**INTER VIVOS** during one's life.
**Example:** Abel makes an *inter vivos* gift of $10,000 to each of 3 children. The children spend the $10,000 and may inherit more money if Abel names them in the will he is preparing.

**INTESTATE** 1. (adj.) having made no valid will 2. (noun) a person who dies leaving no will or leaving one that is defective. Property goes to the legal heirs of the intestate.
**Example:** If Doris dies *intestate,* her heirs under state law will inherit her property. If she leaves no heirs her property will escheat.

**INVENTORY** property held for sale or to be used in the manufacture of goods held for sale. Does not qualify for capital gains tax treatment.
**Examples:** Examples of *inventory* are:
• raw materials
• work-in-progress
• finished goods
To a builder, property under construction and property completed are *inventory.* To a subdivider, vacant lots are *inventory.*

**INVERSE CONDEMNATION** a legal procedure to obtain compensation when a property interest has been taken or diminished in value by a government activity.
**Example:** Abel owns a home near a public airport. The city constructs a new runway that sends air traffic directly over Abel's house, seriously diminishing Abel's enjoyment of his property. Abel may sue for *inverse condemnation* and, if successful, may force the airport authority to take Abel's house in exchange for just compensation.

**INVESTMENT ANALYSIS** a study of the likely return from a proposed real estate investment with the objective of evaluating the amount an investor may pay for it, the investment's suitability to that investor, or the feasibility of a proposed real estate development. Appraised value is based on a synthesis of people in the market whereas *investment analysis* is based on the value to a specific investor.
There are various methods of *investment analysis*, including:
• Cash on cash return
• Payback period
• Internal rate of return
• Net present value
Each provides some measure of the estimated return on an investment, based on various assumptions and investment horizons.

**INVESTMENT LIFE CYCLE** the time span from acquisition of an investment to final disposition.
**Example:** The best way to measure the **rate of return** from an *investment* is over its *life cycle*. All relevant investment contributions, **cash flows**, and resale proceeds are known (Figure 89).

FIGURE 89

**INVESTMENT TAX CREDIT** a reduction in income tax generally based on the cost and life of certain assets purchased.
**Note:** This was abolished by the Tax Reform Act of 1986; but see **rehabilitation tax credit** and **low-income housing (qualified).**

**INVOLUNTARY CONVERSION** **condemnation** or sudden destruction by nature.
**Example:** A property is taken by **eminent domain** for the purpose of constructing a public highway. This *involuntary conversion* of the property is contrasted with a sale that the owner enters into voluntarily.

**INVOLUNTARY LIEN** a lien imposed against property without consent of the owner (unpaid taxes, special assessments, etc.). Compare **mortgage lien.**
**Example:** The **absentee** land **owner** was not notified of the past-due tax bill. The tax **assessor** placed a lien on the property that was an *involuntary lien*, since the owner did not take action to cause the lien.

**INWOOD ANNUITY FACTOR** a number that, when multiplied by the periodic payment from a **level payment income stream,** indicates the present value of the income stream, based on a specific interest rate. Same formula as that for **annuity factor.**
**Example:** An investment is expected to provide income of $100 per month for 10 years. At the end of 10 years the investment has no value. At an interest rate of 10%, the present value (PV) of the investment is

$$PV = \$100 \times 75.67 = \$7,567$$

where 75.67 is the *Inwood annuity factor.*

**INWOOD TABLES** a set of **annuity factors** for various **interest rates** and **maturities.** See **Inwood annuity factor.**
**Example:** The *Inwood tables* show that the right to receive $1.00 at the end of each year for 10 years at 15% interest is worth $5.02 as of the beginning of the first year.

**IRREVOCABLE** incapable of being recalled or revoked; unchangeable.
**Example:** The bank issued an *irrevocable* **letter of credit** stating that if the terms of the **contract** were met the bank would lend the money requested.

**ITALIAN VILLA** a Latin style, massive 2- or 3-story house of masonry with large overhanging eaves.
**Example:** Figure 90.

---

# J

---

**JEOPARDY** danger, **risk.**
**Example:** Property pledged as **security** for a delinquent loan is in *jeopardy* of **foreclosure.**

**JOINT AND SEVERAL LIABILITY** a **creditor** can demand full repayment from any and all of those who have borrowed. Each borrower is **liable** for the full debt, not just the **prorated** share.
**Example:** Abel and Baker are **general partners.** Together they borrow (or the **partnership** borrows) $10,000 from a bank, agreeing to

*joint and several liability*. Upon **default**, the bank can collect the remaining balance of the $10,000 from either party.

**JOINT TENANCY** ownership of **realty** by 2 or more persons, each of whom has an **undivided interest** with the **right of survivorship.** Typically used by related persons.
**Example:** Abel and Baker own land in *joint tenancy*. Each owns half of the entire (undivided) property. Upon Abel's death, Baker will own the entire property, and vice versa.

Massive

2 or 3 story

Some have quoins

Large overhanging eaves

Heavy cornice line

Decorative iron work

Brackets

FIGURE 90

**JOINT VENTURE** an agreement between 2 or more parties who invest in a single business or property. See also **limited partnership, tenancy in common.**
**Example:** Abel and Baker form a *joint venture* to explore for minerals on Cobb's land. Abel and Baker use a **tenancy in common** arrangement for ownership of the mineral rights.

**JUDGMENT** a decree of a court stating that one individual is indebted to another and fixing the amount of the indebtedness.
**Example:** As a result of Abel's failure to pay disputed rent, the landlord obtained a court decision, or *judgment*, against Abel.

**JUDGMENT CREDITOR** one who has received a court decree or **judgment** for money due from the **judgment debtor.**

**Example:** To enforce the judgment awarded by court, the *judgment creditor* filed a **lien** against the **judgment debtor** Abel.

**JUDGMENT DEBTOR** one against whom a **judgment** has been issued by a court for money owed, and that remains unsatisfied.
**Example:** A judgment was entered into against Abel for nonpayment of rent. Abel is the *judgment debtor.*

**JUDGMENT LIEN** the claim upon the property of a debtor resulting from a **judgment.**
**Example:** Abel won't pay his debt to Baker. After establishing the debt in court, Baker may be allowed by the court to put a *judgment lien* on Abel's **real estate.**

**JUDICIAL FORECLOSURE** having a defaulted debtor's property sold where the court ratifies the price paid.
**Example:** Happy Mortgage Company is owed $50,000 on a first mortgage by Mr. Baker. At *judicial foreclosure*, Happy Mortgage Company **bids** $30,000 for the property, which is more than anyone else bids. They then claim the property and are awarded a $20,000 **deficiency judgment** against Mr. Baker.

**JUNIOR MORTGAGE** a **mortgage** whose claim against the property will be satisfied only after prior mortgages have been repaid. See **first mortgage, second mortgage.**
**Example:** Property is purchased for $100,000. A first mortgage is obtained covering $75,000 of the price. To reduce the cash requirements, a *junior mortgage* is arranged to cover $15,000 of the price. The remaining $10,000 is cash **equity.**

**JURISDICTION** geographic or topical area of authority for a specific government entity.
**Example:** The *jurisdiction* of the Lower Valley Consolidated Appraisal District is a 3 county area surrounding the city of Valleyview. The federal district court has *jurisdiction* in all cases involving violation of federal law.

**JUST COMPENSATION** the amount paid to the owner of a property when it is acquired under **eminent domain.** See **condemnation.**
**Example:** Property is condemned to construct a sewage treatment plant. The owner is entitled to *just compensation* equal to the **fair market value** of the property taken.

# K

**KICKER** a payment required by a **mortgage** in addition to normal **principal** and **interest.** See **participation loan.**

**Example:** Abel obtains a loan to purchase a retail store building. The lender requires a *kicker* equal to 10% of gross sales in excess of $100,000 per month, in addition to principal and interest.

---

# L

---

**LACHES** undue delay or negligence in asserting one's legal rights, possibly leading to **estoppel** of the negligent party's suit.
**Example:** Abel was estopped by *laches* after he knowingly delayed telling an **adjacent** property owner of an **encroachment**.

**LAND** the surface of the earth; any part of the surface of the earth. (Note: Legal definitions often distinguish land from water.)
**Example:** Extent of *land* as **real property** (Figure 91). **Air rights** may be limited to some defined altitude. Added **improvements** are distinguished from *land*.

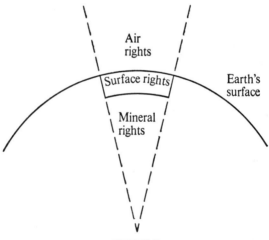

FIGURE 91

**LAND BANKING** the activity of purchasing land that is not presently needed for use.
**Example:** The Burger Company buys 8 **sites** that they plan to use 10 years from now. Wendy Ronald is in charge of *land banking* for The Burger Company.

**LAND CONTRACT** a real estate **installment** selling arrangement whereby the buyer may use, occupy, and enjoy land, but no **deed**

is given by the seller (so no **title** passes) until all or a specified part of the sale price has been paid. Same as **contract for deed** and **installment land contract**.

**Example:** Collins buys a recreational lot. Under the *land contract* she signed, she must pay $500 down and $100 per month for 7 years; then she is to receive a **general warranty deed**.

**LAND LEASE** only the ground is covered by the lease. See **ground lease**.

**Example:** Abel arranges a *land lease* from Baker for 50 years at a net annual rent of $5,000. Abel builds a shopping center on the land. At the end of 50 years the entire property will revert to Baker (Figure 92).

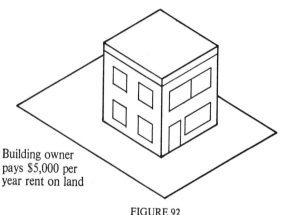

Building owner pays $5,000 per year rent on land

FIGURE 92

**LANDLOCKED** the condition of a lot that has no access to a public thoroughfare except through an **adjacent** lot. See **egress**. Compare **easement, right-of-way**.

**Example:** Figure 93.

**LANDLORD** one who rents property to another; a **lessor**. A property owner who surrenders the right to use property for a specific time in exchange for the receipt of rent.

**Example:** *Landlord*-tenant relationship (Figure 94).

**LANDMARK** a fixed object serving as a **boundary** mark for a tract of land. Same as **monument**.

**Example:** The tree and rail line may serve as *landmarks* in a land description (Figure 95).

**LAND RESIDUAL TECHNIQUE** in **appraisal**, a method of estimating the value of land when given **the net operating income (NOI)** and value of **improvements**. Used for **feasibility** analysis and **highest and best use**. See **income approach**.

**Example:** A property generates $10,000 net operating income ($15,000 rent less $5,000 operating expenses). The improvements cost $70,000 to construct and claim a 12% rate of return (10% interest plus 2% depreciation), which is $8,400. The remaining $1,600 income is capitalized at a 10% rate (divided by .10) to result in a $16,000 land value, using the *land residual technique*. See Table 22.

**Table 22**

| Property NOI | $10,000 |
|---|---|
| Income to improvement | − $8,400 |
| Income to land | $1,600 |
| Divided by required rate (10%) | $16,000 Land value |

FIGURE 93

FIGURE 94

FIGURE 95

**LAND SALE-LEASEBACK** the sale of land and simultaneous leasing of it by the seller, who becomes the **tenant**.

**Example:** Collins owns land and wants to raise cash to build a shopping center on it. She sells the land for $100,000 to Baker and leases it back for 50 years at a $5,000 annual rent. Collins can use the land for the lease **term** provided she pays the annual rent, so she builds the shopping center after the *land sale-leaseback* (Figure 96).

FIGURE 96

**LANDSCAPE ARCHITECT** a professional who designs building sites, subdivisions, and other projects which require work on drainage, grading, vegetation, installation of utilities and site improvements.

**Example:** On the office park project, a *landscape architect* advised the developer on the placement of drainage sewers, parking lots, plantings and other landscaping requirements.

per

LAND, TENEMENTS, AND HEREDITAMENTS a phrase used in early English law to express all sorts of **real estate**.
Example: The **bundle of rights** in real estate is expressed by the phrase *land, tenements and hereditaments*. It includes all **interests** in real estate.

LAND USE INTENSITY a measure of the extent to which a land parcel is developed in conformity with **zoning** ordinances.
Example: Under a local zoning ordinance, **developers** might be allowed a maximum *land use intensity* of 4,000 square feet of **improvements** per **acre** of land.

LAND USE PLANNING an activity, generally conducted by a local government, that provides public and private land use recommendations consistent with community policies. Generally used to guide decisions on **zoning**.
Example: As part of its *land use planning* efforts, the city planning department prepared maps of existing land uses, forecasts of future development, a list of planned new roads, **utility** extensions, and waste disposal facilities, a map of environmentally sensitive areas, and a map showing recommended future land uses.

LAND USE REGULATION government **ordinances**, codes, and permit requirements intended to make the private use of land and natural resources conform to policy standards. See also **zoning**.
Example: Local governments have several types of *land use regulation*. Commonly used types are:
- building codes
- curb-cut permit systems
- historic preservation laws
- housing codes
- subdivision regulations
- tree-cutting laws
- zoning

LAND USE SUCCESSION a change in the predominant use of a **neighborhood** or area over time. See also **neighborhood life cycle**.
Example: As the neighborhood aged, it began to make a transition from large **single-family housing** to **apartment buildings** through the process of *land use succession*.

LATENT DEFECTS flaws that are hidden but are apt to surface later.
Example: A building was found to have *latent defects* in the form of poor construction of subfloors and improper foundation support.

LATE PAYMENTS a fee added to a bill after the expiration of a specific grace period. Such payments are intended to encourage

timely payment of the bill.
**Example:** Largetown Federal Savings requires an additional 5% in *late payments* when a mortgage payment is made after the fifteenth of the month.

**LEASE** a **contract** in which, for a payment called **rent,** the one entitled to the **possession** of real property (**lessor**) transfers those rights to another (**lessee**) for a specified period of time.
**Example:** Abel leases office space from Baker. Under the *lease* signed by the parties, Abel is allowed to conduct business activities within the office space, subject to specified **restrictions**, for a specified period of time. Baker is entitled to receive a specified amount of rent payments according to a specified schedule of payments.

**LEASEHOLD** the **interest** or **estate** on which a **lessee (tenant)** of **real estate** has a **lease.**
**Example:** Mason possesses a long-term lease on a property. She may obtain a loan with the *leasehold* pledged as **collateral.** If the **contract rent** required by the lease is lower than **market rents,** Mason's *leasehold* will have a positive value.

**LEASEHOLD MORTGAGE** a **lien** on the tenant's **interest** in **real estate.**
**Example:** Abel is leasing land from Baker under a 50-year lease. Abel builds a shopping center and borrows money from the Big Money Assurance Company to do so. Big Money Assurance Company secures the loan with a leasehold mortgage. The mortgage will be lower in priority (subordinate) to land lease because the lease was contracted first. Had the mortgage been arranged before the lease, the mortgage would have priority. The holder of a prior **lien** has first claim to the income and assets if in default.

**LEASE WITH OPTION TO PURCHASE** a lease that gives the **lessee** (**tenant**) the right to purchase the property at an agreed-upon price under certain conditions.
**Example:** Abel *leases* property with an *option to purchase*. He must pay $500 per month rent for 5 years; after that he may buy the property (but is not forced to buy) for $100,000.

**LEGAL AGE** the official standard of maturity upon which one is held legally responsible for one's acts. Contracts for the sale or lease of real estate by a minor are voidable by the minor. See **minor.**
**Example:** Young, aged 17, signed a contract to purchase a home. Because Young was not of *legal age,* the seller could not enforce the contract when Young later decided not to go through with the purchase.

**LEGAL DESCRIPTION** legally acceptable identification of **real estate** by one of the following:
- the **government rectangular survey**
- metes and bounds
- recorded **plat (lot and block** number)

**Example:** The seller was required to include a *legal description* in the **deed**.

**LEGAL NAME** the name one has for official purposes.

**Example:** Though friends call him Fast Buck Jones, his *legal name* is Ferdinand Buchanan Jones. He may sign **contracts** with the name Ferdinand B. Jones.

**Example:** The *legal name* of GM is General Motors, Incorporated.

**LEGAL NOTICE** notification of others using the method required by law. See **constructive notice, notice**.

**Example:** Abel wishes to **rescind** an **offer** to buy real estate that has not been accepted by Baker. Abel sends a telegram and registered letter to Baker as *legal notice*.

**Example:** Collins bought land. She recorded the **deed** in the county courthouse as *legal notice* of ownership.

**LEGATEE** one who receives property by **will**. See **devisee**.

**Example:** Garrison wills all her property to Baker. Upon Garrison's death, Baker is the *legatee*.

**LESSEE** a person to whom property is rented under a **lease**. A **tenant**. Compare **lessor**.

**Example:** In the arrangement shown in Figure 97, Baker is the *lessee*.

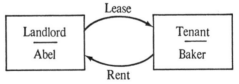

FIGURE 97

**LESSOR** one who rents property to another under a **lease**. A **landlord**. Compare **lessee**.

**Example:** In the arrangement shown in Figure 98, Abel is the *lessor*.

**LET** to rent a property to a tenant.

**Example:** Larry *lets* an apartment to Simon for $300 per month.

**LETTER OF CREDIT** an arrangement, with specified conditions,

whereby a bank agrees to substitute its credit for a customer's.
**Example:** Abel, from Atlanta, wishes to buy property from Baker, in Boston. Abel arranges a *letter of credit* with the Atlanta Trust Company Bank to pay Baker upon **closing** in Boston.

**LETTER OF INTENT** the expression of a desire to enter into a **contract** without actually doing so.
**Example:** After a preliminary meeting, the Five Stars Development Company writes to a landowner, "We wish to enter into a contract to buy your land and will further pursue this matter in coming days. This *letter of intent* does not commit either party to purchase, sell, or lease."

FIGURE 98

**LEVEL PAYMENT INCOME STREAM** see **annuity.**

**LEVEL PAYMENT MORTGAGE** requires the same payment each month (or other period) for full **amortization.** See **mortgage constant, flat.**
**Example:** Abel borrows $50,000 to buy a house. The *level payment mortgage* at 15% interest, payable over 30 years, requires a $632.50 monthly payment for **principal** and **interest.** That payment will be constant over the life of the loan.

**LEVERAGE** use of borrowed funds to increase purchasing power and, ideally, to increase the profitability of an investment. See **positive leverage, reverse leverage.**
**Example:** Collins wishes to invest in real estate. The property costs $100,000 and produces **net operating income** of $10,000 per year. If purchased with all cash, Collin's annual **rate of return** is 10% ($10,000÷$100,000). If she *leverages* the investment by borrowing $75,000, her return may be higher. If the debt cost is 8% ($6,000) annually, the *leverage* results in a return of 16% ($4,000÷$25,000). However, if the debt cost is 12% ($9,000), the *leverage* produces a return of 4% ($1,000÷$25,000).

**LEVY** to legally impose or collect that which is due.
**Example:** A tax assessor *levies* a tax.
**Example:** A judge *levies* a fine.

**LIABILITY** 1. a **debt** or financial obligation. Contrast with **asset**.
**Example:** One who borrows $75,000 for a **mortgage** loan incurs a *liability* to repay that loan.
**Example:** A **general partner** in a **partnership** has a personal *liability* for debts of the partnership in the event the partnership cannot repay its debt.
2. a potential loss.
**Example:** One should purchase sufficient *liability* insurance to protect against possible legal claims of someone who gets injured on one's property.

**LIABILITY INSURANCE** protection for a property owner from claims arising from injuries or damage to other people or property.
**Example:** Abel slipped on a broken step on the walkway in an apartment complex owned by Baker. Baker's *liability insurance* pays Abel for the doctor and hospital fees.

**LIABLE** responsible or obligated. Contrast with **exculpatory clause** and **nonrecourse**.
**Example:** One who borrows a **mortgage** loan generally becomes personally *liable* for its repayment. The lender can look to the **property** or the borrower personally for repayment.

**LICENSE** 1. permission
**Example:** If Abel did not secure *license* to cross Baker's property, it would be a **trespass**.
2. a right granted by a state to an individual to operate as a real estate **broker** or salesperson.
**Example:** The **real estate commission** issued a salesperson *license* to Rollins (Figure 99). Working under the supervision of her broker, Rollins can sell and lease real estate owned by others.

**LICENSEE** one who holds a real estate **license**; a licensed salesperson or **broker**. See **licensing examination**.
**Example:** A pocket card is held by *licensees*. The employing broker displays licenses in the office.

**LICENSE LAWS** laws that govern the activities of real estate salespersons.
**Example:** Abel, an unlicensed individual, sold a farm for Baker and a house owned by Collins. Under state *license laws* each violation subjects Abel to a $10,000 fine and a year imprisonment, or both.

**LICENSING EXAMINATION** a written test given to a prospective real estate **broker** or salesperson to determine ability to represent the public in a real estate transaction. Most states offer examinations on at least 5 dates each year.

**Example:** Educational Testing Services (ETS) in Princeton, New Jersey, and American College Testing (ACT) in Iowa City, Iowa, prepare *licensing examinations* for most states. Some states prepare their own *licensing examination.*

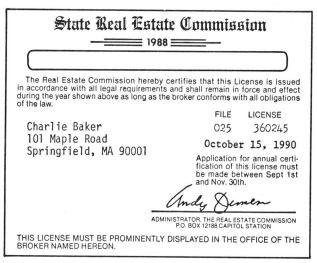

FIGURE 99

**LIEN** a charge against property making it **security** for the payment of a **debt, judgment, mortgage,** or taxes; it is a type of **encumbrance.** A specific lien is against certain property only. A **general lien** is against all of the property owned by the debtor.
**Example:** Abel failed to pay the **contractor** for work performed on his home. The contractor files a **mechanic's lien** against the property for the amount due.

**LIEN, JUNIOR** a **lien** that will be paid after earlier liens have been paid. See **junior mortgage, subordination.**
**Example:** Abel obtains a **mortgage** loan from Solid Savings to finance the acquisition of a property. To reduce the **down payment,** he takes out a **second mortgage** with Baker, an investor. Solid Savings has a first lien and has first **priority** to **foreclosure** sale proceeeds in case of a **default.** Baker has a *junior lien* and is entitled to whatever remains, up to the debt and costs, after Solid Savings is **indemnified.**

**LIEN-THEORY STATES** states whose laws give a **lien** on property to secure debt. Contrasted with **title theory states** in which the

lender becomes the **title** owner. In either case the borrower has the right to use and enjoy the property in the absence of **default**; in the event of default, lenders may **foreclose**.
**Example:** After **closing** the sale of a home in a *lien-theory state*, the lender acquires a **first mortgage** and may foreclose upon certain default.

**LIFE ESTATE** a **freehold** interest (in **real property**) that expires upon the death of the owner or some other specified person (**pur autre vie**).
**Example:** A retired couple purchase a *life estate* in a retirement village apartment unit. Upon death of both husband and wife, ownership of the unit will revert to the owner's association, who may then resell to another couple.

**LIFE OF LOAN CAP** a contractual limitation on the maximum interest rate that can be applied to an adjustable rate mortgage during the term of the loan. See **adjustable rate mortgage**; contrast **annual cap**.
**Example:** An adjustable rate mortgage is offered at the initial interest rate of 7.5% and has a *life of loan cap* of 5 percentage points. At no time during the term of the loan can the interest rate rise above 12.5%, regardless of how much the index rises.

**LIFE TENANT** one who is allowed to use property for life or the lifetime of another designated person. See **life estate**.
**Example:** Graham owns a life estate in a home. As a *life tenant*, Graham may enjoy full ownership rights to the home during her lifetime.

**LIKE-KIND PROPERTY** property having the same nature. See also **Section 1031** and **tax-free exchange**.
**Example:** Under the **Internal Revenue Code**, apartments and land are considered *like-kind property*, but animals of different sexes are not.

**LIMITED LIABILITY** the restriction of one's potential losses to the amount invested. The absence of personal liability. See **at-risk rules**.
**Example:** *Limited liability* is provided to stockholders in a **corporation** and limited partners of a **limited partnership**. Those parties cannot lose more than they contribute to the corporation, unless they agree to become personally liable. For example, if Collins buys stock in a corporation for $1,000, she cannot lose more than that amount. However, many lenders require personal guarantees of major stockholders before lending to corporations.

**LIMITED PARTNERSHIP** one in which there is at least one partner who is passive and limits **liability** to the amount invested, and at least one partner whose liability extends beyond monetary investment. See **general partner**, **partnership**.

**Example:** Abel, a **syndicator**, forms a *limited partnership* with Price, Stone, and Wise. Abel invests his time and talent, is the general partner, and owns 10% of the partnership. Price, Stone, and Wise each invested $30,000 cash and were limited partners. They buy property with a $90,000 **down payment** and a $500,000 mortgage. The property drops in value by $250,000. Price, Stone, and Wise lose their **equity**, and Abel, the general partner, is responsible for additional losses (Figure 100).

Limited partnership

| Abel | Price | Stone | Wise |
|---|---|---|---|
| General partner | Limited partner | Limited partner | Limited partner |
| Entrepreneur and manager | Passive investor | Passive investor | Passive investor |

FIGURE 100

**LINE OF CREDIT** an agreement whereby a financial institution promises to lend up to a certain amount without the need to file another application.

**Example:** Happy Homes Brokers, Inc., has a *line of credit* under which they can borrow up to $50,000 at 3% above the **prime rate** through The Goodmoney National Bank.

**LIQUIDATE** 1. to dissolve a business.

**Example:** A **corporation's** only asset is **real estate** which is encumbered by a **mortgage**. The stockholders decide to *liquidate* the corporation. They may have the corporation sell the real estate, **retire** the mortgage, and distribute the **resale proceeds** to stockholders. The corporation is said to be *liquidated*.

2. to **retire debts**.

**Example:** Abel *liquidates* a $1,000 **debt** by paying it off in full with cash.

**LIQUIDATED DAMAGES** an amount agreed upon in a contract that one party will pay the other in the event of a **breach of the contract**.

**Example:** Abel engages a builder to erect a house. The **contract** says that if the builder fails to complete it by March 1, 1985, the builder will pay $50 per day thereafter until completion, as *liquidated damages*.

**LIQUIDITY** ease of converting **assets** to cash.
**Example:** Common stocks and U.S. savings bonds have good *liquidity*. **Real estate** and many types of collectibles generally have poor *liquidity*.

**LIS PENDENS** Latin: "suit pending." Recorded **notice** of the filing of a suit, the outcome of which may affect **title** to a certain land.
**Example:** The unpaid **mortgage** holder filed a **foreclosure** suit. She gave notice of *lis pendens* to make others aware of the suit pending.

**LIST** to obtain a **listing**.
**Example:** Baker wanted to *list* as many properties as possible under an **exclusive right to sell** so he would earn a commission no matter who sold the property.

**LISTING** 1. a written engagement **contract** between a principal and an **agent**, authorizing the agent to perform services for the principal involving the latter's property. 2. a record of property for sale by a **broker** who has been authorized by the owner to sell. 3. the property so listed.
**Example:** Abel employs Baker to find a buyer for his home by giving Baker a *listing* contract. When prospective buyers visit Baker, they will examine the *listings* in Baker's office. If interested, a prospective buyer may wish to visit the *listing*.

**LISTING BROKER (AGENT)** the licensed real estate **broker** (agent) who secures a **listing** of the property. Contrast with **selling broker (agent)**.
**Example:** For most sales, the *listing broker* and the **selling broker** share **commissions** equally. In some locales, notably for new homes, the *listing broker* earns only 1%, whereas the **selling broker** earns 3% of the selling price.

**LITIGATION** the act of carrying on a lawsuit.
**Example:** *Litigation* is a contest in court to enforce a right.

**LITTORAL** part of the shore zone of a large body of water. Compare **riparian rights**.
**Example:** Lot A has *littoral* land. Lot B has **riparian** land (Figure 101).

**LOAN APPLICATION** document required by a lender prior to issuing a **loan commitment**. The application generally includes the following information:
1. name of the borrower
2. amount and terms of the loan
3. description of the subject property to be mortgaged

4. borrower's financial and employment data
**Example:** Lowry wishes to borrow money to purchase a home. At Friendly Savings, she completes a *loan application* and pays an application fee. Friendly Savings will **appraise** the house, **examine** Lowry's **credit rating**, and verify certain information on the application prior to approving or disapproving the application.
*commitment* from the local **savings and loan association** for permanent financing.

FIGURE 101

**LOAN APPLICATION FEE** a charge required by a loan originator to be paid by the borrower to cover the credit report, property appraisal and other incidental expenses associated with underwriting the loan. The fee is generally not refundable.
**Example:** Home Mortgage Company charges a *loan application fee* of $250 to process a mortgage application. The prospective property buyer/mortgage borrower brings the purchase contract to a loan officer at Home Mortgage Company.

**LOAN CLOSING** see **closing.**

**LOAN COMMITMENT** an agreement to lend money, generally of a specified amount, at specified terms at some time in the future.
**Example:** Before commencing development, Abel obtained a *loan*

**LOAN CORRESPONDENT** see **mortgage correspondent.**

**LOAN ORIGINATION FEE** see **origination fees.**

**LOAN POINTS** see **discount points.**

**LOAN SERVICING** see **servicing.**

**LOAN-TO-VALUE RATIO (LTV)** the portion of the amount borrowed compared to the cost or value of the property purchased.
**Example:** Abel bought a $100,000 house and arranged a $90,000

**mortgage** loan, resulting in a 90% *loan-to-value ratio*. Home mortgages at more than an 80% *LTV* ratio generally require **mortgage insurance**.

**LOG CABIN** an early American style house of unfinished logs.
**Example:** Figure 102.

Chimneys at ends

Shingle covered gable roof

Unfinished logs

FIGURE 102

**LONG-TERM CAPITAL GAIN** for income tax purposes, the gain on a **capital asset** held long enough to qualify for special tax considerations.
**Note:** The Tax Reform Act of 1986 eliminated the favorable treatment for *long-term capital gains*. The highest rate in 1987 for *long-term capital gains* is 28%; thereafter there is no distinction in tax rates as compared with ordinary income.

**LOT AND BLOCK** a method of locating a parcel of land. See **legal description**.
**Example:** The shaded property in Figure 103 is lot 4, block B of Rolling Acres **subdivision**, in Lincoln County, New Mexico.

**LOT LINE** a line bounding a lot as described in a **property survey**.
**Example:** Figure 104

**LOW-INCOME HOUSING (QUALIFIED)** housing that is eligible for special tax credits of up to 9% of their cost (4% in certain situations) under the 1986 tax act. Strict rules must be followed concerning tenant qualification, certification, and project financing.

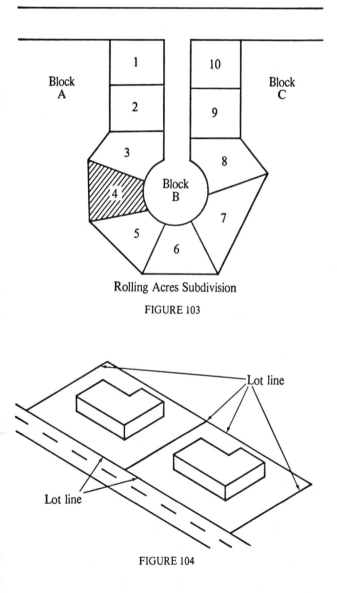

Block
A

Block
C

Block
B

Rolling Acres Subdivision

FIGURE 103

Lot line

Lot line

FIGURE 104

# M

**MAI** (Member, Appraisal Institute) a member of the **American Institute of Real Estate Appraisers,** which is affiliated with the **National Association of Realtors®.**
**Example:** To acquire the designation *MAI*, an **appraiser** must pass several written proficiency examinations, perform acceptable appraisal work for a specific period of time, and prepare a demonstration narrative appraisal report. The *MAI* signifies the appraiser is qualified to appraise a broad range of **real estate** types.
**Address:**
American Institute of Real Estate Appraisers
430 North Michigan Avenue
Chicago, Illinois 60611

**MAINTENANCE** activities required to compensate for **wear and tear** on a property. See **deferred maintenance.**
**Example:** Among the duties of **property management** is *maintenance* of the property. This includes routine upkeep of the building, repair and periodic painting as needed, keeping all mechanical parts in working order, and lawn maintenance.

**MAINTENANCE FEE** an assessment by a **homeowners' association** or a **condominium owners' association,** to pay costs of operating the **common elements.**
**Example:** A condominium association assesses each owner a *maintenance fee* of $100 per month for lawn maintenance and insurance costs.

**MAJORITY** 1. the age at which one is no longer a **minor** and is fully able to conduct one's own affairs; majority (full legal age) is 18 to 21 years, depending on the state.
**Example:** Abel, under 18 years of age, enters into a **contract** to buy land. Because he has not attained *majority,* he may **void** the contract if he chooses. Baker, the seller, is bound to the contract unless Abel voids it.
2. more than half.
**Example:** The bylaws of the **condominium owners' association** require a *majority* of the owners who vote to change to another management firm.

**MALL** a public area connecting individual stores in a **shopping center;** generally enclosed. Also, an enclosed shopping center.
**Example:** A large shopping *mall* was being developed south of town. It was designed to include over 40 stores connected by an

enclosed and air-conditioned *mall*.

**MANAGEMENT AGREEMENT** a **contract** between the owner of property and someone who agrees to manage it. Fees are generally 4-10% of the rental income. See **property management.**
**Example:** Abel has a *management agreement* with Baker for a 200-unit apartment complex. The contract provides that Baker will receive 5% of the rental income, and he will perform all duties concerning leasing, operating, and managing the property. He will maintain a separate bank checking account for receipts and disbursements, provide monthly accounting statements, and manage the property with competence.

**MANSARD ROOF** one having two slopes on all four sides, with the lower slope steeper than the upper, flatter sections.
**Example:** Figure 105

Mansard
FIGURE 105

**MANUFACTURED HOME** see **mobile home, mobile home park.**

**MARGIN** a constant amount added to the value of the **index** for the purpose of adjusting the interest rate on an **adjustable rate mortgage.**
**Example:** An adjustable rate mortgage is indexed to the 1 year Treasury yield and has a *margin* of 3 percentage points. If the index is currently 6%, the fully indexed rate on the loan is 9% (6% index plus 3% *margin*).

**MARGINAL PROPERTY** property that is barely profitable to use.
**Example:** The sale of cotton that has been efficiently raised **yields** $100; yet the cotton cost $99.99 to raise. The land on which the cotton was raised is therefore considered *marginal property*.
**Example:** A tract of undeveloped land is deemed *marginal property* because of lack of access to a roadway.

**MARITAL DEDUCTION** the tax-free amount one transfers by **will**

to one's spouse. The 1981 tax act allows an unlimited amount to be transferred without federal estate tax.

**Example:** The concept of a *marital deduction* is to treat husband and wife as one economic unit. Since 1981, a federal **estate tax** will be due only on taxable property that passes to another generation.

**MARKETABLE TITLE** a **title** so free from defect that a court will enforce the title's acceptance by a purchaser. Compare **cloud on the title.**

**Example:** Through a divorce settlement, Collins obtained certain ownership rights to a property. She now wished to sell the property. To obtain a *marketable title*, she must obtain a **quitclaim deed** from her former husband, thereby curing a defect in her title.

**MARKET ANALYSIS** a study of the supply and demand conditions in a specific area for a specific type of property or service. A *market analysis* report is generally prepared by someone with experience in real estate, economics, or marketing. It serves to help decide what type of project to develop and is also helpful in arranging permanent and construction financing for a proposed development.

**Example:** The developer commissioned a *market analysis* to evaluate the need for luxury apartments in the St. Louis suburban market. Copies of the report were supplied to prospective lenders for this type of development.

**MARKET APPROACH** same as **market comparison approach.**

**MARKET AREA** a geographic region from which one can expect the primary demand for a specific product or service provided at a fixed location.

**Example:** A regional shopping center has a larger *market area* than a neighborhood shopping center.

**Example:** A developer estimates that the *market area* for a **subdivision** covers the northeast section of the metropolitan area.

**MARKET COMPARISON APPROACH** one of 3 **appraisal approaches.** Value is estimated by analyzing sales prices of similar properties (**comparables**) recently sold.

**Example:** The subject property is a 3-bedroom, 2-bath house. Two recently sold comparables are found. The appraiser, using the *market comparison approach*, sets up Table 23.

**MARKET DATA APPROACH** same as **market comparison approach.**

**MARKET DELINEATION** the process of defining the geographic extent of the demand for a specific property.

**Example:** The *market delineation* for a new regional shopping center showed that shoppers are likely to be drawn from a 2 county area.

**TABLE 23**

| Subject | Comparable #1 | Comparable #2 |
|---|---|---|
| Sale price | $70,500 | $69,000 |
| Date of sale | last week | 3 months ago (+$1000) |
| 3 bedrooms | 3 bedrooms | 3 bedrooms |
| 2 baths | 2½ baths (−$500) | 2 baths |
| Adjusted price | $70,000 | $70,000 |

The subject property is appraised for $70,000.

**MARKET PRICE** the actual price paid in a market transaction. Contrast with **market value.**
**Example:** A home was offered for sale at $100,000. It was appraised for $93,000, and actually sold for $95,000 in an **arm's length transaction.** The *market price* is $95,000.

**MARKET RENT** the **rent** that a comparable unit would command if offered in the competitive market. Contrast with **contract rent.**
**Example:** Long rents an apartment to Towns for $400 per month. Similar units are renting for $450 per month. The apartment's *market rent* is $450 per month.

**MARKET SEGMENTATION** the process of defining the socio-economic characteristics of the demand for a specific property or properties.
**Example:** *Market segmentation* shows that the tenants for a new garden apartment complex are likely to be young married couples with incomes between $15,000 and $30,000.

**MARKET STUDY** see **market analysis.**

**MARKET VALUE** the theoretical highest price a buyer, willing but not compelled to buy, would pay, and the lowest price a seller, willing but not compelled to sell, would accept.
**Example:** An **appraisal** of a home indicates its *market value* is $75,000. In a normally active market, the home should sell for this amount if allowed to stay on the market for a reasonable time. The owner may, however, **deed** the home to a relative for $250. The owner may also grow impatient and sell for $70,000. Conversely, an anxious buyer may be found who pays $80,000. Finally, the owner may provide favorable financing and sell for $85,000.

**MASONRY** construction made from brick, cement block, or stone.
**Example:** The ground floor of the house shown in Figure 106 is made of *masonry.* The upper floor is wooden frame with wooden siding.

FIGURE 106

**MASTER DEED** used by a condominium developer or converter for recording a **condominium** development. It divides a single property into individually owned units, includes restrictions on their use and provides for ownership of common areas.
**Example:** When a New York apartment building was converted into a condominium, the converter filed a *master deed* with the city to reflect separate ownership of individual units.

**MASTER LEASE** a controlling **lease.** Contrast with **sublease.** Note that one cannot grant a greater interest in real estate than one has; so if a *master lease* is for a 5-year term, a sublease cannot legally exceed 5 years.
**Example:** Abel leases 10,000 square feet of retail space to Baker. Baker then subleases the space to 5 different **tenants.** The lease between Abel and Baker is the *master lease.*

**MASTER LIMITED PARTNERSHIP** an ownership vehicle, especially used for real estate or oil and gas ventures. It is generally formed by a "roll up" of existing **limited partnerships** that own property, and typically has the advantage of ownership interests that are more marketable than individual limited partnerships.
**Example:** A real estate entrepreneur has syndicated 30 properties over the past 5 years, with each as a separate limited partnership. All were brought together as one large entity, a *master limited partnership*, with interests that were readily marketable.

**MASTER PLAN** a document that describes, in narrative and with maps, an overall development concept. The master plan is used to coordinate the preparation of more detailed plans or may be a collection of detailed plans. The plan may be prepared by a local government to guide private and public development or by a **developer** on a specific project.
**Example:** The city planners checked to see if the **zoning** request complied with the city's *master plan.*
**Example:** The *master plan* for further development of the resort **condominium** is displayed in the sales office.

**MATERIAL FACT** a fact that is germane to a particular situation; one that participants in the situation such as a trial, may reasonably be expected to consider.
**Example:** If *material facts* about the investment property lying in a **floodplain** had been communicated to the buyer, he would not have bought. He is now charging **misrepresentation** against the seller and the **broker.**

**MATERIALMAN** a person who supplies materials used in the construction or repair of a building or other property.
**Example:** Since the *materialman* was not paid for lumber, he filed a **mechanic's lien** against the property.

**MATERIAL PARTICIPATION** a tax term introduced by the 1986 tax act, defined as year-round active involvement in the operations of a business activity on a regular, continuous and substantial basis. Three main factors to consider in determining the presence of *material participation* are:
• Is the activity the taxpayer's principal trade or business?
• How close is the taxpayer to the business?
• Does the taxpayer have knowledge and experience in the enterprise?
**Retired Farmers** A special exception is provided for retired farmers who are considered to continue to participate materially in that activity after retirement, as does the spouse of deceased farmers.
**Limited Partners** Limited partnership interests are considered inherently passive. However, the IRS may draft regulations to prevent persons from using the limited partnership vehicle for any business enterprise simply to generate passive income to offset passive losses.

**MATURITY** the due date of a loan.
**Example:** A **mortgage** loan may have a *maturity* of 30 years. Periodic payments are established so that the loan **principal** will **amortize** by the *maturity* date.
**Example:** A bond may have a *maturity* of 20 years. Generally, **interest** only will be paid, with the full principal repaid at *maturity.*

**MECHANIC'S LIEN** a **lien** given by law upon a building or other **improvement** upon land, and upon the land itself, as **security** for

the payment for labor done and materials furnished for improvement.
**Example:** The unpaid plumber filed a *mechanic's lien* against the property while it was under construction. The builder had to satisfy the lien in order to give **clear title** to the buyer.

**MEETING OF THE MINDS** agreement, by all parties to a **contract,** to the exact terms thereof.
  **Example:** To have a *meeting of the minds* there must be:
  1. an **offer** and **acceptance**
  2. considering the subject property
  3. **consideration**
  4. **terms**

**MERCHANTABLE TITLE** see **marketable title.**

**MERGER** the fusion of 2 or more interests, such as businesses or investments.
  **Examples:** Examples of *mergers* are:
  • conglomerates—corporations that are not customers or suppliers to each other or competitors
  • corporations—union of 2 or more by transferring property to one that survives, and issuing its shares to stockholders of the corporation that ceases to exist

**MERIDIAN** a longitudinal reference line that traverses the earth in a north-south direction; all meridians circle the earth through the equator and converge at the north and south poles; used by **surveyors** in describing property under the **government rectangular**

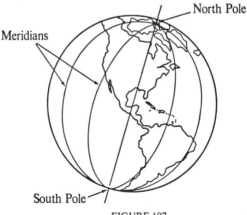

FIGURE 107

survey method.
**Example:** Figure 107

**METES AND BOUNDS** a land **description** method that details all the **boundary** lines of land, together with their terminal points and angles.

**Example:** *Metes and bounds* description: Beginning at a point on the northeasterly corner of the intersection of South St. and West Rd.; running thence northerly along West Rd. 200 feet; thence easterly parallel to South St. 150 feet; thence southerly parallel to West Rd. 200 feet; thence westerly along South St. 150 feet to the point of beginning (Figure 108).

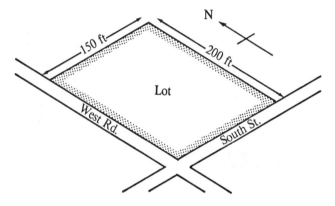

FIGURE 108

**METROPOLITAN AREA** generally the developed region economically attached to a large central city; same as **standard metropolitan statistical area.**

**Example:** The *metropolitan area* of Atlanta, Georgia covers 15 counties and contains over 2 million people.

**MILL** one tenth of a cent. Used in expressing tax rates on a per-dollar basis.

**Example:** A tax rate of 60 *mills* means that taxes are 6 cents per dollar of **assessed valuation.**

**MILLAGE RATE** a tax rate applied to property. Each **mill** represents $1 of tax **assessment** per $1,000 of assessed property value.

**Example:** The *millage rate* for property taxes in the Bumpton school district is 20 mills. A home with assessed value of $100,000 pays $2,000 a year in property taxes to the district.

**MINERAL RIGHTS** the privilege of gaining **income** from the sale of oil, gas, and other valuable resources found on land.
**Example:** Abel purchases a property that contains underground oil deposits. Abel may:
• develop these *mineral rights* by drilling a well
• sell the rights for a price to an oil company
• **lease** the rights to an oil company in exchange for a **royalty**

**MINIMUM LOT AREA** the smallest building lot area allowed in a **subdivision,** generally specified by a **zoning ordinance.**
**Example:** Baker owns land that is zoned "R-4." If Baker develops the land, it must be used for residential purposes and lots must have a *minimum lot area* of ¼ acre.

**MINOR** a person under the age of **majority** specified by law (18 to 21 years, depending on the state).
**Example:** Contracts for the sale or use of real estate, entered into by a *minor*, are voidable by the minor. Note that the other party is bound; only the minor may void them.

**MISREPRESENTATION** an untrue statement, whether unintentional or deliberate. It may be a form of nondisclosure where there is a duty to disclose or the planned creation of a false appearance. Where there is misrepresentation of **material fact,** the person injured may sue for **damages** or **rescind** the **contract.** See **false advertising.**
**Example:** The **broker** represented the home as being structurally sound. The broker did not know that **termites** were destroying the wood. The buyer sued the broker for *misrepresentation.*

**MISSION HOUSE** a nineteenth century style house that looks like the old mission churches and houses of Southern California. The doors and windows are arch-shaped.
**Example:** Figure 109

**MISTAKE** an unintentional error made in preparing a **contract;** may be corrected by mutual consent of all parties without voiding contract.
**Example:** Abel and Baker agree to a sales contract for a property located at 100 Main Street. In preparing the contract the address is listed as 100 Main Blvd. The *mistake* is discovered at the **closing,** and correction is made with the consent of both parties.

**MOBILE HOME** a dwelling unit (Figure 110) manufactured in a factory and designed to be transported to a **site** and semipermanently attached.
**Example:** One option for low-cost housing is purchase of a *mobile home,* which generally costs much less than site-built housing. *Mobile homes* may be placed on the purchaser's lot or in a **mobile home park** for a monthly rental.

Looks like old mission church

Arch-shaped doors and windows

Pyramid-shaped roof   Parapet   Tile roof   Stucco walls

FIGURE 109

Up to 72 ft long   Metal roofing and siding
Removable wheels   Relocatable   About 12 ft wide   Factory made

FIGURE 110

**MOBILE HOME PARK** a **subdivision** of plots designed for siting of mobile homes. Plots are generally leased to mobile home owners and include **utilities,** parking space, and access to utility roads. Many parks also include such **amenities** as swimming pools and clubhouses.
**Example:** A typical *mobile home park* design (Figure 111).

**MODEL UNIT** a representative home, apartment, or office space used as part of a sales campaign to demonstrate the design, structure, and appearance of units in a development.

**Example:** A **developer** constructs a *model unit* in an effort to **pre-lease** units in a development. Prospective tenants are invited to tour the *model unit* to gain an appreciation for the design and appearance of the development.

**MODERNIZE** to alter a property by installing up-to-date equipment, making contemporary cosmetic improvements, and deleting obsolete facilities.
   **Example:** The redeveloper *modernized* the apartment building by installing dishwashers, wall-to-wall carpeting, a new gas furnace and by removing the coal storage bin.

FIGURE 111

**MODULAR HOUSING dwelling** units constructed from components **prefabricated** in a factory and erected on the **site**.
   **Example:** In a *modular housing* project, site preparation may be performed while structural panels are being fabricated by mass production techniques in a factory. The panels are then shipped to the site and erected in place.

**MOISTURE BARRIER** a layer of foil, plastic, or paper used in the construction of exterior walls, ceilings, and foundations to prevent moisture penetration into wooden members or insulation.
   **Example:** The *moisture barrier* in an exterior wall (Figure 112).

**MONETARY INSTITUTION DEREGULATION ACT** same as **Depository Institutions Deregulation and Monetary Control Act.**

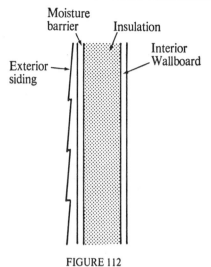

FIGURE 112

**MONTEREY ARCHITECTURE** a nineteenth century style, 2-story house with a balcony across the front at the second floor level.
**Example:** Figure 113

Balcony across front at second floor

Shingle roof

2 stories

Rail simple iron or wood

FIGURE 113

**MONTH-TO-MONTH TENANCY lease** agreement extendable or cancelable each month.
**Example:** Abel rents an apartment from Baker on a *month-to-month tenancy* basis. Abel may remain as long as he pays rent and Baker does not give notice to cancel the lease. Abel may also cancel the lease upon giving notice.

**MONUMENT** a fixed object and point established by **surveyors** to determine land locations.
**Example:** See **landmark.**

**MORATORIUM** a time period during which a certain activity is not allowed.
**Example:** Fair City passes an **ordinance** that establishes a 6-month *moratorium* on condominium **conversions.** During the period, no one may legally convert an apartment complex into **condominium** units.

**MORTGAGE** a written **instrument** that creates a **lien** upon **real estate** as **security** for the payment of a specified debt.
**Example:** Lowry wants to buy a home. She needs a loan to complete the purchase. As **collateral,** Lowry offers a *mortgage* on the property to the lender.
Note that the borrower gives the mortgage, which pledges the property as collateral. The lender gives the loan.

**MORTGAGE ASSUMPTION** same as **assumption of mortgage.**

**MORTGAGE BACKED SECURITY** a bond or other financial obligation secured by a pool of mortgage loans. See **collateralized mortgage obligations, REMICs.**
**Example:** The Sachs Mortgage Broker Company purchased $100 million worth of mortgage loans on private homes. To fund the purchase, Sachs created a *mortgage backed security* secured by the pool of mortgages and sold the security to investors.

**MORTGAGE BANKER** one who originates, sells, and services **mortgage** loans. Most loans are insured or guaranteed by a government agency or private mortgage insurer. See **mortgage insurance.**
**Example:** The Mortgage Store, a *mortgage banker,* originates 100 loans totaling $5,000,000. They sell this package of loans to an out-of-state investor for $5,010,000. They continue to collect monthly payments from homeowners and assure that property taxes are paid and insurance is maintained. They charge the investor an annual fee of ⅜ of 1% of the loan **principal,** each month remitting to the investor the rest of the monthly payments from homeowners.

**MORTGAGE BANKERS ASSOCIATION (MBA)** an organization that provides educational programs and other services for **mortgage bankers.** Offers the Certified Mortgage Banker (CMB) designation. Publishes *Mortgage Banker* magazine.
**Address:** Mortgage Bankers Association of America
1125 Fifteenth Street, N.W.
Washington, D.C. 20005

**MORTGAGE BONDS** tax-exempt securities sold by municipal and state authorities for the purpose of providing low-interest rate **mortgage** loans to qualified individuals. For most programs, mortgage borrowers must be first-time home buyers with moderate income.
**Example:** Local Housing Finance Agency, a creation of the city of Local, sold $50 million of *mortgage bonds*. The proceeds from the sale were used to originate loans through local mortgage lenders for first-time home buyers within the city. Interest on the bonds was tax-exempt to the bond-holders, thereby allowing the agency to borrow money at an **interest rate** below 8%. The mortgage loans could be originated at rates below 9% at a time when market mortgage interest rates were above 10%.

**MORTGAGE BROKER** one who, for a fee, places loans with investors, but does not service such loans.
**Example:** The Ace Development Company wants to build a shopping center. A *mortgage broker* charges a 1% fee for each construction loan (placed with a commercial bank) and the permanent loan (placed with an insurance company).

**MORTGAGE COMMITMENT** an agreement between a lender and a borrower to lend money at a future date, subject to the conditions described in the agreement.
**Example:** Baker wishes to build a home. Construction will require 6 months. Baker obtains a *mortgage commitment* from Home Town Savings and Loan for permanent financing of the home at the time of its completion.

**MORTGAGE CONSTANT** the percentage ratio between the annual **debt service** and the loan **principal.** The formula is

$$\frac{\text{Ann. debt serv.}}{\text{Loan prin.}} = \text{mort. const.}$$

**Example:** A loan of $10,000 at 12% interest for 5 years requires annual payments of $2774. The *mortgage constant* is

$$\frac{2,774}{10,000} = .2774 \text{ or } 27.74\%$$

**Annual debt service** for the loan is

$$0.2774 \times \$10,000 = \$2,774$$

**MORTGAGE CORRESPONDENT** one who services loans for a fee. Compare **mortgage broker.**
**Example:** The Good Money Savings Association bought a package of 1,000 loans in another state. They arrange with a *mortgage correspondent* to collect monthly payments, pay real estate taxes, and assure that the property is insured. The *mortgage correspondent* keeps as a fee ⅜ of 1% of the mortgage balance each year.

**MORTGAGE DISCOUNT** amount of **principal** that lenders deduct at the beginning of the loan. See **discount points.**
**Example:** Abel obtains a mortgage loan in the amount of $50,000. The loan is discounted by 2 **points,** each point equaling 1% of the **principal.** At **closing** Abel will receive $49,000, yet will owe $50,000. The $1,000 difference is the *mortgage discount.*

**MORTGAGEE** one who holds a **lien** on property or **title** to property, as **security** for a debt.
**Example:** Abel obtains a **mortgage** loan from Homebuyers Savings. Homebuyers Savings serves as the *mortgagee.*

**MORTGAGE GUARANTEE INSURANCE CO. (MGIC)** a private company that insures, to lenders, loan repayment in the event of **default** and/or **foreclosure.** See **mortgage insurance.**
**Example:** Collins wants to arrange a loan for 90% of the cost of the home she is buying. The lender applies to *MGIC* for **private mortgage insurance.** MGIC accepts and, for a **premium,** stands willing to accept any losses on the mortgages up to 25% of the **principal.**

**MORTGAGE INSURANCE** 1. a policy that guarantees repayment of a mortgage loan in the event of death or, possibly, disability of the **mortgagor.** 2. protection for the lender in the event of **default,** usually covering the top 25% of the amount borrowed. See **private mortgage insurance.**
**Example:** Manning obtains a mortgage loan and, for an additional monthly **premium,** purchases *mortgage insurance.* Should Manning die before loan **maturity,** the policy will pay the remaining balance of the loan. This protects Manning's survivors from losing the property because of inability to continue the loan payments, and also protects the **mortgagee.**

**MORTGAGE LIEN** an **encumbrance** on property used to secure a loan. The holder of the **lien** has a claim to the property in case of loan **default.** The **priority** of the claim depends on the order of **recording** and any **subordination** agreements. Thus a **first mortgage** generally has prior claim to all other mortgage lien holders. See also **second mortgage.**
**Example:** Minton obtains a mortgage loan to purchase a house. Minton signs a **note** and mortgage contract. The lender obtains a

*mortgage lien* on the house. Should Minton default on the loan, the lender may **foreclose** and exercise the lien to force a sale, the proceeds of which are used to satisfy Minton's debt.

**MORTGAGE OUT** to obtain financing in excess of the cost to construct a project. In the early 1970's **developers** could mortgage out by obtaining a permanent **loan commitment** based on a high percentage of the completed project's value. This enabled the developer to borrow more than the cost of developing the project. Since then opportunities to mortgage out have been virtually eliminated by lower **loan-to-value ratios,** higher **capitalization rates** and higher construction costs.

**Example:** A proposed office building is projected to produce annual **net operating income** of $100,000. At a capitalization rate of 10%, the building is worth $1,000,000. A **takeout** loan commitment is obtained for 80% of value, or $800,000. The developer requires only $750,000 to purchase the land and construct the building. The $50,000 excess represents the results of the developer *mortgaging out.*

**MORTGAGE POOL** a collection of loans of similar nature which are sold as a unit in the secondary market or used to back a security which is then sold in the capital markets.

**Example:** Lenders Mortgage Company packaged a *mortgage pool* consisting of $50 million worth of VA guaranteed loans. The package was sold to a group of investors who each put up a minimum of $25,000.

**MORTGAGE RELIEF** acquired freedom from mortgage debt, generally through **assumption of mortgage** by another party or **debt** retirement. In a tax-free exchange, mortgage relief is considered **boot** received.

**Example:** Collins exchanged her mortgaged office building, receiving land worth $25,000 and *mortgage relief* of $75,000. The total value received was $100,000.

**MORTGAGOR** one who pledges property as **security** for a loan.
**Example:** Abel obtains a mortgage loan from Homebuyers Savings. Abel serves as a *mortgagor.*

**MULTIFAMILY HOUSING** a type of residential structure with more than one **dwelling** unit in the same building.
**Example:** *Multifamily housing* is divided into 2 categories:
2-4 dwelling units: **duplexes,** triplexes, and quadraplexes
5 or more units: apartment buildings
*Multifamily housing* may be tenant-occupied, owner-occupied (as in a **condominium** or cooperative project), or mixed (as many duplexes with the owner occupying one side).

**MULTIPLE LISTING** an arrangement among a group of real estate **brokers;** they agree in advance to provide information about some or all of their **listings** to the others and also agree that **commissions** on sales of such listings will be split between listing and selling brokers.

**Example:** A broker lists a home under an **exclusive right to sell.** The broker belongs to a *multiple listing* association. After 5 days the broker turns in a description of the home to the association. Any cooperating broker can sell the home and will receive half of the commission. The broker who obtained the **exclusive right to sell** is assured of earning half the commission upon the sale.

**MULTIPLE LISTING SERVICE (MLS)** an association of real estate **brokers** that agrees to share **listings** with one another. The listing broker and the selling broker share the **commission.** The MLS usually distributes a book with all listings to its members, updating the book frequently. Prospective buyers benefit from the ability to select from among many homes from any member broker.

**Example:** Abel and Baker, both brokers, are members of the *multiple listing service.* A home that was listed by Abel under an **exclusive right to sell** is sold by Baker. The two brokers share the commission.

**MUNIMENTS OF TITLE** documents, such as **deeds** or **contracts,** one uses to indicate ownership.

**Example:** In order to register **title** under the **Torrens system,** the owner offered *muniments of title.*

**MUTUAL SAVINGS BANKS** mostly in the northeastern U.S., these state-chartered banks are owned by the depositors and operated for their benefit. Most of these banks hold a large portion of their **assets** in home mortgage loans.

**Example:** Abel deposits his savings in a *mutual savings bank* in New York. As a depositor-shareholder, Abel receives a proportionate distribution of the bank's earnings.

# N

**NATIONAL APARTMENT ASSOCIATION (NAA)** an organization of apartment owners, with local chapters in metropolitan areas, that provides information and services for members concerning apartment rentals, **lease** forms, occupancy rates, and other matters.

**Address:**
National Apartment Association
1825 K Street, N.W.
Washington, D.C. 20006

**NATIONAL ASSOCIATION OF CORPORATE REAL ESTATE EXECUTIVES (NACORE)** membership includes those active with purchasing, selling, and managing **real estate** held by **corporations.**
Address:
National Association of Corporate Real Estate Executives
7799 Southwest 62nd Avenue
South Miami, Florida 33143, N.W.

**NATIONAL ASSOCIATION OF HOME BUILDERS (NAHB)** an organization of home builders, providing educational, political information and research services. Publishes a monthly magazine, *Builder.*
Address:
National Association of Home Builders
15th and M Street, N.W.
Washington, D.C. 20005

**NATIONAL ASSOCIATION OF REAL ESTATE BROKERS (NAREB)** an organization mostly of minority real estate salespersons and **brokers** who are called **Realtists.**
Address:
National Association of Real Estate Brokers
9th floor, Suite 900
1101 14th Street, N.W.
Washington, D.C. 20005

**NATIONAL ASSOCIATION OF REAL ESTATE LICENSE LAW OFFICIALS (NARELLO)** membership is composed of commissioners from state real estate licensing agencies.
Address:
National Association of Real Estate License Law Officials
2580 South 90th Street
Omaha, Nebraska 68124

**NATIONAL ASSOCIATION OF REALTORS® (NAR)** an organization of **Realtors®,** devoted to encouraging professionalism in **real estate** activities. There are over 600,000 members of NAR, 50 state associations, and several affiliates. Members are required to abide by the **Code of Ethics** of the NAR.
Address:
National Association of Realtors®
430 N. Michigan Avenue
Chicago, Illinois 60611

**NATIONAL SOCIETY OF REAL ESTATE APPRAISERS** an affiliate of the National Association of Real Estate Brokers that offers the professional designations RA, CRA, MREA.

**Address:**
National Society of Real Estate Appraisers
1265 East 105th Street
Cleveland, Ohio 44108

**NEGATIVE AMORTIZATION** an increase in the **outstanding balance** of a loan resulting from the failure of periodic **debt service** payments to cover required interest charged on the loan. Generally occurs under **indexed loans** for which the applicable **interest rate** may be changed without affecting the monthly payments. *Negative amortization* will occur if the indexed interest rate is increased.

**Example:** A loan is originated at 15% interest with a **maturity** of 30 years. The interest rate may be adjusted each 6 months, but monthly payments remain a constant $632. After 6 months, the interest rate is raised to 16.5%, which would require a monthly payment of $692 to fully amortize the loan. At the new interest rate, $687 is required to pay interest. The $55 difference between the payment and interest due is added to the principal in month 7 as *negative amortization* (Figure 114).

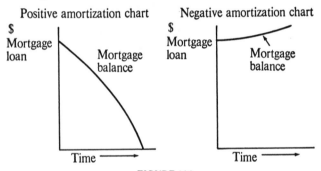

FIGURE 114

**NEGATIVE CASH FLOW** situation in which a property owner must make an outlay of funds to operate a property.
**Example:** Baker acquires an apartment building with the first year income statement shown in Table 24.

Baker must spend $5,000 to operate the building for the first year, because of a *negative cash flow*.

**NEGATIVE LEVERAGE** same as **reverse leverage.**

**NEGOTIABLE INSTRUMENT** a promise to pay money, transferable from one person to another.
**Example:** Abel gave Baker a *negotiable instrument* that contained

a promise to pay $1000 on July 22 of this year. Baker sold the note for $900 cash to Collins by endorsing and delivering it. Collins became a **holder in due course.**

## TABLE 24

| | |
|---|---:|
| Potential **gross income:** | $50,000 |
| Vacancy loss | − 5,000 |
| Effective gross income | 45,000 |
| **Operating expenses** | −30,000 |
| **Net operating income** | 15,000 |
| **Debt service** | −20,000 |
| Negative cash flow before tax | $5,000 |

**NEGOTIATION** the process of bargaining that precedes an agreement. Successful negotiation generally results in a **contract** between the parties.
**Example:** Nelson wishes to purchase a property from Newman. Nelson is willing to pay up to a certain price and desires certain **conditions** placed on the sale. Newman will accept anything over a certain price and may be willing to help finance the purchase for a higher price. In *negotiation* Nelson and Newman attempt to come to an agreement over the price and conditions. When they agree, a sales contract is **executed.**

**NEIGHBORHOOD** a district or locality characterized by similar or compatible land uses. Neighborhoods are often identified by a place name and have boundaries composed of major streets, barriers, or abrupt changes in land use.
**Example:** Residential *neighborhoods* are often identified with a **subdivision,** an elementary school attendance zone, a major public facility, such as a college, or a small town within a larger urban area. Homes in the neighborhood are of similar style, age, and value.
**Example:** Commercial *neighborhoods* are generally associated with a major road, shopping center, or **central business district.**
**Example:** Industrial *neighborhoods* are generally identified by common use of a transportation linkage.

**NEIGHBORHOOD LIFE CYCLE** a generalized pattern that describes the physical and social changes that residential areas experience over time. See also **abandonment, filtering down, urban renewal, land use succession.**
**Example:** Richard Andrews' *neighborhood life cycle* (Figure 115).

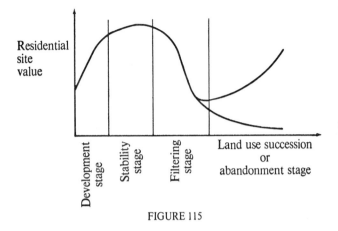

Residential site value

Development stage

Stability stage

Filtering stage

Land use succession or abandonment stage

FIGURE 115

**NET INCOME** 1. in accounting, the amount remaining after all expenses have been met.
**Example:** Table 25
2. in **appraisal,** same as **net operating income.**

TABLE 25

| | | |
|---|---:|---:|
| Rental income | | $10,000 |
| Less: | | |
|   Utilities | $1,500 | |
|   Property taxes | 1,000 | |
|   Management fee | 500 | |
|   Maintenance expenses | 2,000 | |
|   Interest | 2,000 | |
|   Depreciation | 1,000 | |
|   Income taxes | 1,000 | |
|   Subtotal | | − 9,000 |
| Net income | | $1,000 |

**NET LEASABLE AREA** in a building or project, floor space that may be rented to tenants. The area upon which rental payments are based. Generally excludes common areas and space devoted to the heating, cooling, and other equipment of a building.
**Example:** A building with 10 floors, each containing 3,000 square feet of space, may have a *net leasable area* of 25,000 square feet. Elevators, hallways etc. absorb the remaining 5,000 square feet.

**NET LEASE** a **lease** whereby, in addition to the rent stipulated, the **lessee** (tenant) pays such expenses as taxes, insurance, and **maintenance.** The landlord's rent receipt is thereby "net" of those expenses.
**Example:** Baker leases retail space from Abel on a *net lease*. Abel can expect to receive the full rent without deducting for **operating expenses,** which are paid by Baker. In practice, various levels of net leases are often used to designate arrangements where the tenant pays only some types of expenses and the landlord pays other types.

**NET LISTING** a listing in which the brokers's **commission** is the excess of the sale price over an agreed-upon (net) price to the seller; illegal in some states.
**Example:** Abel agrees to sell Baker's house on a *net listing*. They set the net price at $70,000. Abel finds a buyer willing to pay $75,000. Abel's commission is $5,000. Note that should Abel find a buyer offering $70,000, Abel would earn no commission.

**NET OPERATING INCOME (NOI)** income from property or business after **operating expenses** have been deducted, but before deducting income taxes and financing expenses (**interest** and **principal** payments). The formula is:

NOI = gross income − operating expenses

**Example:** A property produces rental income of $100,000 during the year. The expenses incurred are shown in Table 26.

**TABLE 26**

| Operating expenses: | |
|---|---|
| Maintenance | $20,000 |
| Insurance | 5,000 |
| Property taxes | 10,000 |
| Management | 10,000 |
| Utilities | 15,000 |
| | $60,000 |

| Debt service:* | |
|---|---|
| Interest | $18,000 |
| Principal | 2,000 |
| | $20,000 |
| Income taxes* | ($5,000) |

*Excluded from the computation.

NOI = $100,000 − $60,000 = $40,000 (*net operating income*)

**NET PRESENT VALUE** a method of determining whether expected

performance of a proposed investment promises to be adequate.
See also **internal rate of return, present value of one.**
**Example:** A proposed land investment requires $10,000 of cash
now, and is expected to be resold for $25,000 in 4 years. For the
**risks** involved, the investor seeks a 20% **discount rate** (same as
**compounded rate of return**). The $25,000 amount to be received in
4 years, when discounted by 20% annually, is worth $12,056 now.
Since the investment costs $10,000, the *net present value* is
$2,056.

$$\frac{\$25,000}{(1 + 0.20)^4} - \$10,000 = \$2,056$$

**NET WORTH** the excess of **assets** over **liabilities.** The amount of
equity.
**Example:** Table 27:

**TABLE 27**

| Balance Sheet | | | |
|---|---|---|---|
| Assets | | Liabilities | |
| Land | $10,000 | Mortgage | $75,000 |
| Buildings | 90,000 | Net worth | 25,000 |
| Total | $100,000 | Total | $100,000 |

**NET YIELD** the return on an investment after subtracting all
expenses. See also **current yield, yield to maturity.**
**Example: Equity** paid for an investment is $10,000. **Net income** is
$1,000. Therefore, the investment generates a $1,000 *net yield.*

**NEW ENGLAND COLONIAL** an early American style, 2½ story
boxlike house that is generally symmetrical, square, or rectangular with side or rear wings. The traditional material is narrow clapboard siding. The roof is usually the gable type covered with shingles.
**Example:** Figure 116.

**NEW ENGLAND FARM HOUSE** an early American style of house
that is simple and box-shaped. The traditional material for the
exterior siding is white clapboard. A steep pitched roof is used to
shed heavy snow.
**Example:** Figure 117.

**NEW TOWN** a large mixed-use development designed to provide
residences, general shopping, services, and employment. The
basic concept of a new town is to construct a community in a
previously undeveloped area under a central plan, to avoid

Cornice with dentils

Chimney at each end

Gable roof

2½ stories

Small pane double-hung windows

Side lights

Wing

Working wood shutters

FIGURE 116

White clapboard

Steep, pitched roof simple box shape

FIGURE 117

unplanned development. Some European and South American countries use new towns to attract population into less developed regions.

**Example:** The popularity of *new towns* reached a peak in the early 1970's under financial assistance from the federal government.

Possibly the most famous modern *new towns* in the U.S. are Columbia, Maryland and Reston, Virginia. *New towns* have been developed to serve as national capitals, such as Washington, D.C., Brasilia, Brazil, and Canberra, Australia.

**NOMINAL LOAN RATE** same as **face interest rate.**

**NOMINEE** one who, in a limited sense, acts for or represents another.
**Example:** Davis with consent, used her secretary's name as the **grantee** to property she buys. Her secretary was considered her *nominee.* Simultaneously, her secretary **deeded** the property to Davis. There was a **mortgage** on the property. Davis acquired the property from the *nominee* **subject to** the mortgage. By doing so, Davis is not personally liable for the mortgage loan.

**NO MONEY DOWN** general term referring to real estate acquisition strategies based on seller provided financing and/or existing loan assumption and minimal use of cash down payments. It is a method of achieving maximum profits from real estate investments.
**Example:** Allen purchased three houses using a *no money down* strategy. In one transaction, Allen assumed the existing mortgage of $55,000, gave the seller a note for an additional $30,000 and transferred ownership of an automobile worth $5,000 to finance the $90,000 house with no cash down payment.

**NONCONFORMING USE** a use that violates **zoning** regulations or codes but is allowed to continue because it began before the zoning **restriction** was enacted.
**Example:** Carter owns a commercial building constructed in 1920. In 1935, the city enacted a **zoning ordinance** that prescribes residential use for the area in which the building is located. Under *noncomforming use,* the building may remain, but Carter is restricted in the extent to which he may improve or restore the building.

**NONDISTURBANCE CLAUSE** 1. an agreement in mortgage contracts on income-producing property that provides for the continuation of **leases** in the event of loan **foreclosure.**
**Example:** The tenant was concerned that he would be **evicted** if the landlord went **bankrupt.** He insisted on a *nondisturbance clause* so the lease would continue in the event of foreclosure.
2. an agreement in a sales contract, when the seller retains **mineral rights,** that provides that exploration of minerals will not interfere with surface development.
**Example:** When the seller negotiated the **oil and gas lease,** she was assured by the oil company that the property could be **conveyed** with a *nondisturbance clause.*

**NONEXCLUSIVE LISTING** same as **open listing.**

**NONRECOURSE** no personal **liability.** Lenders may take the property pledged as **collateral** to satisfy a **debt,** but have no **recourse** to other **assets** of the borrower.
**Example:** Downing purchases a property with a *nonrecourse* loan. Should Downing **default,** the lender may **foreclose** and acquire the property but is barred from seeking a **judgment** against other properties held by Downing.

**NORMAL WEAR AND TEAR** physical **depreciation** arising from age and ordinary use of the property.
**Example:** An **appraiser** estimates that a certain type of carpeting, subject to *normal wear and tear,* should have a physical life of 5 years.

**NOTARIZE** to attest, in one's capacity as a **notary public,** to the genuineness of a signature.
**Example:** Before a county clerk will record certain types of documents, they must be *notarized* to assure the signature is not forged.

**NOTARY PUBLIC** an officer who is authorized to take **acknowledgments** to certain types of documents, such as **deeds, contracts,** and **mortgages,** and before whom **affidavits** may be sworn.
**Example:** Eakins and Finwick agree to transfer a piece of property. At the **closing,** a *notary public* serves to witness the signing of all documents.

**NOTE** a written **instrument** that acknowledges a **debt** and promises to pay.
**Example:** Greer borrows money from Thrifty Savings to purchase a home. Greer signs a *note* to acknowledge the debt, to promise to pay under specified terms, and to prescribe a procedure for curing **default.** A **mortgage** will also be signed that pledges the home to the lender as **security** for the note.

**NOTICE** official communication of a legal action or one's intent to take an action. See also **public offering, public sale.**
**Example:** A landlord may be required to give a tenant 30 days *notice* before terminating the **lease.**
**Example:** A lender may be required to give a debtor *notice* that a **default** has occurred before initiating **foreclosure** proceedings. See **notice of default.**
**Example: Recording** a deed serves to give **constructive notice** to the public of one's ownership of a property.

**NOTICE OF DEFAULT** a letter sent to a defaulting party as a reminder of the **default.** May state a **grace period** and the **penalties**

for failing to cure the default.
**Example:** Vacation Lot Sales Corp. sent a *notice of default* to Abel. It offered a 7-day grace period, after which they would consider his **interest** as forfeited unless he paid the delinquent **installment.**

**NOTICE TO QUIT** 1. a notice to a tenant to **vacate** rented property.
**Example:** After the lease expired the tenant remained in **possession.** The landlord sent a *notice to quit* by January 31.
2. sometimes used by a tenant who intends to vacate on a certain date.

**NOTORIOUS POSSESSION** generally acknowledged **possession of real estate.** One of the requirements to gain ownership of real estate through **adverse possession.**
**Example:** A squatter, who was in *notorious possession* of land, was thought by neighbors to be the owner of record.

**NOVATION** a 3-party agreement whereby one party is released from a **contract** and another party is substituted.
**Example:** Baker wants to buy Abel's home and assume the mortgage. Abel wants to be released from all mortgage **liability.** Good Money Savings Association cooperates. The 3 sign a *novation* whereby Baker is substituted for Abel on the mortgage.

**NUISANCE** a land use whose associated activities are incompatible with surrounding land uses.
**Example: Zoning** laws and private **deed restrictions** are used to prevent the development of *nuisances,* such as:
• activities that produce noxious fumes or air pollution in residential areas
• commercial uses that generate large volumes of automobile traffic in residential areas
• junkyards in highly visible areas
• activities considered socially offensive, such as sale of pornographic materials, in residential areas

**NULL AND VOID** that which cannot be legally enforced, as with a **contract** provision that is not in conformance with the law.
**Example:** Ivenson sells a property and places in the **deed** a **covenant** that the property may never be sold to someone of a minority race. Since this provision is in defiance of the U.S. Constitution, it could never be enforced and is thereby *null and void.*

# O

**OBLIGEE** the person in whose favor an obligation is entered into.
**Example:** Jackson promises to manage the property of Kindall, an out-of-town investor. In this arrangement, Kindall is the *obligee;* Jackson is the **obligor.**

**OBLIGOR** the person who binds himself or herself to another; one who has engaged to perform some obligation; one who makes a **bond.**
**Example:** See obligee.

**OBSOLESCENCE** a loss in value due to reduced desirability and usefulness of a structure because its design and construction has become obsolete; loss due to a structure's becoming old-fashioned, not in keeping with modern needs, with consequent loss of income. See **economic depreciation, functional depreciation, functional obsolescence.**
**Example:** An old house may suffer from the following examples of *obsolescence:*
• rooms of improper size
• features no longer useful, such as a coal chute with a gas-fired furnace
• out-of-date plumbing, heating, and electrical fixtures and systems
• inadequate insulation
• unsuitable architectural style
• construction materials that require excessive **maintenance**
• undesirable location

**OCCUPANCY AGREEMENT, LIMITED** one that allows a prospective buyer to obtain **possession** under a temporary arrangement, usually prior to **closing.**
**Example:** Abel, the seller, signs a *limited occupancy agreement* with Baker that allows Baker possession of the property at rent of $25 per day for up to 30 days or the day of closing, whichever occurs first.

**OCCUPANCY LEVEL** percentage of currently rented units in a building, city, neighborhood, or complex. Contrast with **vacancy rate.**
**Example:** Today the Holiday Hotel has 90 of its 100 rooms booked and filled. Its *occupancy level* is 90%. Conversely, its vacancy rate is 10%.

**OFFER** an expression of willingness to purchase a property at a specified price.
**Example:** Lincoln places a property on the market. Murray makes an *offer* to buy the property for $150,000. Lincoln may accept the offer, reject the offer, or propose a **counteroffer.**

**OFFER AND ACCEPTANCE** see **agreement of sale.**

**OFFEREE** one who receives an offer. Generally a buyer offers a purchase contract to an owner, which makes the owner the *offeree*. When the seller offers a contract to a buyer, the buyer is the *offeree*.
**Example:** Brewster offers Smithton a contract in which Brewster offers to pay $120,000 for a property. Smithton is the *offeree*.

**OFFEROR** one who extends an offer to another.
**Example:** Brewster offers Smithton $120,000 for a property. Brewster is the *offeror*.

**OFFICE OF INTERSTATE LAND SALES REGISTRATION (OILSR)** a division of the U.S. Department of **Housing and Urban Development** that regulates offerings of land for sale across state lines. See **Interstate Land Sales Act.**
**Example:** Norwood **subdivides** a large land parcel in Arizona and wishes to market the lots to investors across the nation. Norwood is required to register the offering with *OILSR* and follow certain procedures intended to inform buyers of the characteristics of their investment.

**OFF-SITE COSTS** expenditures related to construction that are spent away from the place of construction.
**Example:** Owens is developing a **subdivision.** Certain *offsite costs* are incurred, such as the costs of extending roads, sewers, and water lines to the **site.** Site costs include landscaping and other site **improvements.**

**OFF-SITE IMPROVEMENTS** the portions of a **subdivision** or development that are not directly on the lots to be sold.
**Example:** Access streets, curbs, sewers, and utility connections are common examples of *off-site improvements*.

**OIL AND GAS LEASE** an agreement that gives the right to explore for oil, gas, and sometimes other minerals and to extract them from the ground. Provisions include the granting of subsurface and surface rights, **lease** duration, **extension** terms, **royalties**, surface damages, **assignments**, and **warranties.** See **mineral rights.**
**Example:** In an *oil and gas lease*, the owner is to receive $100 per acre as a bonus payment, and one eighth of the value of minerals found on the property.

**ONE-HUNDRED-PERCENT LOCATION** a point in space where a

retail establishment would achieve maximum sales volume compared to other locations in the local market area.
**Example:** The corner of First and Main is the busiest intersection downtown. It represents the *hundred-percent location* for a department store.

**OPEN-END MORTGAGE** a **mortgage** under which the **mortgagor** (borrower) may secure additional funds from the **mortgagee** (lender), usually stipulating a ceiling amount that can be borrowed.
**Example:** Poole obtains an *open-end mortgage* to purchase a home. Under the mortgage agreement, Poole may borrow additional funds over the **maturity** of the loan as long as the unpaid **principal** does not exceed 80% of the home's **appraised** value.

**OPEN HOUSE** a method of showing a home for sale whereby the home is left open for inspection by interested parties.
**Example:** A **broker** advertises an *open house* to promote the sale of a **listing.** On the specified date, prospective buyers may inspect the house during the hours of the *open house.*

**OPEN HOUSING** a condition under which housing units may be purchased or **leased** without regard for racial, ethnic, color, or religious characteristics of the buyers or tenants.
**Example:** The intent of government antidiscrimination laws applied to housing is to provide *open housing* under which anyone with sufficient funds may purchase or rent available housing units.

**OPEN LISTING** a **listing** given to any number of **brokers** without liability to compensate any except the one who first secures a buyer who is ready, willing, and able to meet the terms of the listing or secures the seller's **acceptance** of another **offer.** The sale of the property automatically terminates all open listings.
**Example:** Quarry offers an *open listing* to 2 brokers, Ridley and Sims. Ridley presents a buyer who eventually purchases the property. Ridley is entitled to a **commission;** Sims is not.

**OPEN MORTGAGE** a **mortgage** that has **matured** or is overdue and is therefore open to **foreclosure** at any time.
**Example:** Towns sells a property to Udall. Towns provides financing for the sale in the form of a 5-year, **interest-only** loan. At the end of 5 years, Udall does not pay the **principal** and Towns allows the loan to become an *open mortgage.* This arrangement allows Udall to pay off the loan at any time or Towns to call the loan at any time.

**OPEN SPACE** land, within a developed area, that is left undeveloped and serves as an **amenity** to surrounding occupants.
**Example:** A 20-acre **planned unit development** contains 12 acres

that are covered by structures and pavement. The remaining **8** acres are left in *open space*.

**OPERATING EXPENSES** amounts paid to maintain property, such as **property taxes, utilities, hazard insurance.** Excludes **financing** expenses and **depreciation.**
**Example:** The following are expenses incurred in operating a property:
Operating expenses
- maintenance
- management
- real estate taxes
- hazard and liability insurance
- utilities
- supplies

The following are not categorized as operating expenses:
debt service
- principal payments
- interest
- loan fees
- participation payments

depreciation
income taxes

**OPERATING LEASE** a **lease** between the **lessee** and the **sublessee** who actually occupies and uses the property. See **sublease.**
**Example:** Figure 118.

FIGURE 118

**OPINION OF TITLE** a certificate, generally from an attorney, as to the validity of **title** to property being sold. See **title abstract.**
**Example:** Based upon the attorney's *opinion of title*, the **title insurance** company insured title to the property.

**OPTION** the right to purchase or **lease** a property upon specified terms within a specified period.

**Example:** Moore purchases an *option* on a piece of land. The option runs 90 days and costs $500 per acre. If Moore wishes to purchase the land, she has 90 days to exercise her right and may buy the land for $5,000 per acre. If she decides not to purchase, she **forfeits** the $500 per acre.

**OPTIONEE** one who receives or purchases an option.
**Example:** Brewster pays Smithton $5,000 for the right to purchase a property for $120,000 within the next year. Brewster is the *optionee*.

**OPTIONOR** one who gives or sells an option.
**Example:** Brewster pays Smithton $5,000 for the right to purchase a property for $120,000 within the next year. Smithton is the *optionor*.

**ORAL CONTRACT** a verbal agreement. With few exceptions, verbal agreements for the sale or use of **real estate** are unenforceable. In most states, contracts for the sale or rental of real estate are, unless they are in writing, unenforceable under the **Statute of Frauds.** Verbal leases for a year or less are often acceptable.
**Example:** Abel agrees to sell property to Baker. Their contract is oral. Abel changes his mind. He faces no **penalty** because *oral contracts* for the sale of real estate are unenforceable.

**ORDINANCES** municipal rules governing the use of land.
**Examples:** Local governments may pass *ordinances* to:
• specify certain land uses in certain areas
• regulate **nuisances**
• specify the manner in which structures are constructed or maintained
• specify the manner in which **subdivisions** are designed
• regulate rental practices
• regulate condominium **conversion** practices

**ORDINARY AND NECESSARY BUSINESS EXPENSES** a tax term that allows a current deduction for business expenses. Contrasted with **capital expenditures** and unreasonable expenses.
**Example:** Each day the apartment manager enjoyed a 3-martini lunch with his friend. He claimed a tax deduction for the lunch expense. The **Internal Revenue Service** contests the deductions because they were not *ordinary and necessary business expenses*.

**ORDINARY ANNUITY** a series of equal payments, each payment occurring at the end of each equally spaced period.
**Example:** For a lender the **income stream** from a standard, fixed rate mortgage loan provides an *ordinary annuity* (Figure 119).

**ORDINARY INCOME** defined by the **Internal Revenue Code** to include salaries, fees, **commissions,** interests, dividends, and many

other items. Taxed at regular tax rates. Contrasted with long-term
**capital gains,** which receive more favorable tax treatment.
**Example:** Abel would prefer to convert *ordinary income* into long-
term capital gains. He wants to change the nature of property he
has from **inventory** to investment.

FIGURE 119

**ORDINARY LOSS** for income tax purposes a loss that is deductible
against **ordinary income.** Usually more beneficial to a taxpayer
than a **capital loss,** which has limitations on deductibility.
**Example:** The sale of **inventory** at a loss results in an *ordinary
loss,* whereas the sale of an investment at a loss results in a capital
loss.

**ORIENTATION** the position of a structure on a **site** relative to sunlight angles and prevailing winds.
**Example:** A house in Figure 120 has a north-south *orientation*
designed to maximize the natural heating effect of the sun in the
winter:

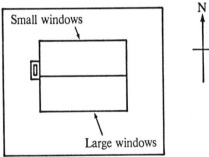

FIGURE 120

**ORIGINATION FEES** charges to a borrower to cover the costs of
issuing the loan, such as **credit** checks, **appraisal,** and **title**
expenses.
**Example:** The lender issued a $50,000 **mortgage** loan and charged
a 1% *origination fee* ($500).

**OUTSTANDING BALANCE** the amount currently owed on a debt.
**Example:** Whitman borrowed $10,000. She then paid $1,200 of interest and $500 toward **principal.** Her *outstanding balance* is $9,500 ($10,000 minus $500).

**OVERAGE** in leases for retail stores, amounts to be paid, based on gross sales, over the **base rent.** See **percentage lease.**
**Example:** Winfield leases retail space in a shopping center. The lease calls for a base rent of $2,500 per month plus 5% of gross sales over $10,000. The first month, Winfield has sales of $20,000. In addition to the $2,500 base rent, Winfield pays an *overage* of $500 [.05 × ($20,000 − $10,000)].

**OVER AGE 55 HOME SALE EXEMPTION** in taxation, an individual over age 55 can sell principal residence at a gain and exclude up to $125,000 of the gain from taxation. Allowed regardless of the purchase of another home. Must have used the property as a **principal residence** for 3 of the last 5 years.
**Example:** Abel, *over age 55,* sells his principal residence, which he has lived in for the last 3 years, at a $150,000 gain. He may exclude $125,000 of the gain from taxation. The rest of the gain is taxable as a **capital gain.**

**OVERALL RATE OF RETURN (OAR)** the percentage relationship of **net operating income** divided by the purchase price of property. See **capitalization rate.**
**Example:** Property that sells for $1,000,000 is anticipated to produce a net operating income of $100,000 per year. The indicated *overall rate of return* is 0.10 or 10% $\left(\dfrac{\$100,000}{\$1,000,000}\right)$.

**OVERIMPROVEMENT** a land use considered too intense for the land.
**Example:** A proposed house costs $100,000 to construct on a **site** valued at $20,000. It is estimated that the completed house would have a market value of only $110,000. The proposed house is an *overimprovement* of the site.

**OVERRIDE** 1. a fee paid to someone higher in the organization, or above a certain amount.
**Example:** In the agreement the salesman was required to pay an *override* of 10% of his gross **commissions** to the managing **broker.**
2. an **estate** carved out of a working interest in an **oil or gas**

lease.
**Example:** The *overriding* **royalty** required 2% of the production of the well be paid to the attorney who negotiated the oil lease.

**OWNER OCCUPANT**  a tenant of a residence who also owns the property.
**Example:** Homer lives in a home that he also owns. Landon owns a home but rents it to Renton. Homer is an *owner occupant*, Landon is an **absentee owner**, and Renton is a rental tenant.

**OWNERSHIP FORM** methods of owning **real estate,** which affect income tax, **estate tax,** continuity, **liability, survivorship,** transferability, disposition at death and at **bankruptcy.**
**Example:** *Ownership* forms include:
• **corporation**
• joint tenancy
• **limited partnership**
• **partnership**
• **Subchapter S corporation**
• tenancy by the entireties
• **tenancy in common**
• **tenancy in severalty**

**OWNERSHIP RIGHTS TO REALTY** **possession,** enjoyment, control, and disposition. See also **fee tail, interest, tenancy.**
**Example:** By virtue of **title** to the property, Overton enjoys full *ownership rights to realty*. This enables Overton to use the property, **lease** out the property, pledge it as **security** on loans, and sell the property within the restrictions of the law.

---

# P

---

**PACKAGE MORTGAGE** a **mortgage** arrangement whereby the **principal** amount loaned is increased because **personalty** (e.g., appliances), as well as **realty** serve as **collateral.**
**Example:** Simmons applied for a *package mortgage* in order to spread the cost of appliances over 25 years and to pay for them with her home mortgage payment.

**PAPER** **credit** given, evidenced by a written obligation that is backed by **property.**
**Example:** Dunn sells his property for $100,000. He receives $20,000 cash and $80,000 of *paper* that is payable over 20 years at 10% interest.

**PARCEL** a piece of property under one ownership; a lot in a **subdivision.**

**Example:** In order to construct the highway, the state must acquire parts of *parcels* A and C in Figure 121. *Parcels* B and D are unaffected.

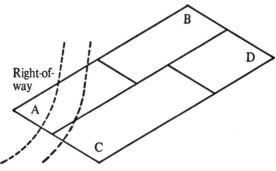

FIGURE 121

**PAROL EVIDENCE** oral evidence, rather than that contained in documents. The parol evidence rule states that when parties put their agreement in writing, all previous oral agreements merge into the written agreement. The written agreement cannot be contradicted by oral testimony, unless there was a **mistake** or **fraud.**
**Example:** Carter agrees to buy a house from Dooley, and both sign a written agreement. Carter later argues that Dooley said he'd pay all the loan **discount points.** Under the *parol evidence* rule, courts will interpret the **contract** as it is written.

**PARTIAL RELEASE** a provision in a **mortgage** that allows some of the property pledged to be freed from serving as **collateral.**
**Example:** Baker sold 3 acres of land (Figure 122), and accepted a $30,000 purchase money mortgage. *Partial releases* in the mortgage require that, upon each $10,000 **principal** payment, one acre be freed from serving as collateral. The sequence of release was **platted,** and described in the mortgage.

**PARTIAL TAKING** acquisition by **condemnation** of only part of the property or some property rights.
**Examples:** Situations calling for *partial takings* (Figure 123).

**PARTICIPATION MORTGAGE** one that allows the lender to share in part of the income or resale proceeds.
**Example:** A loan is given on an office building. In addition to a fixed payment of **principal** and **interest,** the lender is entitled to 2% of gross rental income. This is a *participation loan* in which the lender participates in the **income stream** provided by the property.

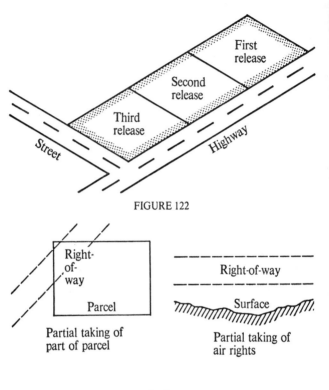

FIGURE 122

Partial taking of
part of parcel

Right-of-way

Surface

Partial taking of
air rights

Surface

Right-of-way

Partial taking of
underground rights

FIGURE 123

**PARTITION** the division of **real property** between those who own it
with **undivided interest.**
**Example:** Abel and Baker own land by **tenancy in common** until
they *partition* it. Thereafter, each owns a particular tract of land
(Figure 124).

| Before partition | After partition | |
|---|---|---|
| Abel and Baker, as tenants in common, are owners of one parcel. | Abel owns this half. | Baker owns this half. |

FIGURE 124

**PARTNERSHIP** an agreement between 2 or more entities to go into business or invest. Either partner may bind the other, within the scope of the partnership. Each partner is liable for all the partnership's debts. A partnership normally pays no taxes, but merely files an information return. The individual partners pay personal income tax on their share of **income**. See also **general partner, limited partnership**. Compare **corporation**.
**Example:** Abel and Baker form a *partnership* to buy land. The partnership owns the property, rather than Abel and Baker.

**PARTY WALL** a wall built along the line separating 2 properties, partly on each **parcel**. Either owner has the right to use the wall and has an **easement** over that part of the **adjoining** owner's land covered by the wall.
**Example:** The structures built on lots A and B in Figure 125 are separated by a *party wall*.

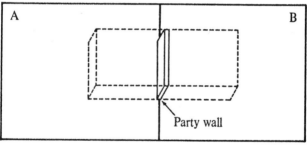

FIGURE 125

**PASSIVE ACTIVITY INCOME** under the 1986 tax act, is generated by: 1. Any trade or business conducted for profit in which the taxpayer does not materially participate. 2. Any rental activity, whether or not the taxpayer materially participates.

Rental activities are presumed to be passive. These include all activities that generate income from payments for the use of property rather than for the performance of services. Rental activities include long-term rentals of apartments, net leased property, office equipment, and automobiles. In contrast, the rental of hotel rooms or transient apartments and short-term car rentals are not passive because of the extent of services provided.

Because rental real estate is a passive activity, owners may not use losses to shelter other types of income. These are exceptions:

1. Phase-out for property acquired before October 22, 1986, the enactment date of the 1986 tax act. Losses on property acquired before then are allowed as follows:

1987  65%
1988  40%
1989  20%
1990  10%

Property acquired after the October 22, 1986 date is not eligible for the phase-out.

2. Real estate dealers.

3. **"Active" participants** in rental real estate are allowed to shelter up to $25,000 per year of losses against nonpassive income. A less stringent definition of active participation is provided as compared to **material participation**.

4. Mortgage interest on a principal or second residence is not subject to these rules even when the residence is rented out.

5. A closely held *C* corporation (other than a personal services corporation) may use passive losses and credits to offset its net active income, but not portfolio income. An *S* corporation may not apply passive losses and credits against other income.

**Example:** Paul bought an apartment complex in 1988, which generated a $30,000 tax loss. If Paul meets the test of an active investor, up to $25,000 of the loss may be used to offset active or portfolio income. If not, the entire loss remains suspended until Paul earns passive income.

**PASSIVE INCOME** 1. generally, income from **rents, royalties**, dividends, interest, and gains from the sale of securities. 2. A new meaning created by the Tax Reform Act of 1986, distinguishes *passive income* or loss from **active income** and **portfolio income**. See **passive activity income**.

**PASSIVE INCOME GENERATOR** a business or investment that produces **passive income** which can be used to offset passive losses.

**Example:** Perry owns rental real estate which provides a tax loss. Under the 1986 tax act, the loss may be offset by passive income, but not by **portfolio income** or **active income**. Without a *passive income generator* to offset the loss, the loss will be carried forward in a suspense account.

**PASSIVE INVESTOR** 1. one who invests money but does not manage the business or property. 2. See **passive income, portfolio income**.

**Example:** Dooley has neither time nor skills to manage the property that he wants to invest in. He forms a **partnership** with a real estate syndicator who will devote time and expertise to manage the property for profit. Dooley contributes money but not effort, so he is a *passive investor*.

**PASSIVE SOLAR HEATING** a system of features incorporated into a building's design to use and maximize the effects of the sun's natural heating capability. See **active solar heating.**

Example: *Passive solar heating* systems use some type of collection and storage element, such as a water-filled partition, which is exposed to the sun during the day and radiates heat to the structure at night. Other features, such as south-facing windows, site **orientation,** roof overhangs, are included to enhance the effects of the sun's heat.

**PASS-THROUGH CERTIFICATES** interests in a pool of mortgages sold by **mortgage bankers** to investors. Money collected as monthly mortgage payments is distributed to those who own certificates. Often **guaranteed** by **Ginnie Mae.**

Example: A mortgage banker sells $5,000,000 of *pass-through certificates* in $10,000 denominations, supported by an equal amount of **VA** and **FHA mortgages.** Monthly collections of **interest** and **principal** are remitted to certificate holders, except for $44/100$ of 1% of the annual principal, kept by the mortgage banker as a **servicing** fee (Figure 126).

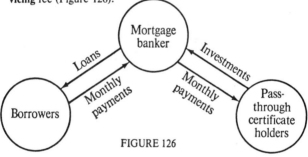

FIGURE 126

**PATENT** conveyance of **title** to government land.

Example: The federal government grants a *patent* on land they sell to a mining company.

**PAYBACK PERIOD** the amount of time required for cumulative estimated future income from an investment to equal the amount initially invested. It is used to compare alternative investment opportunities.

Example: Purchase of an apartment building requires an equity investment of $20,000. Annual cash flow is expected to be $2,000. The *payback period* for the investment is 10 years.

**PAYMENT CAP** a contractual limit on the percentage amount of adjustment allowed in the monthly payment for an adjustable rate mortgage at any one adjustment period. Generally it does not affect the interest rate charged. If the allowable payment does not cover interest due on the principal at the adjusted rate of interest, **negative amortization** will occur.

**Example:** An adjustable rate mortgage has a *payment cap* of 7% a year. The monthly payment in year 1 is $500.00. When the interest rate is adjusted in year 2, the new payment would be $550.00 to pay interest and amortize the principal. However, due to the *payment cap*, the maximum payment for year 2 is $535.00.

**PENALTY** money one will pay for breaking a law or violating part or all of the **terms** of a **contract.**

**Example:** *Penalties* are often imposed for:
• prepaying a loan
• failing to complete a contract of sale
• breaking a lease

**PENTHOUSE** a luxury housing unit located on the top floor of a high-rise building.

**Example:** A *penthouse* (Figure 127).

Penthouse

High rise
building

FIGURE 127

**PERCENTAGE LEASE** a **lease** of property in which the rental is based on a percentage of the volume of sales made upon the leased premises. It usually stipulates a minimum rental and is regularly used for retailers who are **tenants**. See **overage.**
**Example:** The *percentage lease* required the jewelry store to pay as additional rent 6% of annual sales in excess of $100,000. The **base rent** is $6,000 per year.

**PERCOLATION TEST** a procedure to measure the drainage characteristics of the soil on a lot. Required in the proper design of septic tank drainfields.
**Example:** Carter is developing a **subdivision** in the county. As part of site preparation, Carter runs *percolation tests* on the soil. From this information, the engineer can determine the proper size of the lots and placement of septic tanks.

**PERFORMANCE BOND** issued by an insurance company; posted by a party who is to perform certain work. If the work is not performed, the insurer promises to complete the work or pay damages up to the amount of the bond. Contrast with **completion bond.**
**Example:** The contract requires the **contractor** to put up a $10,000 *performance bond*. If the contractor fails to do the job, the property owner has assurances of compensatory payment from the insurance company.

**PERMANENT MORTGAGE** a mortgage for a long period of time (over 10 years).
**Example:** The **savings and loan association** promises to originate a 25-year **self-amortizing** *permanent mortgage* when construction is completed. A permanent **mortgage commitment** is often needed before a **construction** loan can be arranged.

**PERMIT** a document, issued by a government regulatory authority, that allows the bearer to take some specific action.
**Example:** An occupancy *permit* allows the owner of a building to occupy or rent the building.
**Example:** A building *permit* allows a builder to construct or modify a structure.

**PERPETUITY** the condition of being never ending. Most states attempt to outlaw perpetuities because of potential problems. A perpetual income stream may cause bankruptcy. A **deed** that keeps property in a family in *perpetuity* can cause financial hardship.
**Example:** A bank offers to pay a 10% interest rate in *perpetuity*. A $10,000 deposit should receive $1,000 annual income for as long as the deposit remains in the account.

**PERSON** in law, an **entity** having legal responsibility. Legally, a natural person is a human being who has reached **majority.** (Compare **minor.**) An artificial person may be a **corporation;** in some instances **partnerships,** governments, and certain other bodies are considered persons.
**Example:** When negotiating a contract it is important to deal with a **person;** otherwise the contract may be unenforceable.

**PERSONAL PROPERTY** same as **personalty.**

**PERSONALTY** personal property, i.e., all **property** that is not **realty.** Property that is movable, not fixed to land. See **chattel**
**Example:** The following are *personalty:*
• appliances not permanently attached to **real property**
• cash and securities
• furniture and household items
• **mobile homes** not permanently affixed to a **site**
• vehicles

**PER STIRPES** a legal method of distributing an **estate** to include the descendants of a deceased legatee, whose share is apportioned among linear descendants.
**Example:** A person dies intestate. State law requires a *per stirpes* distribution of assets. The decedent had 4 children. Three are surviving; the fourth child died as an adult and left 5 children. The estate is divided into 4 equal parts. Each surviving child of the decedent gets one fourth, and the 5 orphaned grandchildren, as a group, share one fourth.

**PHOTOVOLTAIC** the process of converting light directly into electricity using specially designed silicon cells.
**Example:** The house has a *photovoltaic* system which supplies power to the filter pumps of the swimming pool.

**PHYSICAL DEPRECIATION OR DETERIORATION** the loss of value from all causes of age and action of the elements.
**Example:** Sources of *physical depreciation:*
• breakage
• deferred maintenance
• effects of age on construction material
• normal wear and tear

**PIGGYBACK LOAN** 1. a combination of the **construction loan** with the permanent **loan commitment.**
**Example:** The permanent lender would issue a commitment at a 15% rate, effective upon completion of construction. As assurance that the loan will be borrowed even if rates are lower later, the commitment is *piggybacked* to the construction loan, and must be drawn down upon **retiring** the construction loan.

2. one mortgage held by more than one lender, with one lender holding the rights of the others in **subordination.**
**Example:** A loan is made for 90% of the home price; 80% of the price is supplied by a **savings and loan association,** 10% by an individual, who then has a *piggyback loan.* The piggyback agreement allows the S&L to have priority in **foreclosure.**

**PITI** principal, interest, taxes and insurance. Refers to the monthly payment required for most home mortgage loans. The tax and insurance portion of the payment is the monthly deposit to the escrow account used to pay property taxes and hazard insurance premiums.
**Example:** A mortgage loan requires monthly payments of principal and interest of $600. In addition, monthly deposits to maintain the escrow account are $150. *PITI* is $750.

**PLAINTIFF** the person who brings a lawsuit. Contrast with **defendant.**
**Example:** A *plaintiff* sued for **specific performance** to force the owner of land to sell at the agreed upon terms.

**PLANNED UNIT DEVELOPMENT (PUD)** a **zoning** classification that allows flexibility in the design of a **subdivision.** Planned Unit Development zones generally set an overall **density** limit for the entire subdivision, allowing the dwelling units to be clustered to provide for common open space. See also **cluster housing, common areas.**
**Example:** A typical *planned unit development* (Figure 128).

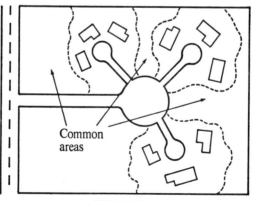

FIGURE 128

**PLANNING COMMISSION** a group of citizens appointed by local government officials to conduct hearings and recommend amendments to the **zoning ordinance.** The planning commission generally oversees the work of a professional planning department, which prepares a comprehensive plan. May also be called a planning board, zoning commission, or zoning board, depending on locality.

**Example:** Moore wishes to have her land **rezoned** from low **density** to high density **residential.** She submits her request to the *planning commission.* The commission holds a public hearing and asks the planning department to evaluate the change. Following the review, the commission makes a recommendation to the city council on whether or not to grant the request.

**PLAT** a plan or map of a specific land area. See also **description, government rectangular survey.**
   **Example:** *Plat* of a **subdivision** (Figure 129).

**PLAT BOOK** a public record containing maps of land, showing the division of the land into streets, blocks, and lots and indicating the measurements of the individual **parcels.**
   **Example:** Sample entry in a *plat book* for property number 001 in district 07-510-AZ (Figure 130).

FIGURE 129

**PLEDGED ACCOUNT MORTGAGE (PAM)** a type of home purchase loan under which a sum of cash contributed by the owner is set aside in an account pledged to the lender. The account is drawn down during the initial years of the loan to supplement periodic mortgage payments. The effect is to reduce the payment amounts in early years. See **graduated payment mortgage.** Compare **collateral.**
   **Example:** Abel obtains a *pledged account mortgage.* The loan

07-510-AZ

FIGURE 130

**principal** is $40,000 and Abel makes a down payment of $10,000. $5,000 of this amount is put in a pledged account. Abel makes payments based on a mortgage principal of $45,000 but the payments are reduced in the first 3 years by drawing upon the $5,000 pledged account.

**PLOT PLAN** a diagram showing the proposed or existing use of a specific **parcel** of land.
**Example:** A *plot plan* submitted to a **zoning** review board (Figure 131).

**PLOTTAGE VALUE** increment in the value of land comprised by **assemblage** of smaller plots into one ownership.
**Example:** A and B are **adjacent** lots, each worth $10,000 (Figure 132). By combining them under one owner the entire **tract** becomes large enough for use as a restaurant **site,** worth $50,000. The *plottage value* is $30,000.

**POCKET CARD** required for salespersons and **brokers** in most states. Issued by the state licensing agency, it identifies its holder as a **licensee** and must be carried at all times.
**Example:** Figure 133

**POINTS** fees paid to induce lenders to make a **mortgage** loan. Each point equals 1% of the loan **principal.** Points have the effect of reducing the amount of money advanced by the lender. Same as *discount points.*

**Example:** Mortgage lenders commonly charge one *point* as a loan **origination fee.** Additional points may be charged to raise the loan **yield** to current **market interest rates.** If only one point is required, a borrower requesting a loan of $50,000 would actually receive only $49,500. The $500 cost of the point is a **closing** cost.

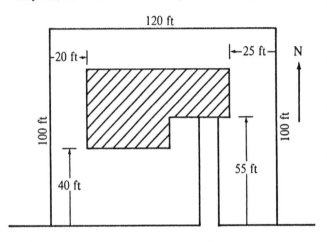

FIGURE 131

**POLICE POWER** the right of any governmental body to enact and enforce regulations for the order, safety, health, morals, and general welfare of the public.

**Example:** Types of *police power* mechanisms applied to **real property:**
- **condemnation** proceedings
- **housing codes**
- public **nuisance** ordinances
- **rent controls**
- special operating **licenses**
- **subdivision** regulations
- **zoning**

**PORTFOLIO INCOME** interest, dividends, royalties (unless earned in the ordinary course of business) and gains from the sale of property that generates this type of income. Under the Tax Reform Act of 1986 this type of income cannot be used to offset passive activity losses. See **passive income.**

**POSITIVE LEVERAGE** the use of borrowed funds that increases the return on an investment.
**Example:** See **leverage.**

100 ft

50 ft     50 ft

Two lots valued at $10,000 each

100 ft

100 ft

Lots combined with value of $50,000

FIGURE 132

Real Estate Broker Identification Card

Expires 3-1-92

Charlie Baker
101 Maple Road
Springfield, MA 90001

FILE   025        LICENSE   360245

(NOT A LICENSE — FOR IDENTIFICATION ONLY)

FIGURE 133

**POSSESSION** the holding, control, or custody of property for one's use, either as owner or person with another right. See also **ownership rights to realty, title.**
Example: Actual *possession:* within immediate occupancy
Adverse *possession:* see definition
Constructive *possession:* as stated in the public record

**POTENTIAL GROSS INCOME** the amount of income that could be produced by a real property assuming no vacancies or collection losses. Does not include miscellaneous income. Contrast **cash flow, net operating income.**
Example: An office building has 10,000 square feet of rentable space and rents for an average of $12 per square foot. *Potential gross income* for the building is $120,000 per year. Concessions on the ground floor that contribute $1,000 of annual revenue, and a 5% vacancy and collection allowance are not included in *potential gross income.*

**POWER OF ATTORNEY** an **instrument** authorizing a person to act as the **agent** of the person granting it. See **attorney-in-fact.**
Example: Abel is going on a 6-month vacation to China. He wants to sell his house in Colorado for $75,000 but will not be present to sign the **deed.** He gives his trusted friend Baker the *power of attorney* so Baker may deed the property to a **grantee** while Abel is in China.

**POWER OF SALE** a clause sometimes inserted in **mortgages** or **deeds of trust;** grants the lender (or **trustee**) the right to sell the property upon certain **default.** The property is to be sold at **auction** but court authority is unnecessary.
Example: The **savings and loan association** exercises the *power of sale* clause in the mortgage by selling the defaulted property at public auction for $100,000. Since the debt was $60,000 and expenses of sale $5,000, the $35,000 surplus belongs to the borrower.

**PRAIRIE HOUSE** an early twentieth century style house with a long, low roof line, continuous row of windows and an unornamented exterior. Designed to satisfy the physical and psychological needs of the inhabitants, it is unlike the traditional concept of a house that is a box subdivided into smaller boxes (rooms), each with some doors and windows.
Example: Figure 134.

**PRECLOSING** a rehearsal of the **closing** whereby **instruments** are prepared and signed by some or all parties to the **contract.** Used when closings are expected to be complicated.
Example: *Preclosings* are used when there are many parties to an agreement. This sometimes occurs when there are multiple loans

Continuous row of windows
Long, low roof line
Unornamented exterior

FIGURE 134

to be arranged and/or multiple buyers or sellers, as when **syndicating** property or converting an apartment complex to a **condominium.**

**PREEXISTING USE** See **nonconforming use.**

**PREFABRICATED** 1. constructed, as building components, **in a** factory prior to being erected or installed on the construction site. 2. constructed, as a house, of prefabricated components. See **modular housing.**
Example: The **subdivision** is developed with *prefabricated* housing. The roof, exterior walls, and interior partitions are *prefabricated* in a factory in Dallas.

**PRELEASE** to obtain **lease** commitments in a building or complex prior to its being available for occupancy.
Example: As a requirement for obtaining a **permanent mortgage, a** developer must *prelease* 50% of the space in the office building.

**PREMISES** land and **tenements;** an **estate;** the subject matter of a **conveyance.**
Example: In selling the property, Carter **deeds** the *premises* **to** Dawson. Dawson later **leases** the *premises* to Enwright.

**PREMIUM** 1. the cost of an insurance policy.
Example: Annual or monthly *premiums* are generally required for **hazard insurance, liability insurance,** and life insurance. **Title** insurance *premiums* are paid only once.
2. the value of a **mortgage** or bond in excess of its **face amount.**
Example: When the face rate of a mortgage exceeds the prevailing **market interest rate,** the mortgage may be worth a *premium* over its **face value.**

**PREPAID EXPENSES** amounts that are paid prior to the period they cover.
Example: Simmons pays the full **premium** on a 3-year insurance policy. When her accountant prepares Abel's financial statement, the proportionate value of the unused premium is presented as a *prepaid expense.*

**PREPAID INTEREST** interest paid in advance of the time it is earned.
Example: Prior to 1968, up to 5 years of prepaid interest could be deducted from taxable income; until 1976 up to one year could be deducted. Since then *prepaid interest* has not been deductible. An exception is for **points** paid to purchase one's residence, provided that the practice and amount is customary in the local area.

**PREPAYMENT CLAUSE** a clause in a **mortgage** that gives a **mortgagor** (borrower) the privilege of paying the mortgage indebtedness before it becomes due. Sometimes there is a **penalty** for prepayment, with **waiver** of the interest that is not yet due.
Example: The *prepayment clause* in the mortgage allows the unpaid **principal** to be **retired** by the owner with a 1% penalty.

**PREPAYMENT PENALTY** fees paid by borrowers for the privilege of **retiring** a loan early.
Example: Abel borrowed $50,000 last year at 15% interest on a 30-year mortgage. If he pays the remaining **principal** now, in one lump sum, there will be a 5% *prepayment penalty* that amounts to $2,500.

**PREPAYMENT PRIVILEGE** the right of a borrower to **retire** a loan before **maturity.**
Example: A loan on **commercial property** is closed (no *prepayment privilege*) for the first 5 years. Afterwards it can be prepaid without **penalty.**

**PREPAYMENTS** advance payments of expenses such as insurance and taxes, often into an escrow account.
Example: At the closing of a residence they bought, the Pollards made *prepayments* equal to 14 months of hazard insurance and 6 months of property taxes.

**PRESALE** sale of proposed properties, such as **condominiums,** before construction begins.
Example: The developer *presold* 40% of the condominium units at a $5,000 **discount** for each unit before construction began. Based on the *presales*, the developer was able to get a favorable **construction loan.**

**PRESCRIPTION** acquiring rights through **adverse possession.**

**Example:** For years, Fulson, owner of a **landlocked** parcel, has continually and openly crossed the property of Grissom to reach the highway. Fulson eventually acquires an **easement** by *prescription* to the access route, thus preventing Grissom from blocking his way.

**PRESENT VALUE OF ANNUITY** the value now of a level stream of income to be received each period for a finite number of periods. See **ordinary annuity.**

$$\text{Present value of annuity} = \frac{1 - \frac{1}{(1 + i)^n}}{i}$$

where $i$ = interest rate
$n$ = number of periods

**Example:** The *present value of an annuity* of $1.00 per year for 10 years, discounted at 12%, is $5.65. Selected present values of annuity factors for annual income of 1 are shown in Table 28.

**Table 28**

| Life of the Annuity (years) | Discount Rates | | | |
|---|---|---|---|---|
| | 5% | 10% | 15% | 20% |
| 1 | .952 | .909 | .870 | .833 |
| 2 | 1.859 | 1.736 | 1.626 | 1.528 |
| 3 | 2.723 | 2.487 | 2.283 | 2.016 |
| 4 | 3.546 | 3.170 | 2.855 | 2.589 |
| 5 | 4.329 | 3.791 | 3.352 | 2.991 |
| 10 | 7.722 | 6.144 | 5.019 | 4.192 |
| 15 | 10.380 | 7.606 | 5.847 | 4.675 |
| 20 | 12.462 | 8.514 | 6.259 | 4.870 |
| 25 | 14.094 | 9.077 | 6.464 | 4.948 |
| 30 | 15.372 | 9.427 | 6.566 | 4.979 |

**PRESENT VALUE OF ONE** the value today of an amount to be received in the future, based on a **compound interest** rate.
**Example:** At a 12% interest rate, the receipt of one dollar one year from now has a *present value* of $.89286 (slightly more than 89 cents). One dollar to be received in 2 years has a *present value* of $.79719 (under 80 cents). Factors are based on the following formula:

$$\text{Present worth (1 factor)} = \frac{1}{(1 + i)^n}$$

where $i$ = interest rate
$n$ = number of periods
See Table 29.

**TABLE 29**

| | Number of Years until $1 Is Received | | | |
|---|---|---|---|---|
| | Rates | | | |
| | 5% | 10% | 15% | 20% |
| 1 | .952381 | .909091 | .869565 | .833333 |
| 2 | .907029 | .826446 | .756144 | .694444 |
| 3 | .863838 | .751315 | .657516 | .578704 |
| 4 | .822702 | .683014 | .571753 | .482253 |
| 5 | .783526 | .620921 | .497177 | .401878 |
| 10 | .613913 | .385543 | .247185 | .161506 |
| 15 | .481017 | .239392 | .122894 | .0649055 |
| 20 | .376889 | .148644 | .0611003 | .0260841 |
| 25 | .295302 | .092296 | .0303776 | .0104826 |
| 30 | .231377 | .057308 | .015103 | .004212 |

**PRICE LEVEL ADJUSTED MORTGAGE** a loan whose payment is adjusted according to the rate of inflation. The payments are generally quite low, typically 3 to 5% annually of the debt. This type of mortgage is not commonly used in the U.S.

**Example:** A *price level adjusted mortgage* is made for $100,000. Monthly payments in the first year are $400. After the first year, the principal balance is reduced to $98,000. The inflation rate for the year was 10%. The principal balance is adjusted to $107,800 and the payments for the second year are increased to $440 per month.

**PRIMARY LEASE** a lease between the owner and a tenant whose **interest,** all or in part, has been sublet.
**Example:** Figure 135.

**PRIMARY MORTGAGE MARKET** that portion of the credit market that originates mortgage loans, including institutional lenders, such as savings and loan associations and banks, and mortgage bankers and brokers. Contrast with **secondary mortgage market.**

The *primary mortgage market* originates and services mortgage loans. Many of these loans are packaged and sold in the secondary mortgage market.

**PRIME CONTRACTOR** see **general contractor.**

**PRIME RATE** the lowest commercial **interest rate** charged by banks on short-term loans to their most credit-worthy customers. The prime rate is not the same as the long-term mortgage rate, though it may influence long-term rates. Also, it is not the same as the consumer loan rate that is charged on personal property loans and credit cards. Mortgage rates and consumer loan rates are generally

higher than the prime rate, but exceptions occur at times.
**Example:** The Chemical Bank and the Chase Manhattan Bank offer a *prime rate* of 12%. Gulf Oil is a prime customer and at that rate may borrow loans up to 270 days. Chemical Bank offers construction loans at 4 **points** over the *prime rate.*

**PRIME TENANT** in a shopping center or office building, the tenant who occupies the most space. Prime tenants are considered credit worthy and attract customers or traffic to the center. See also **anchor tenant.**
**Example:** Huntley is developing an office building with 40,000 square feet of leasable space. Of this, 20,000 square feet are **preleased** to a *prime tenant,* Diesoil. The **credit rating** and prestige of the prime tenant allow Huntley to obtain **financing** and prelease the remaining space to other tenants.

**PRINCIPAL** 1. the one who owns or will use property.
**Example:** The *principals* to the **lease** are the **landlord** and **tenant;** *principals* to a sale are the buyer and seller.
2. One who contracts for the services of an **agent** or **broker,** the broker's or agent's **client.**
**Example:** Grey wishes to purchase a shopping center. Grey engages Jamison, a mortgage broker, to arrange **financing.** Jamison arranges a loan in the name of the *principal,* Grey. The loan is payable as **interest** only for 5 years, with the *principal* payable as a **balloon payment** at the end of year 5.
3. the amount of money raised by a mortgage or other loan, as distinct from the **interest** paid on it.

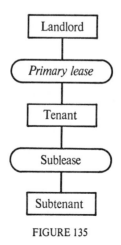

FIGURE 135

**Example:** Abel arranged a loan with $100,000 principal on his home. The first monthly payment is $1,200 including $1,000 interest and $200 that **amortized** the *principal*.

**PRINCIPAL AND INTEREST PAYMENT (P&I)** a periodic payment, usually paid monthly, that includes the **interest** charges for the period plus an amount applied to **amortization** of the **principal** balance. Commonly used with amortizing loans. See **mortgage constant, amortization.**
**Example:** A $1,200 annual *principal and interest payment* is required by a $10,000 **face value** amortizing mortgage at a 10% **interest rate.** $1,000 of the first year payment is required for interest; $200 reduces the outstanding balance to $9,800.

**PRINCIPAL BROKER** the licensed broker responsible for the operations conducted by the **brokerage** firm.
**Example:** As *principal broker*, Collins receives a 10% **override** on all sales **commissions** earned by the other **agents.**

**PRINCIPAL, INTEREST, TAXES and INSURANCE PAYMENT (PITI)** the periodic (typically monthly) payment required by an amortizing loan that includes **escrow** deposits. Each periodic payment includes a **principal and interest payment** plus a contribution to the escrow account set up by the lender to pay insurance premiums and property taxes on the mortgaged property.
**Example:** Abel's monthly *PITI payment* is $950. This includes $750 for **principal and interest,** $150 for **ad valorem taxes** and $50 for insurance.

**PRINCIPAL MERIDIAN** one of the prime **meridians** used in the **government rectangular survey** method of land **description** to locate **range lines.**
**Example:** *Principal meridians* within the state of California are shown in Figure 136.

**PRINCIPAL RESIDENCE** the place one lives in most of the time. May be a single-family house, **condominium,** trailer, or houseboat. To defer **capital gain** taxes on the profit from a home, the home must be used as the taxpayer's *principal residence.*
**Example:** Collins spends 10 months each year living in a rented apartment in downtown Seattle. She spends 2 months in a home she owns in San Diego. The rented apartment is her *principal residence.*

**PRIORITY** legal precedence; having preferred status. Generally, upon **foreclosure,** lenders are repaid according to priority.
**Example:** Abel's home was foreclosed and sold for $25,000. Unpaid taxes and attorney's fees were accorded *priority,* and paid in full. The rest of the sales proceeds was applied against the **first**

**mortgage.** There was nothing for the **second mortgage,** because it was lower in *priority*.

**PRIVATE MORTGAGE INSURANCE** **default** insurance on conventional loans, provided by private insurance companies. See **mortgage insurance.**
**Example:** Lawton wishes to obtain a home purchase loan covering 90% of value. The lender requires Lawton to acquire *private mortgage insurance* as a condition for granting any loan for more than 80% of value.

Humboldt meridian   Mt. Diablo meridian   San Bernardino meridian

FIGURE 136

**PRIVATE OFFERING** an investment or business offered for sale to a small group of investors, generally under exemptions to registration allowed by the **Securities and Exchange Commission** and state securities registration laws.
**Example:** The **syndicator** prepared a *private offering* of the **equity** in the apartments. Up to 35 persons are allowed to participate in the purchase. If more persons are allowed, the **syndicator** must register a **public offering** with the state securities commissioner or the U.S. Securities and Exchange Commission (SEC).

**PROBATE OR PROVE** to establish the validity of the **will** of a
deceased person.
**Example:** Hughes died. The **executor** appealed to the *probate*
court that a certain document was the **valid** will that Hughes
left.

**PROCEEDS FROM RESALE** same as **resale proceeds.**

**PROCURING CAUSE** a legal term that means the cause resulting in
accomplishing a goal. Used in **real estate** to determine whether a
**broker** is entitled to a **commission.**
**Example:** A real estate broker introduced parties and they agreed
to enter into a transaction to sell a home. The broker claimed she
was entitled to a commission but had to show in court that she was
the *procuring cause*.

**PRO-FORMA STATEMENT** according to form. Financial statements showing what is expected to occur.
**Example:** The **broker** prepared a *pro-forma* statement for the prospective purchaser (Table 30). It showed expected cash flows for
the property:

**TABLE 30**

| Pro-forma Cash Flow Statement Next Year, Projected | | |
|---|---:|---:|
| Rental income | | $10,000 |
| Taxes | −$2,000 | |
| Utilities | −1,000 | |
| Miscellaneous | − 500 | |
| Subtotal expenses | | −3,500 |
| Cash flow | | $6,500 |

**PROGRESS PAYMENTS** in construction, loan payments issued to
the builder as building is completed. See **draw.**
**Example:** For the $100,000 **construction loan,** the *progress pay-
ments* were $20,000 upon buying the lot and a like amount upon
pouring the foundation, roofing, wiring, and completion of all
work.

**PROMISSORY NOTE** a promise to pay a specified sum to a specified **person** under specified **terms.** See also **note.**
**Example:** Figure 137.

**PROPERTY** 1. the rights that one individual has in lands or goods to
the exclusion of all others; rights gained from the ownership of

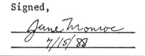

Promissory Note

I, June Monroe, do promise to pay City Finance Co. the sum of $50,000. Repayment is to be made in the form of 300 equal payments at 12% interest, or $526.61 payable on the 1st of each month, beginning 8/1/88 until the total debt is satisfied.

Signed,

June Monroe
7/15/88

FIGURE 137

wealth. See **real property, personalty; possession, title.**
**Example:** An individual may own *property* with the associated rights to enjoyment, control over others' use of the property, and disposition, subject to government-imposed **restrictions.** Groups of individuals may own *property,* with ownership rights shared collectively. Governments may also own *property,* held for public use.
2. real estate
**Example:** The appraiser needed to inspect the *property* prior to establishing its value.

**PROPERTY LINE** the recorded **boundary** of a plot of land.
  **Example:** Figure 138.

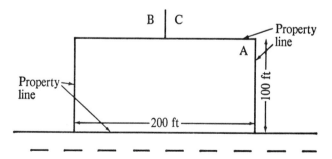

FIGURE 138

**PROPERTY MANAGEMENT** the operation of property as a business, including rental, rent collection, **maintenance,** etc.

**Example:** The following tasks are often required in the ownership of property:

Property management
- accounting and reporting
- leasing
- maintenance and repair
- paying taxes
- provision of utilities and insurance
- remodeling
- rent rate setting and collection

Investment management
- acquisition and disposition
- development and rehabilitation feasibility
- financing
- income tax accounting

**PROPERTY REPORT** required by the **Interstate Land Sale Act** for the sale of **subdivisions** of 50 lots or more, if the subdivisions are not otherwise exempt. Filed with HUD's **Office of Interstate Land Sales Registration (OILSR).**

**Example:** A **subdivider** wishes to sell lots in a 55-lot development, through an interstate commerce promotional plan. She is required to file a *property report* with OILSR.

**PROPERTY RESIDUAL TECHNIQUE** in **appraisal,** a method for estimating the value of property based on estimated future income and the **reversionary value** of the building and land. See **income approach.**

**Example:** Table 31.

### TABLE 31

| | | |
|---|---:|---:|
| Level annual **net operating income** | | $10,000 |
| Multiplied by: **annuity factor** of appropriate rate for number of years (say 12%, 30 years) | | × 8.0552 |
| Value of income | | $80,552 |
| Estimated *property residual* in 30 years | $50,000 | |
| Multiply by: Present worth of one factor at 12% | × .03338 | |
| Present worth of reversion | | $1,669 |
| Estimated property value | | $82,221 |

**PROPERTY TAX** a government levy based on the **market value** of privately owned property. Sometimes referred to as **ad valorem tax** or real estate tax.

**Example:** Homeville assesses a *property tax* at the rate of $.50 per $100 of market value. Kilmer pays a tax of $500 on a property valued at $100,000.

**PROPRIETARY LEASE** in a cooperative apartment building, the lease a corporation provides to the stockholders which allows them to use a certain apartment unit under the conditions specified.
**Example:** The Coopers purchase a unit in a cooperative on Fifth Avenue. Their ownership provides 450 shares of stock in the cooperative and a *proprietary lease* to a unit in the apartment building.

**PRORATE** to allocate between seller and buyer their proportionate share of an obligation paid or due; for example, to prorate real **property taxes** or insurance.
**Example:** Property taxes were $730, assessed for the calendar year and paid by the seller on April 30. The property was sold on September 15 (Figure 139). It is necessary to *prorate* property taxes so that the buyer and seller each pay a proportionate share for his or her ownership period. There are 107 days from September 15 to December 31. Therefore the buyer must pay $214 at **closing,** based on a daily rate of $2.00.

FIGURE 139

**PROSPECT** a **person** considered likely to buy. A prospective purchaser.
**Example:** All of the persons who request further information about the advertised property are considered *prospects*.

**PROSPECTUS** a printed descriptive statement about a business or investment that is for sale, to invite the interest of prospective investors.
**Example:** A **syndicator** prepared a *prospectus* that disclosed all **material facts** about the property being offered. Before it is approved by the SEC or state securities commissioner, it is called **a red herring.** If it need not be approved, it is called a **descriptive memorandum.**

**PROXY** a person who represents another, particularly in some meeting. Also, the document giving to another the authority to represent.
**Example:** Abel could not be at the **cooperative** apartment association's annual meeting, so he cast his vote by *proxy*.

**PUBLIC HOUSING** government-owned housing units made available to low-income individuals and families at no cost or for nominal rental rates. Contrast to **low-income housing.**
**Example:** The Metropolitan Housing Authority operates several *public housing* projects for those who cannot afford decent housing on the rental market.

**PUBLIC LANDS** acreage held by the government for conservation purposes. Public lands are generally undeveloped, with limited activities such as grazing, wildlife management, recreation, timbering, mineral development, water development, and hunting.
**Example:** Many western states, such as Alaska and Nevada, have large amounts of *public lands*. A part of this area is held by the federal government and is dedicated to national parks, wilderness, and wildlife refuges. Some oil and mineral exploration is allowed under **lease** to private firms.

**PUBLIC OFFERING** soliciting the general public for the sale of investment units. Generally requires approval by the SEC and/or state securities agencies. Contrast with **private offering.**
**Example:** The **syndicator** who wishes to sell **limited partnership** interests to over 35 investors should register this *public offering* with the SEC or state securities commissioner.

**PUBLIC RECORD** usually refers to land transaction records kept at the county courthouse.
**Example:** Documents that are evidence of real estate transactions should be taken to the county courthouse to be officially entered in the *public record*. Recording gives **constructive notice** of a document's existence.

**PUBLIC SALE** an **auction** sale of property with **notice** to the general public.
**Example:** After **foreclosure**, a *public sale* was effected. It was advertised in the local newspaper in advance. The property was auctioned off on the courthouse steps to the highest bidder.

**PUEBLO OR ADOBE** an early twentieth century house that is made of adobe brick or some other material made to look like adobe brick. The characteristic projecting roof beams are called viga.
**Example:** Figure 140.

**PUFFING** overstating the qualities of a property.
**Example:** "This house has the most efficient floor plan of any home in the world" is an example of a salesperson's *puffing*.

**PUNCH LIST** an enumeration of items that need to be corrected prior to a sale.

**Example:** The buyer refuses to close the purchase until the builder fixes the leaky roof and replaces the defective carpeting—the 2 items on the buyer's *punch list.*

**PUR AUTRE VIE** for the life of another. An **estate** one person grants to another, only for the duration of the life of a third person.
**Example:** Abel grants a **life estate** to Baker to use Abel's ranch until Baker's wife dies. Baker has a life estate *pur autre vie.*

**PURCHASE AGREEMENT** same as **contract of sale.**

Projecting roof beams (viga)

Real or simulated adobe brick

Flat roof

Massive looking

FIGURE 140

**PURCHASE MONEY MORTGAGE** a **mortgage** given by a **grantee** (buyer) to a **grantor** (seller) in part payment of the purchase price of **real estate.**
**Example:** Lamar wishes to purchase a house from Murphy. The sale price is $75,000. Lamar will assume Murphy's existing mortgage in the amount of $50,000. In addition, Lamar gives Murphy a *purchase money mortgage* of $15,000, plus $10,000 in cash to close the sale.
(note: a purchase money mortgage can be a **first mortgage** or junior **lien,** depending on its **priority**).

# Q

**QUADRANGLE** a square-shaped land area, 24 miles on each side, used in the **government rectangular survey** method of land **description**. Each quadrangle contains 16 **townships**.
**Example:** See example for **government rectangular survey**.

**QUANTITY SURVEY** a method used by **appraisers** to estimate **reproduction cost** (new) of an **improvement**; detailed cost estimate of all materials, labor, and overhead required to reproduce a structure. See **cost approach**.
**Example:** A simplified *quantity survey* estimate of reproduction cost (new) is shown in Table 32.

TABLE 32

| Item | Cost |
| --- | --- |
| site preparation | $5,000 |
| cement | 10,000 |
| masonry | 15,000 |
| lumber | 25,000 |
| fasteners | 5,000 |
| siding | 15,000 |
| roof cover | 10,000 |
| labor | 30,000 |
| fees | 5,000 |
| financing | 10,000 |
| Total cost | $130,000 |

**QUEEN ANNE HOUSE** a nineteenth century style house that is unique-looking, multi-story, and irregular in shape with a variety of surface textures, materials, and colors. The term Queen Anne has come to be applied to any Victorian house that cannot be otherwise classified.
**Example:** Figure 141.

**QUIET ENJOYMENT** the right of an owner or any other **person** legally entitled to **possession** to the use of property without interference.
**Example:** The landlord, unhappy with a low rental rate, continually blocks the driveway of the tenant. The tenant sues for *quiet enjoyment*.

**QUIET TITLE (ACTION)** court action to settle a title dispute.
**Example:** People may use quiet **title** action to:
• substantiate the **title** of a squatter

- extinguish **easements**
- release a **dower** interest
- remove any **cloud on title**

**QUIET TITLE SUIT (OR ACTION)** a suit in court to remove a defect, **cloud on the title,** or suspicion regarding legal rights of an owner to a certain **parcel** of **real property.**
**Example:** In an *action to quiet title*, the landowner of record brought the **adverse possessor** to court that required him to establish his claim or be forever barred from claiming the property.

**QUITCLAIM DEED** a **deed** that conveys only the **grantor's** rights or interest in real estate, without stating the nature of the rights and with no **warranties** of ownership. Often used to remove a possible **cloud on the title.** Contrast with **general warranty deed.**
**Example:** It is discovered during a **title** search that a certain property was at one time held by a **partnership** that later **abandoned** the property. To obtain a **marketable title,** the current owner obtains *quitclaim deeds* from all partners in the old partnership.

FIGURE 141

# R

**RANGE LINES** lines parallel to a **principal meridian,** marking off the land into 6-mile strips known as ranges; they are numbered east or west of a principal meridian in the **Government Rectangular Survey.** See **base line.**
**Example:** Figure 142.

Range lines

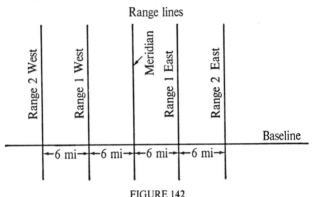

FIGURE 142

**RATE OF RETURN** the percentage relationship between the earnings and the cost of an investment. See **internal rate of return, overall rate of return.**
**Example:** Nickson deposits $100 in a savings account. At the end of the year Nickson receives a payment of $10. Nickson's *rate of return* is 10%.

**RATE OF RETURN OF INVESTMENT** same as **recapture rate.**

**RAW LAND** acreage with no added **improvements,** such as landscaping, drainage, streets, **utilities,** and structures.
**Example:** The developer bought 50 acres of *raw land* upon which to develop a **subdivision.**

**READY, WILLING, AND ABLE** capable of an action and disposed to act.
**Example:** A home is listed with a **broker** who finds a *ready, willing and able* person who agrees to buy under the terms of the **listing.** The seller refuses to sell. The broker has earned a **commission** because she fulfilled the requirements of the listing.

**REAL ESTATE** 1. in law, land and everything more or less attached to it. Ownership below to the center of the earth and above to the heavens. Distinguished from **personal property.** Same as **realty.**
**Example:** Figure 143.

2. in business, the activities concerned with ownership and use transfers of the physical property.
**Example:** The following are engaged in *real estate* business activities:
- **accountants**
- **appraisers**
- attorneys
- **brokers**
- counselors
- government regula'ors
- **mortgage brokers**
- mortgage lenders
- salespersons
- **surveyors**
- **title** companies

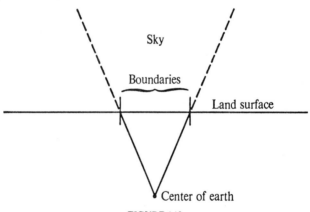

FIGURE 143

**REAL ESTATE COMMISSION** state agency that enforces **real estate license** laws.
**Example:** The *Real Estate Commission* is usually comprised of between 5 and 15 members who are appointed for a term (2 to 6 years) by the governor, generally confirmed by the state senate. They enforce the real estate laws and regulations, subject to judicial authority. The real estate **commissioner,** a full time employee of the Real Estate Commission, conducts the routine activities of licensing, collecting fees, and other matters.

**REAL ESTATE INVESTMENT TRUST (REIT)** a real estate mutual fund, allowed by income tax laws to avoid the corporate income tax. It sells shares of ownership and must invest in real estate or mortgages. It must meet certain other requirements, including minimum number of shareholders, widely dispersed ownership, asset and income tests. If it distributes 95% of its income to shareholders, it is not taxed on that income, but shareholders must include their share of the *REIT's* income in their personal tax returns.

**Example:** During the early 1970's, many *real estate investment trusts were created*. They raised money from investors for investment in mortgages and real estate equities. An individual could buy shares on the stock market in such a trust. Its unique feature is to allow small investors to participate, without double taxation, in large real estate ventures. The trust is not subject to corporate income tax as long as it complies with the tax requirements for a *REIT*.

**REAL ESTATE MARKET** the potential buyers and sellers of real property at the current time, and the current transaction activity for real property. It includes markets for various property types, such as housing market, office market, condominium market, land market.

**Example:** The local *real estate market* is very active. There have been a record number of sales and there still are many properties on the market.

**REAL ESTATE MORTGAGE INVESTMENT CONDUIT (REMIC)** The Tax Reform Act of 1986 created a new entity, the *REMIC*. The purpose of a *REMIC* is to hold a fixed pool of mortgages and issue interests in itself to mortgage investors. A *REMIC* may be a partnership, corporation, trust, or separate pool of assets. *REMICs* are intended to become the exclusive means for issuing multiple-class mortgage backed securities in a form that avoids the corporate double tax.

Substantially all of a *REMIC's* assets must be qualified mortgages (mortgages secured by real estate) but it may also hold some short-term liquid assets that produce interest income, and assets held in a special reserve fund, and foreclosed properties.

All interests in a *REMIC* must be classified as regular or residual. Regular interests entitle the holder to interest and principal income, through debt, stock or some other ownership form. Residual interests provide income that is more contingent in nature.

A *REMIC* will not, in general, be a taxable entity, although it must comply with tax requirements and is subject to a 100% tax on prohibited transactions. Regular interest holders will be taxed as if their interests were debt obligations subject to their share of the *REMIC's* income on an accrual basis. Gain or loss on the sale of a regular interest will be ordinary to the extent of their share of original issue discount. Residual interest holders generally receive their share of *REMIC* income as ordinary. (Although the Tax

Reform Act of 1986 makes no distinction in rates for capital gains after 1987, the character of capital gains remains in the tax code, perhaps paving the way for a rate distinction in the future.)

**REAL ESTATE OWNED (REO)** property acquired by a lender through foreclosure and held in inventory. Commonly referred to as REO.

**Example:** Because of a large number of recent mortgage foreclosures, the bank's *real estate owned* has grown to 5% of all assets, or $25 million.

**REAL ESTATE SECURITIES AND SYNDICATIONS INSTITUTE (RESSI)** an organization of **syndicators** affiliated with the **National Association of Realtors®.** Offers a newsletter, *RESSI Review,* on current developments affecting **syndications,** and educational courses.

**Address:** Real Estate Securities and Syndications Institute
430 N. Michigan Avenue
Chicago, Illinois 60611

**REAL ESTATE SETTLEMENT PROCEDURES ACT (RESPA)** a law that states how **mortgage** lenders must treat those who apply for federally related real estate loans on property with 1-4 dwelling units. Intended to provide borrowers with more knowledge when they comparison shop for mortgage money.

**Example:** Within 3 days after Abel applies for a loan on a house he wants to buy, the lender is to provide a **good faith** estimate of settlement **(closing)** costs, and a booklet about *RESPA.* In addition, one day before closing, the borrower is entitled to review the closing papers, including all amounts that are known at that time.

**REALIZED GAIN** in a tax-free exchange, a gain that has occurred financially, but is not necessarily taxed. See **boot, recognized gain, Section 1031.**

**Example:** Abel's land has a tax **basis** of $10,000. Its **market value** is $75,000. He exchanges the land, tax-free under Section 1031, for Baker's warehouse, which was appraised at $75,000. Abel's *realized gain* is $65,000. None of Abel's *realized gain* is recognized, because he did not receive boot.

**REAL PROPERTY** the rights to use real estate.    Sometimes also defined as **real estate.**

**Example:** *Real property* includes, but is not limited to:
• personal residence owned in **fee simple**
• a **life estate** to a farm
• rights to use land under a **lease**
• **easements** and other partial interests

**REALTIST** a member of the **National Association of Real Estate Brokers,** a group comprised of mainly minority brokers.

**Example:** Abel, a black real estate broker, paid dues to the National Association of Real Estate Brokers and subscribed to its code of ethics. Abel is a *Realtist.*

**REALTOR®** a professional in real estate who subscribes to a strict **Code of Ethics** as a member of the local and state boards and of the **National Association of Realtors®.**
**Example:** Much of the general public are surprised to discover that only about 40% of licensed real estate **brokers** are eligible to use the designation *Realtor®.*

**REALTOR®-ASSOCIATE** a licensed salesperson (not **broker**) who is a member of the **National Association of Realtors®.**
**Example:** Downing passed the salesman's **licensing exam** and is sponsored by a **Realtor®**-broker. Upon being sworn in to the national and state association, Downing is appropriately described as a *Realtor®-Associate.*

**REALTORS® NATIONAL MARKETING INSTITUTE (RMNI)** an affiliate of the **National Association of Realtors®;** mainly concerned with educational programs and literature for members. Publishes *Real Estate Today* (monthly) and *Real Estate Perspectives* (bimonthly).
**Address:**
Realtors® National Marketing Institute
430 N. Michigan Avenue
Chicago, Illinois 60611

**REALTY** same as **real estate.**

**REAPPRAISAL LEASE** a **lease** where the rental level is periodically reviewed by independent **appraisers.** Often, the **lessor** and **lessee** will each select an appraiser; if they do not agree on a value, they will choose a third appraiser.
**Example:** In the 20-year *reappraisal lease,* Big Buy Foods agrees to pay the landlord an annual rent of 12% of the property value. Every 5 years the property will be reappraised to determine the rent.

**REASSESSMENT** the process of revising or updating the value estimate of property for **ad valorem tax** purposes.
**Example:** Local **property tax** assessors are required to periodically conduct a *reassessment* of all property. Value estimates are revised based on recent sales and other data, and tax **assessments** are based on the new estimates.

**REBATE** 1. a refund resulting from a purchase or tax.
**Example:** To encourage sales of the **condominium** project, the developer offered a $2,500 *rebate* to each purchaser.
2. a kickback of a charge, often illegal if done without knowledge of all parties.
**Example:** the broker accepted a $50 *rebate* from the insurer each time he sold a home carrying a homeowner's **warranty.**

**RECAPTURE CLAUSE** in a contract, a clause permitting the party who grants an **interest** or right to take it back under certain conditions.
**Example:** Carter grants a **lease** to Frank's Furniture, with rent set at 6% of retail sales. The lease contains a *recapture clause* whereby Carter can regain the property unless sales are over $1 million per year.

**RECAPTURE OF DEPRECIATION** same as **depreciation recapture.**

**RECAPTURE RATE** in **appraisal,** a term used to describe the rate of recovery of an investment in a **wasting asset.** This rate is added to the **discount rate** to derive a **capitalization rate** in appraisal terminology. May be based on the straight line, **sinking fund,** or annuity method.
**Example:** A building with a 50-year estimated **useful life** has a 2% straight-line *recapture rate.* At a discount rate of 10%, the capitalization rate is 12%.

**RECASTING** the process of adjusting a loan arrangement, especially under the threat of **default.** See **workout.**
**Example:** Pope owns an apartment building with a **mortgage** loan requiring **debt service** of $25,000 per year. Because of a period of high vacancies, Pope's **net operating income** falls to $20,000 per year. To eliminate the **negative cash flow,** Pope appeals to the lender to *recast* the loan by extending the **maturity** and reducing the **interest rate** for the next 2 years.

**RECIPROCITY** mutual agreement to accept, such as a state's **acceptance,** as **valid** the real estate **license** one has earned in another state.
**Example:** In the absence of *reciprocity,* Moore must take a new examination to obtain a real estate license in the state which she moves. With *reciprocity* she needs only to present her previously earned license.

**RECOGNIZED GAIN** in a **tax-free exchange,** the portion of gain that is taxable. A **realized gain** will generally be recognized to the extent of **boot** received. See **Section 1031.**
**Example:** Abel's land has a tax **basis** of $10,000. It is worth $75,000. He exchanges the land under Section 1031 for Baker's warehouse worth $70,000 and $5,000 of cash. Of Abel's $65,000 realized gain, $5,000 will be *recognized.*

**RECONCILIATION** in **appraisal,** the process of adjusting **comparables** to estimate the value of the subject being appraised.
**Example:** An **appraiser** arrives at the market value estimates shown in Table 33 following application of the 3 traditional approaches.

**TABLE 33**

| | |
|---|---|
| **market comparison:** | $85,000 |
| **cost approach:** | $89,000 |
| **income approach:** | $84,000 |

In *reconciliation,* the appraiser considers the appropriateness of each approach to the subject, the quality of available data, and the amount of judgmental **adjustment** required to reach each estimate. Following this review, the appraiser settles on an estimate of $85,000 as her opinion of **market value.**

**RECONVEYANCE** occurs when a **mortgage** debt is **retired.** The lender **conveys** the property back to the **equity** owner, free of the debt.
**Example:** The *reconveyance* took place after Abel paid off the loan; Abel promptly **recorded** the *reconveyance* **instrument.**

**RECORDING** the act of entering in a book of public records **instruments** affecting the **title** to **real property.** Recording in this manner gives **notice** to the world of facts recorded. See **constructive notice, ownership rights to realty.**
**Example:** By *recording* the **deed** from a sale of property, the purchaser assumes that all subsequent interested parties are given notice of the purchaser's ownership **interests** in the property. **Leases** and **liens** may also be recorded.

**RECOURSE** the ability of a lender to claim money from a borrower in **default,** in addition to the property pledged as **collateral.**
**Example:** Ross obtains a **mortgage** loan from Local Savings. Should Ross default on the loan, Local Savings may **foreclose** and force the sale of the mortgaged property. Should the sale fail to satisfy the unpaid loan **principal,** Local Savings has *recourse* to other assets of Ross.

**RECOVERY FUND** generally administered by the **Real Estate Commission.** Requires **licensees** to contribute, then reimburses aggrieved persons who are unable to collect from **brokers** for wrongdoings.
**Example:** A typical state's *recovery fund* law requires all new licensees to contribute $10 to the fund. Anytime the fund account balance drops below $500,000, all licensees will be assessed. Payments from the fund to an aggrieved person may not exceed $10,000; total payments on behalf of any licensee may not exceed $25,000. The recovery fund pays only when the broker does not.

**RECTANGULAR SURVEY** same as **government rectangular survey method.**

**REDEMPTION, EQUITY OF** same as **equity of redemption.**

**REDEMPTION PERIOD** the period during which a former owner
can reclaim **foreclosed** property. See **equity of redemption.**
**Example:** Collins' property was foreclosed. If she acts within her
state's *redemption period,* she can reclaim her property by paying
the **debt** and legal fees.

**REDEVELOP** the process of demolition of the existing improvements and construction of new improvements on a site. The new
improvements are often of a different type from the old.
**Example:** Since the old building has outgrown its usefulness, the
owner plans to *redevelop* the site as the location of a new office
tower.

**RED HERRING** a proposed **prospectus** that has not been approved
by the **Securities and Exchange Commission** (SEC) or state securities commission. See **public offering.**
**Example:** A *red herring* is shown in Table 34.

**TABLE 34**

Proposed Prospectus

A registration statement has
been filed with the Securities
and Exchange Commission
but is subject to change. The
securities described herein
may not be sold until approval
becomes effective.

**REDISCOUNT RATE** the rate of interest charged to member banks
when they borrow from the **Federal Reserve System.** Also called
**discount rate.**
**Example:** The First and Citizens Banks borrows funds from the
Federal Reserve for one day and is charged interest at the *rediscount rate.*

**REDLINING** the illegal practice of refusing to originate **mortgage**
loans in certain **neighborhoods** on the basis of race or ethnic com-
position.
**Example:** A **savings and loan association** may be accused of prac-
ticing *redlining* if it is found that no loans have been originated in
predominantly nonwhite neighborhoods. The term derives from
the alleged practice of drawing a red line on a map around certain
neighborhoods to designate them as off limits for loan approvals.

**REDUCTION CERTIFICATE** a document in which the **mortgagee** (lender) acknowledges the sum due on the **mortgage** loan. Used when mortgaged property is sold and the buyer assumes the debt.
**Example:** Abel buys Baker's home and agrees to assume the existing mortgage. They obtain a *reduction certificate* from the mortgage lender stating that the remaining balance is $34,567.89.

**REFERRAL** the act of suggesting the use of a certain **broker.**
**Example:** Smith receives several **listings** based on *referrals* from former customers.
**Example:** A broker agrees to pay a 1% *referral* fee to out-of-state brokers who suggest families that are moving into the area.

**REFINANCE** the substitution of an old loan(s) with a new loan(s).
**Example:** Garner has a $30,000 loan against her house. She desires cash to pay for a college education. By *refinancing* the home with a new $40,000 loan, she will realize $9,000 in cash after paying $1,000 in **transaction costs.** See Table 35.

**TABLE 35**

|  |  |
|---|---|
| New loan | $40,000 |
| Old debt | -30,000 |
| Cost of loan | - 1,000 |
| Refinancing: cash proceeds | $9,000 |

**REGENCY** an English style 2- or 3-story, symmetrical house with a hip roof. A small octagonal window over the front door is traditional.
**Example:** Figure 144

**REGISTRAR** the person who is to maintain accurate official records, such as for **deeds, mortgages,** and other recorded **documents.**
**Example:** After **closing,** the buyer brought the deed to the *registrar* of deeds for **recording** in the county records.

**REGRESSION** a statistical technique used to estimate mathematical models of economic and other processes. It is used to find a mathematical expression which best fits the relationship between a group of random variables as indicated by a sample of data.
**Example:** An appraiser wants to find the relationship between sales prices for homes and their physical characteristics. Data are collected on the prices of a group of homes and their size, number of rooms, location and age. Linear *regression* is used to analyze

the relationship expressed by the data. The *regression* model can then be used to estimate prices for other similar houses on the market.

**REGULATION D** a regulation of the **Securities and Exchange Commission** that sets forth conditions necessary for a **private offering** exemption.
**Example: Syndicator** Stuart wants to sell 35 **limited partnership** interests in an office building. He applies for an exemption under *Rule 146* to avoid the need of registering a **public offering**; he thereby saves over $100,000 and avoids a 4-month delay.

Simple informal style

Brick

Small octagonal window

Double-hung windows    Hip roof

1 chimney at side

FIGURE 144

**REGULATION Q** a federal law that specified the maximum interest rates that banks and **savings and loan associations** could pay on various types of deposits. It was phased out by the **Depository Institutions Deregulations and Monetary Control Act of 1980.**
**Example:** Under *Regulation Q*, Hometown Savings could offer no more than a 5% yield on its passbook accounts. Today, it can offer any rate required to attract deposits.

**REGULATION Z** a federal regulation requiring **creditors** to provide full disclosure of the terms of a loan. Compliance is compulsory for anyone who arranges **credit** for more than 5 sales of **residential real estate** in a year. **Terms** of the loan must be disclosed. The **interest rate** must be stated as an **annual percentage rate** (APR).

See also **rescind, rescission.**
**Example:** Figure 145.

Convenient Savings and Loan                    Account number: 4862-88

  Michael Jones
  500 Walnut Court, Little Creek, U.S.A.

| Annual Percentage Rate The cost of your credit as a yearly rate | Finance Charge The dollar amount the credit will cost you | Amount Financed The amount of credit provided to you or on your behalf | Total of Payments The amount you will have paid after you have made all payments as scheduled |
|---|---|---|---|
| 15.37% | $177,970.44 | $43,777 | $221,548.44 |

Your payment schedule will be:

| Number of Payments | Amount of Payments | When Payments Are Due |
|---|---|---|
| 12 | $446.62 | Monthly beginning 6/1/88 |
| 12 | $479.67 | "  "  6/1/89 |
| 12 | $515.11 | "  "  6/1/90 |
| 12 | $553.13 | "  "  6/1/91 |
| 12 | $593.91 | "  "  6/1/92 |
| 300 | varying from $637.68 to $627.37 | "  "  6/1/93 |

**Security:** You are giving a security interest in the property being purchased.

**Late Charge:** If a payment is late, you will be charged 5% of the payment.

**Prepayment:** If you pay off early, you
☒ may    ☐ will not    ☐ have to pay a penalty.
☒ may    ☐ will not    ☐ be entitled to a refund of part of the finance charge.

**Assumption:** Someone buying your home cannot assume the remainder of the mortgage on the original terms.

See your contract documents for any additional information about nonpayment, default, any required repayment in full before the scheduled date, and prepayment refunds and panalties.

---
e means an estimate

FIGURE 145

**REHABILITATE** to restore a structure to a condition of good repair.
**Example:** An old building has deteriorated to the point of prohibiting profitable operation. The owner faces the choice of **demolition** of the structure and rebuilding or *rehabilitation* to restore the building to a competitive position.

**REHABILITATION TAX CREDIT** the Tax Reform Act of 1986 provides a 20% tax credit for rehabilitating certified historic structures, and a 10% credit for other buildings that were placed in service after 1936. However, there are certain conditions or requirements that are imposed.
  • The credit may be used to offset a maximum of $25,000 of non-passive income, but is phased out on a 50% basis between $200,000 and $250,000 of adjusted gross income. Thus, the credit is not of use to high income investors.
  • The tax basis of the property is reduced by the full amount of the credit.
  • Transition rules are provided for those with binding contracts for rehabilitations between March 1, 1986 and October 22, 1986; these rules require such property be placed in service before 1994.

**RELEASE** to free real estate from a **mortgage.** See **partial release.**
  **Example:** Reynolds owns 100 **acres** of land that is mortgaged for $10,000. If she pays the $10,000, the land will be *released* from the lender's **lien** on the property.

**RELEASE CLAUSE** in a **mortgage,** a clause that gives the owner the privilege of paying off a portion of the mortgage indebtedness, thus freeing a portion of the property from the mortgage.
  See **partial release.**
  **Example:** Smith, a **developer,** is **subdividing** land that is **financed** under a mortgage. A *release clause* in the mortgage allows Smith to sell individual lots from the **tract** by retiring portions of the loan. Without the clause, Smith would have to **retire** the entire loan before selling any lots.

**RELICTION** gradual subsidence of waters, leaving dry land.
  **Example:** As the Great Salt Lake in Utah becomes smaller by evaporation, *reliction* occurs. Generally the new land belongs to the party who owned the rights to the water area (Figure 146).

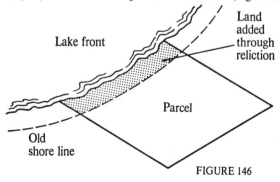

FIGURE 146

**RELOCATION CLAUSE** a **lease** stipulation that allows the landlord to move the tenant within the building.
**Example:** The landlord of an office building requires *relocation clauses* in all leases for space that does not include an entire floor. When a new client wishes to lease an entire floor, the landlord may relocate tenants in such a way as to provide the desired space.

**RELOCATION NETWORK** a geographically diversified group of independent real estate brokerage companies, generally not members of a franchise, that share information with one another concerning potential customers.
**Example:** A broker in Atlanta, Georgia lists a home for sale which is owned by a family who is moving to Dallas, Texas. The broker, who is a member of a certain *relocation network,* finds a counterpart member/broker in Dallas and refers the family to the Dallas broker. If they buy a home through the Dallas broker, the Atlanta broker will receive a referral fee.

**RELOCATION SERVICE** a company which contracts with other firms to arrange the relocation of employees from one city to another. The service generally handles the sale of the employee's home and purchase of a new home. Furniture moving services may be included also.
**Example:** The Beeker Company wishes to open a new office in Denver. Most of the staff for the new office will be relocated from Miami. Beeker hires a *relocation service* to sell the employees' homes and to help them find new homes in the Denver area.

**REMAINDER** an **estate** that takes effect after the termination of a prior estate, such as a **life estate.**
**Example:** At the death of her husband, Polly Rowen inherits a **life estate** in their home. The *remainder* is **devised** to their son, Paul Rowen. When Polly dies, Paul will gain **title** to the house. Paul is the **remainderman.**

**REMAINDERMAN** the person who is to receive **possession** of the property after the death of a **life tenant.**
**Example:** See example under **remainder.**

**REMODEL** to change the appearance and functional utility of a building. This may include painting, repairing and replacing of fixtures and equipment.
**Example:** The Moodys wish to *remodel* the kitchen in their home. They plan to refinish the cabinets, repaint the walls, install a new floor covering and replace the range and sink.

**RENEGOTIATE** to legally revise the **terms** of a **contract.**
**Example:** Abel owes $10,000 to Baker at 7% interest. Abel and Baker *renegotiate* so that Baker agrees to lend $15,000 at 13% interest instead of the original loan.

**RENEWAL OPTION** the right, but not the obligation, of a **tenant to** continue a **lease** at specified **term** and **rent**.

**Example:** Abel leases property from Baker for 20 years at $500 monthly rent. A *renewal option* in the lease gives Abel the right to continue leasing for 5 years beyond the original term (Figure 147).

FIGURE 147

**RENOVATE** general term applied to the process of upgrading an existing improvement. Usually there is an attempt to keep the same general appearance of the building with new materials or to return the building to its original appearance.

**Example:** The city bought several dilapidated homes in the neighborhood. They plan to *renovate* the homes by bringing them up to the current housing code standards. The renovated homes will be sold to city residents.

**RENT** a charge for the use of space. See **contract rent, economic rent.**

**Example:** Abel allows Baker to use property, provided that Baker pays $500 per month (Figure 148). The charge is *rent*.

**RENTABLE AREA** same as **net leasable area.**

**RENTAL RATE** the periodic charge per unit for the use of a property. The period may be a month, quarter or year. The unit may be a dwelling unit, square foot or other unit of measurement.

**Example:** The *rental rate* for the 2-bedroom apartments is $400 per month. The *rental rate* for office space is $12 per square foot per year.

**RENT BID MODELS** a conceptual tool used to explain how land is allocated in competitive markets. The model is based on the assumption that space is controlled by the activity which offers the highest bid for the site.

**Example:** A simple *rent bid model* of urban land is formulated. The model predicts that commercial uses will occupy land near the city's center, while residential land will spread around the core.

**RENT CONTROL** laws that govern the rate that may be charged for space.
**Example:** Since the 1940's, apartment owners in New York City have been restricted by law in the rent that they may charge. *Rent control* laws have been adopted by Boston, Washington, D.C., Los Angeles, and many cities in New Jersey, among others.

**RENT-FREE PERIOD** a portion of the term of a lease when no rent is required. It is offered by a landlord as a rental concession to attract tenants.
**Example:** In order to attract tenants to the new office building, the landlord is offering a 3-month *rent-free period* to all tenants who sign a 2-year lease.

**RENT-UP PERIOD** the time it takes for newly constructed properties to be fully occupied.
**Example:** Figure 149.

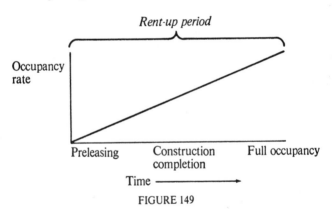

FIGURE 149

**REO** see **real estate owned.**

**REPAIRS** work performed to return property to a former condition without extending its **useful life**, as distinguished from **capital improvements.** In **income property**, repairs are an **operating expense** for accounting and tax purposes.
**Examples:** Patching a hole in the roof (but not replacing the roof) and mending (but not rebuilding) a fence are *repairs*.

**REPLACEMENT COST** the cost of erecting a building to replace or serve the functions of a previous structure. See **reproduction cost.**

**Example:** Abel wishes to insure a building against accidental destruction. The policy should be written so that in the event of destruction of the building, Abel may replace it with a structure that serves an identical function. Therefore, Abel should insure the building in an amount equal to its *replacement cost*, which is likely to be greater than its **market value.**

**REPLACEMENT RESERVE** an amount set aside from **net operating income** to pay for the eventual wearing out of short-lived **assets.** See **reserve fund.**

**Example:** Singer buys new apartments, each containing $1,000 worth of carpeting and appliances that have a 10-year **useful life.** Each year she deposits $100 in a *replacement reserve* account to pay for recarpeting in 10 years.

**REPRODUCTION COST** the cost of exact duplication of a property as of a certain date. Reproduction differs from replacement in that replacement requires the same functional utility for a property, whereas reproduction is an exact duplication. See **replacement cost.**

**Example:** In the **cost approach** to property valuation, the **appraiser** estimates the *reproduction cost* of the subject structure. Various deductions are then made to account for **depreciation** in value from the time the building was constructed. These deductions reflect the fact that the building is not new, may not be of modern design, and may have suffered adverse effects due to its location.

**RESALE PROCEEDS** the amount a former owner receives upon a sale after paying **transaction costs,** remaining debt, and, sometimes, income taxes. Same as **proceeds from resale.**

**Example:** Table 36.

**TABLE 36**

| | | |
|---|---:|---:|
| Selling price | | $100,000 |
| Less: Commissions | $5,000 | |
| Closing costs | 1,000 | |
| Unpaid mortgage | 60,000 | |
| Capital gains tax | $14,000 | − $80,000 |
| Resale proceeds | | $20,000 |

**RESCIND** to withdraw an **offer** or contract. **Regulation Z** allows a 3-day period in which to *rescind* certain credit transactions.

**Example:** Abel offers to buy a certain house from Baker. Before Baker accepts, Abel *rescinds* the offer and, therefore, is not obligated to follow through on the purchase.

**RESCISSION** the act of cancelling or terminating a **contract.** Rescission is allowed when the contract was induced by **fraud, duress, misrepresentation,** or **mistake. Regulation Z** allows one to **rescind** certain credit transactions within 3 business days (not applicable to **first mortgages** on a home); purchasers of certain land that must be registered by **Department of Housing and Urban Development** (HUD) may rescind within 3 business days. See **rescind.**

**Example:** *Rescission* was allowed by the court for a contract that Abel was induced to enter on the threat of death.

**RESERVE FUND** an account maintained to provide funds for anticipated expenditures required to maintain a building. A reserve may be required by a lender in the form of an **escrow** to pay upcoming taxes and insurance costs. A **replacement reserve** may be maintained to provide for **replacement cost** of short-lived components, such as carpets, heating equipment, or roofing. Deposit of money into such a fund does not achieve a tax deduction.

**Example:** A **property management** firm anticipates that property taxes will be due in 6 months, insurance must be renewed in 2½ years, and carpeting must be replaced in 6 years. Accordingly, she establishes a *reserve fund* by depositing a portion of monthly revenues in an account. Monies from the fund will be used at the appropriate time to meet the future expenditures.

**RESIDENCE** the place where one lives, particularly the **dwelling** in which one lives. See **domicile.**

**Example:** Baker owns several houses, one of which is Baker's *residence,* another is a vacation home, and the others are **income properties** rented to tenants.

**RESIDENTIAL** pertaining to housing. See **residential property.**

**RESIDENTIAL BROKER** one who **lists** and sells houses or **condominiums.** Contrast **commercial broker.**

**Example:** Baker earned a livelihood as a *residential broker* selling **single-family housing.**

**RESIDENTIAL MEMBER (RM)** a professional designation offered by the **American Institute of Real Estate Appraisers.**

**Example:** Collins passed several examinations, prepared demonstration **appraisal** reports, and acquired several years of experience in the appraisal of **residential property.** She has been awarded the *RM* designation, which acknowledges her skills as a residential appraiser.

**RESIDENTIAL PROPERTY** 1. in real estate **brokerage** terminology, owner-occupied housing.

**Example:** Rollins is in *residential* real estate. She secures **listings** for **single-family housing** and sells homes.

2. in income taxation terminology, rental units used for **dwelling** purposes, not of a transient (hotel, motel) nature. To qualify as residential, at least 80% of a building's income should be derived from dwelling units.

**Example:** *Residential* rental *property* owners may be subject to different methods of **depreciation (accelerated cost recovery)** and/or **depreciation recapture** than **commercial property** owners.

**RESIDENTIAL SERVICE CONTRACT** an insurance **contract** or home **warranty**, generally for one year, covering the plumbing, mechanical, and electrical systems of a home. It is available in most areas upon the purchase of an existing home. Either the buyer or seller can pay for the contract.

**Example:** Ricky and Rebecca Miller purchase a home. The sellers paid $300 for a *residential service contract*. Three months later, the air-conditioner compressor breaks and costs $800 to repair. The Millers must pay the $100 deductible, and the contract covers the balance of the cost of repair.

**RESIDENT MANAGER** one who supervises the care of an apartment complex while living in one of the units in the complex.

**Example:** Carter employs Downs as a *resident manager*. Downs' duties include showing vacant units to prospective tenants, making sure the building is kept clean, and providing entry to repair persons. In return, Downs receives an apartment rent-free.

**RESIDUAL** value or income remaining after deducting an amount necessary to meet fixed obligations.

**Example:** After deducting **operating expenses, debt service,** and income taxes from **gross income,** the **equity** investor is entitled to the *residual*. Note, there is no assurance that a residual will exist.

In **appraisal,** a portion of stabilized **net operating income** is deducted to support the value of the **improvements.** The *residual* net operating income is then left to support the value of the **site.**

**RESPONDEAT SUPERIOR** in **agency** law, the doctrine that a **principal** is liable for the acts of an **agent.**

**Example:** A real estate **agent** misrepresented the facts about property that was offered for sale. The injured party sued the **agent** and the **broker.** The **broker** was held liable under the doctrine of *respondeat superior*.

**RESTORE** to return a building to its original quality and appearance. While modern materials are used, the emphasis is on faithful reproduction of the original style.

**Example:** The Hollys bought an old Victorian style home which had been converted into a duplex. They plan to *restore* the home by removing partitions, refinishing the hardwood floors, repairing the fireplaces and other improvements to return the building to its original style.

**RESTRAINT ON ALIENATION** a limiting condition on the right to transfer property. If the condition is against public policy or is unreasonable, courts will void the condition.
**Example:** The deed that Lowell received when she bought property specifies that she may not resell the property to certain ethnic minorities. Since the clause is illegal, she went to court to remove this *restraint on alienation*.

**RESTRICTION** a limitation placed upon the use of property, contained in the **deed** or other written **instrument** in the **chain of title** or in local **ordinances** pertaining to land use. See **encumbrance.**
**Example:** The ownership of property is subject to several *restrictions*. A deed **covenant** may restrict development alternatives, as may a local **zoning ordinance. Easements** may restrict use of parts of the property. **Liens** may restrict sales. **Building** codes may restrict construction practices.

**RESTRICTIVE COVENANT** see **restriction.**

**RETAIL GRAVITATION** the drawing power of a shopping center; generally, the larger the center, the greater its ability to draw from distant areas.

**RETAINAGE** in a construction **contract,** money earned by a **contractor** but not paid to the contractor until the completion of construction or some other agreed-upon date.
**Example:** The **general contractor** earns $5,000 upon pouring the foundation, plus $15,000 upon completion of the frame, plus $10,000 upon completion of the roof. Of each payment, 10% is held back as *retainage*. It is paid after a **certificate of occupancy is** issued.

**RETALIATORY EVICTION** the requirement that a tenant vacate a unit in response to a complaint from the tenant concerning the condition of the building. Landlord-tenant laws in many states forbid such **evictions** if proper channels are taken to lodge the complaint.
**Example:** Six months after Romney moved into an apartment, the heating system stopped operating. The landlord failed to repair the system, and Romney filed a formal complaint with the city **housing code** enforcement office. When the landlord received notice from the city to repair the system, he evicted Romney in a *retaliatory eviction*. The eviction was stopped in court.

**RETIRE (A DEBT)** to pay off the **principal** on a loan, thereby fulfilling the obligation under the loan contract. See also **amortization.**
**Example:** When Smith made the last monthly payment on his mortgage loan, he *retired* the debt.

**Example:** Jones arranged to *retire* her home improvement loan by paying an amount equal to the remaining principal balance.

**REVALUATION CLAUSE** see **reappraisal lease.**

**REVERSE ANNUITY MORTGAGE** a type of **mortgage,** designed for elderly homeowners with substantial **equity,** by which a lender periodically (monthly, for example) pays an amount to the borrower. The loan balance increases with interest and periodic payments, causing **negative amortization.**
**Example:** Roper, age 70, who retired from his job, owns his home **free and clear** of any **liens.** His pension is inadequate to pay expenses. He seeks a *reverse annuity mortgage* that will pay him $200 per month. At a 15% interest rate, he will owe $55,043 in 10 years.

**REVERSE LEVERAGE** a situation in which financial benefits from ownership accrue at a lower rate than the mortgage interest rate. See **leverage.**
**Example:** Net-leased property is purchased for $100,000 with a $75,000 mortgage at 12% interest and $25,000 of **equity.** The net rent is $10,000 per year; interest expense is $9,000 per year. The $1,000 difference (**cash flow**) provides a 4% return to the equity owner. In the absence of debt, the owner would receive a 10% return. *Reverse leverage* works against the property owner.

**REVERSION** the right of a **lessor** to **possess** leased property upon the termination of a **lease.**
**Example:** Evans purchases the home of Felker, a senior citizen, and leases the home back to Felker for life. Evans has the right to receive rental payments from Felker plus a *reversion* in the property at Felker's death.

**REVERSIONARY FACTOR** the mathematical factor that indicates the present worth of one dollar to be received in the future. Same as **present value of one.** The formula is

$$\text{Reversionary factor} = \frac{1}{(1 + i)^n}$$

where $i$ = interest rate
       $n$ = number of years (or periods)

**Example:** The *reversionary factor* for 30 years at 12% is .03338. The present value of the receipt of land that will be worth $50,000 in 30 years is $1,690 (.03338 x $50,000).

**REVERSIONARY VALUE** the value of property at the expiration of a certain time period.

**Example:** A **lease** will expire in 30 years. The landlord estimates that the *reversionary value* of the property will be $50,000; that is, the property can be sold in 30 years for $50,000.

**REVERSIONARY INTEREST** the **interest** a person has in property upon the termination of the preceding **estate.**
**Example:** Abel is the **remainderman** in property that was granted to Baker for life. Abel has a *reversionary interest* in the property.

**REVOCATION** an act of recalling a power of authority conferred, as a revocation of a **power of attorney,** a **license,** an **agency,** etc.
**Example:** The *revocation* of Abel's broker's license, caused by his fraudulent acts, prevented him from earning a living in **real estate.**

**REZONING** an action to change the designation of a subject **parcel** or group of parcels on the **zoning** map. The effect of a rezoning is to change the permitted uses for the affected parcels. See **downzoning.**
**Example:** Brown, whose property was zoned for low-**density** residential, petitioned the city for a *rezoning* to allow construction of an **apartment building.**

**RIDER** an amendment or **attachment** to a **contract.**
**Example:** A *rider* to Owen's **homeowner's policy** insured the valuable paintings against fire and theft losses.

**RIGHT OF FIRST REFUSAL** the opportunity of a party to match the **terms** of a proposed contract before the contract is **executed.**
**Example:** In some states, tenants whose apartments are converted to **condominium** are given a *right of first refusal* for the unit when it is sold. This means the tenant may purchase the unit at the same price and terms of any outside purchaser.

**RIGHT OF SURVIVORSHIP** the right of a surviving joint tenant to acquire the **interest** of a deceased joint owner; the distinguishing feature of both **joint tenancy** and **tenancy by the entirety.**
**Example:** Frank Adams and Anna Adams own property as joint tenants with the *right of survivorship*. When either dies, the entire property will pass to the other without **probate.**

**RIGHT-OF-WAY** 1. the right to use a particular path for **access** or passage; a type of **easement.**
**Example:** Lot A has acquired a *right-of-way* across lot B (Figure 150).
2. the areas of subdivisions **dedicated** to government for use for streets, roads, and other public access to lots.
**Example:** A section of a subdivision with a *right-of-way* for a public road (Figure 151).

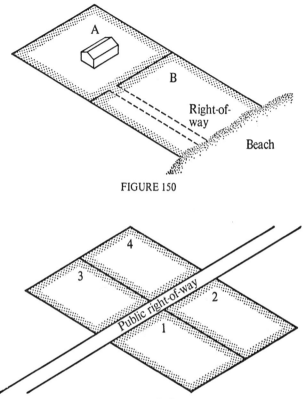

FIGURE 150

FIGURE 151

**RIPARIAN OWNER** one who owns land bounding upon a lake, river, or other body of water. See also **littoral.**
**Example:** The owner of lot A in Figure 152 is a *riparian owner,* whose ownership rights include access to the river and use of its waters, or **riparian rights.** The owner of lot B has no riparian rights.

**RIPARIAN RIGHTS** rights pertaining to the use of water on, under, or **adjacent** to one's land. May be qualified to avoid **nuisance** and pollution. Riparian rights are recognized in most eastern states but rarely in western states, where they recognize **usufructory rights.**
**Example:** See **riparian owner.**

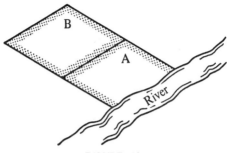

FIGURE 152

**RISK** 1. uncertainty or variability. The possibility that returns from an investment will be greater or less than forecast. Diversification of investments provides some protection against risk.
**Example:** Types of *risk* in real estate:
- business risk—rents, vacancies, or **operating expenses** vary from projected amounts
- interest risk—property may be subject to a higher rate **mortgage** than the **market rate**
- market rental rate—a long-term lease may lock the owner into low rents
- principal risk—resale proceeds may be less than anticipated

2. the possibility of a loss. Insurance can offer protection against certain risks.
**Example:** Owners insure buildings against *risk* of loss caused by fires, storms, and other hazards by taking out a **hazard insurance** policy.

**ROD** a linear unit of measurement equal to 16½ feet.
**Example:** A certain lot has 165 feet, or 10 *rods,* of road **frontage.**

**ROLLOVER LOAN** a type of **mortgage** loan, commonly used in Canada, in which the **amortization** of **principal** is based on a long **term** but the **interest rate** is established for a much shorter term. The loan may be extended, or rolled over, at the end of the shorter term at the current market interest rate.
**Example:** Abel obtains a *rollover loan.* The amortization term is 30 years. The interest rate is 14% for 2 years. After 2 years, Abel must renew the loan at the going interest rate or **refinance** with a new loan.

**ROW HOUSE single-family** dwelling units attached to one another by common walls, generally with a common **facade.** See **town-**

**house.**
**Example:** A group of *row houses* (Figure 153).

A group of *row houses*

FIGURE 153

**ROYALTY** money paid to a property owner for extraction of some valuable resource from the land.
**Example:** Richman owns a 500-**acre** ranch in west Texas. An oil company negotiates a **lease** with Richman to explore for oil on the ranch. Under the agreement, Richman will receive a *royalty* in proportion to the number of barrels of oil pumped from the ranch.

**RULE OF 72's** an approximation of the time it takes for money to double when earning **compound interest.** Divide the percentage rate into 72 to derive the number of years to double the **principal.**
**Example:** A $1,000 **certificate of deposit** pays a 9% interest rate with annual compounding. In about 8 years the balance will be $2,000. ($72 \div 9\% = 8$ years)

**RULE OF 78's** a method for computing unearned interest used on installment loans with **add-on interest.** The number 78 is based on the sum of the digits from 1 to 12.
**Example:** A 12-month loan is made for $1,000 with 8% add-on interest. The loan payments are based on a total of $1,080, payable at the rate of $90 per month for 12 months. If the borrower prepays the loan at the end of 1 month, $\frac{12}{78}$ of the $80 interest is charged; the balance of interest is refunded. If the borrower prepays at the end of the second month, $\frac{12+11}{78} = \frac{23}{78}$ is charged. Prepayment at the end of the eleventh month results in a $\frac{1}{78}$ refund.

RUN WITH THE LAND

RUN WITH THE LAND an expression indicating a right or **restriction** that affects all current and future owners of a property. Contrasted to an agreement, between a current owner and other parties, that is not passed on to future owners in a **deed.**
Example: A **covenant,** written into the **deed,** prohibits the property from being used as a liquor store. The restriction *runs with the land,* and all future owners are restrained from violating the covenant.

RURBAN areas, on the fringe of urban development, that are in the process of being developed for urban uses.
Example: Figure 154.

FIGURE 154

RURAL pertaining to the area outside the larger and moderate-sized cities and surrounding population concentrations. Generally characterized by farms, ranches, small towns and unpopulated regions. Compare **suburb.**
Example: Garrison grew up on a farm in a *rural* area of Indiana. She later moved to Chicago and lived in a suburban town nearby. Garrison invested in *rural* land, hoping to be able to return at retirement.

R VALUE a measure of the heat conductivity of material. The higher the *R value*, the better the material serves as insulation from heat

transfer. *R value* generally applies to insulating materials, roofs, exterior walls and windows and doors.

**Example:** The walls in a building have an estimated *R value* of 20. Fiberglass insulation with an *R value* of 34 was installed in the walls to make the building more energy efficient.

---

# S

---

**SALES CONTRACT** a **contract** by which the buyer and seller agree to the **terms** of sale. Same as **agreement of sale, earnest money** contract.

**Example:** Carter and Dooley sign a *sales contract,* which specifies the property to be sold, type of **deed, closing date,** price, **financing** conditions, and other details.

**SALE-LEASEBACK** the simultaneous purchase of property and **lease** back to the seller. The lease portion of the transaction is generally long-term. The seller-lessee in the transaction is converted from an owner to a tenant.

**Example:** ABC Corporation owns an office building. It arranges a *sale-leaseback* for the building **site** with the Carpenters Pension Fund. ABC receives cash and a 25-year lease to the site. In addition, ABC might **depreciate** the value of the building for income taxes. The Fund receives an **income stream** for 25 years and a **reversion** to the property at the end of the lease.

**SALESPERSON** one who is licensed to deal in real estate or perform any other act enumerated by state real estate **license** laws, while under the supervision of a **broker** licensed by the state.

**Example:** A *salesperson* arranges a 90-day **listing** on a house, which is accepted by the broker. Another *salesperson* shows the home to a prospective buyer. The sale is closed, and **commissions** are collected by the broker and shared with the *salespersons.*

**SALT BOX COLONIAL OR CATSLIDE (IN SOUTH)** an early American style, 2 or 2½-story house that is square or rectangular with a steep gable roof that extends down to the first floor in the rear.

**Example:** Figure 155:

**SALVAGE VALUE** the estimated **value** that an **asset** will have at the end of its **useful life.**

**Example:** An appraiser estimates the useful life of a building at 40 years; she also estimates that the building's *salvage value* would be $10,000 in 40 years. Consequently, all but $10,000 of the building cost is to be **depreciated** over 40 years.

Large central chimney

Steep gable roof extended to first floor in rear

2 or 2½ stories

Square or rectangular shape

No windows in rear

Small glass panes in double-hung windows

FIGURE 155

**SANDWICH LEASE** lease held by a **lessee** who becomes a **lessor** by subletting. Typically, the sandwich leaseholder is neither the owner nor the user of the property. See **sublease.**
**Example:** Figure 156

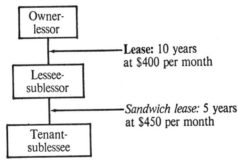

Owner-lessor

**Lease:** 10 years at $400 per month

Lessee-sublessor

*Sandwich lease:* 5 years at $450 per month

Tenant-sublessee

FIGURE 156

**SATISFACTION PIECE** an **instrument** for recording and acknowledging final payment of a **mortgage** loan.
**Example:** After the mortgage loan was paid off, the borrower received a *satisfaction piece*, which she promptly **recorded,** officially.

**SAVINGS & LOAN ASSOCIATIONS (S&Ls)** depository institutions that specialize in originating, servicing, and holding **mortgage** loans, primarily on owner-occupied, **residential property.** See **Federal Savings and Loan Association.**
**Example:** Most home buyers finance the purchase with a mortgage loan from a *savings and loan association.* Such associations receive most of their investment funds from the deposits of small individual savers. All savings and loan associations are subject to regulation from federal or state government.

**SCALE** the proportional relationship between the dimensions of a drawing, plan, or model to the dimensions of the physical object it represents.
**Example:** A **subdivision** plan is prepared at a *scale* in which one inch equals 1,000 feet. A distance of one inch on the drawing is intended to signify 1,000 feet on the **site.**
**Example:** A *scale* model of a building has a *scale* of one to 25. Each inch on the model represents 25 inches on the actual building.

**SCENIC EASEMENT** an **encumbrance** on the **title** to a property to preserve it in a more-or-less natural or undeveloped state. See **easement.**
**Example:** Smith owns a house with a view of the ocean (Figure 157). Snyder owns the property between the Smith house and the beach. To preserve the view of the ocean, Smith purchases a *scenic easement* to Snyder's property. Snyder is then prevented from developing the property in such a manner as to obstruct Smith's view.

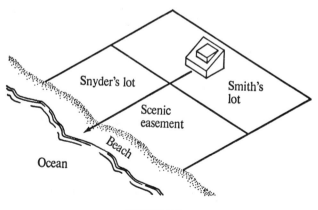

FIGURE 157

**SEASONED LOAN** a loan on which several payments have been collected.
**Example:** The seller accepts a **second mortgage** on the property sold. After he collects 12 months of payments, the loan is considered *seasoned* and can more easily be sold to a second mortgage investor.

**SECONDARY FINANCING** see **junior mortgage, second mortgage.**

**SECONDARY MORTGAGE MARKET** the mechanisms available to buy and sell mortgages, mainly residential **first mortgages.** There is no set meeting place for the secondary mortgage market. **FNMA** and **Freddie Mac** hold **auctions** weekly to buy those mortgages offered at the highest **effective rate. Bids** are collected from all over the country.
**Example:** The Good Money Mortgage Bankers originated 100 residential first mortgages with a total **face value** of $5 million. They sell the mortgages in the *secondary mortgage market* for a $1,000 profit on each.

**SECOND HOME** a residence that is not one's **principal residence.** Under the Tax Reform Act of 1986, a taxpayer may deduct interest on 2 personal residences.
**Example:** Senator Goodwill maintains his principal residence in Hometown, Iowa and a *second home* in Washington, D.C. He is allowed to deduct interest paid on both as an itemized deduction.

**SECOND MORTGAGE** a **subordinated lien,** created by a mortgage loan, over the amount of a **first mortgage.** Second mortgages are used at purchase to reduce the amount of a cash **down payment** or in **refinancing** to raise cash for any purpose. See **subordination.**
**Example:** A house costs $100,000. Available **financing** is a mortgage loan covering 80% of value, or $80,000. The required cash **down payment** is $20,000. A *second mortgage* is available for an additional $10,000 of value, reducing the down payment to $10,000. The *second mortgage* will generally carry a higher **interest rate** than the first mortgage to reflect the inferior position and greater **risk** of the second mortgage.

**SECTION (OF LAND)** one square mile in the **government rectangular survey.** There are 36 sections in a 6-mile square **township.**
**Example:** A township, containing 36 *sections* (Figure 158).

**SECTION 8 HOUSING** privately owned rental **dwelling** units participating in the low-income rental assistance program created by 1974 amendments to Section 8 of the 1937 Housing Act. Under the program, landlords receive rent subsidies on behalf of qualified low-income tenants, allowing the tenants to pay a limited proportion of their incomes toward the rent.

**Example:** A **landlord** elects to participate in the *Section 8 housing* program. A prospective tenant's income is $800 per month—low enough to qualify for the program. A **fair market rent** for the unit is established by the **Department of Housing and Urban Development** as $200 per month. The tenant pays 20% of income, or $160 per month, and HUD supplements $40 per month to the landlord.

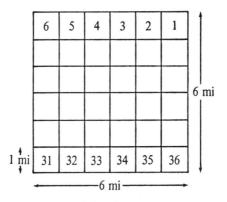

FIGURE 158

**SECTION 167** the part of the **Internal Revenue Code** that deals with depreciation.

**Example: Improvements** to **real estate** are depreciable in accordance with *Section 167* of the Internal Revenue Code.

**SECTION 1031** the section of the **Internal Revenue Code** that deals with **tax-free exchanges** of certain property. General rules for a **tax-free exchange** of real estate are:

The properties must be:

1. exchanged
2. **like-kind property** (real estate for real estate)
3. held for use in a trade or business or held as an investment

See also **tax-free exchange, boot, delayed exchange.**

**Example:** Under *Section 1031*, Lowell trades her **appreciated** land for Baker's shopping center. **Equities** are the same. Lowell's **adjusted tax basis** in the land becomes her **adjusted tax basis** in the shopping center.

**SECTION 1034** the section of the **Internal Revenue Code** dealing with sales of personal residences. Generally, there is no **recognized gain** or loss on the sale of a personal residence, provided another one is purchased within 2 years of the sale date of the old one. The new one must cost at least as much as the adjusted sales price of the old one (sales price, less expenses of sale, less fixing-up expenses).

**Example:** Under *Section 1034,* Abel can defer tax on the $10,000 gain on the home he sold for $65,000 by buying a new one that costs more.

**SECTION 1221** the part of the **Internal Revenue Code** that defines a **capital asset.** It actually states what is not a capital asset.

**Examples:** Under *Section 1221* the following are not **capital assets:**
• inventory (such as lots of a subdivider)
• receivables collected in the course of business (such as **notes** received from the sale of lots by a **subdivider)**
• copyrights and the like held by the creator or certain other parties
• certain U.S. securities

The following are capital assets:
• the personal **residence** that one owns
• **raw land** held as an investment
• **mortgages** held as investments

**Note:** The importance of capital gains has been diminished by the Tax Reform Act of 1986 which applies the same tax rate to capital gains after 1987 as it does to ordinary income. However, there remain important distinctions as to capital loss limitations, so *Section 1221* remains relevant.

**SECTION 1231** the section of the **Internal Revenue Code** that deals with **assets** used in a trade or business. Generally, gains on Section 1231 assets are taxed at **capital gains** rates (except for **depreciation recapture**) and losses are **tax deductible** as **ordinary income.** See also **Section 1245, Section 1250.**

**Example:** *Section 1231* assets include:
• vehicles used in business
• machinery used in business
• hotels, office buildings, warehouses, apartments

**SECTION 1245** the section of the **Internal Revenue Code** dealing with **gains** from **personal property** on which **depreciation** had been claimed. Generally, gains are taxed at **capital gains** rate except to the extent of depreciation claimed.

**Note:** The Tax Reform Act of 1986 provides the same tax rate for ordinary income as for capital gains after 1987. Therefore the nature of the gain has diminished in importance, though *Section 1245* remains in the Internal Revenue Code.

**SECTION 1250** the section of the **Internal Revenue Code** dealing with **gains** from **real estate** on which **accelerated depreciation** had been claimed. Under the Tax Reform Act of 1986, the tax rate for ordinary income is the same as for capital gains after 1987, and straight-line depreciation is mandated for most buildings. Consequently, the importance of *Section 1250* has been minimized. Under prior law, gains on **residential property** were generally treated as **capital gains** except to the extent of accelerated depreciation claimed (Figure 159 and Table 37). Gains on nonresidential property on which accelerated depreciation was claimed were all **recaptured** to the extent of gain or depreciation, whichever is less.

**TABLE 37**

TREATMENT OF GAIN
AFTER USE OF DEPRECIATION METHOD

1. Accelerated Method

|                 | Nonresidential | Residential |
|-----------------|:--------------:|:-----------:|
| Capital gain    | A — B          | A — C       |
| Ordinary income | B — D          | C — D       |

2. Straight-line

|                 | Nonresidential | Residential |
|-----------------|:--------------:|:-----------:|
| Capital gain    | A — B          | A — C       |
| Ordinary income | none           | none        |

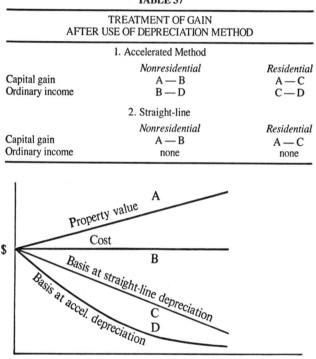

FIGURE 159

**SECURITIES AND EXCHANGE COMMISSION (SEC)** the federal agency created in 1934 to carry out the provisions of the Securities Exchange Act. Generally, the agency seeks to protect the investing public by preventing **misrepresentation, fraud,** manipulation, and other abuses in the securities markets.

**Example:** The **Securities and Exchange Commission** requires their review of proposed **public offerings** of securities, registration of listed securities, and other matters. They do not, however, guarantee the investor against loss.

**SECURITIZATION** the process of creating a security marketable in the capital markets and backed by a package of assets such as mortgage loans. See **real estate mortgage investment conduit, mortgage pools, collateralized mortgage obligation.**
**Example:** Mortgage loans insured by the Federal Housing Administration are good assets for *securitization*. A lender can organize a pool of such loans and create a collateralized mortgage obligation for sale to investors.

**SECURITY** 1. property that serves as **collateral** for a **debt.**
**Example: Real estate** serves as *security* for a **mortgage** loan. In the event of **default** on the loan, the lender may sell the property to satisfy the debt.
2. a document that serves as evidence of ownership.
**Examples:** The following are securities:
• common and preferred stocks
• **bonds**
• **mortgages**
   The **Securities and Exchange Commission** defines **limited partnership** interests and **condominiums** and **cooperatives** in certain situations as *securities*.

**SECURITY DEPOSIT** a cash payment required by a landlord, to be held during the **term** of a **lease** to offset damages incurred due to actions of the tenant. Such damages may include physical damage to the property, theft of property, failure to pay back rent and breaking the lease. **Forfeiture** of the deposit does not absolve the tenant of further financial **liability.** Laws in most states require landlords to hold the deposit in a separate account and refund the amount within a specified time after termination of the lease.
**Example:** A landlord requires a *security deposit* equal to one month's rent, payable at the signing of the lease. An additional deposit is required for tenants with pets. At termination of the lease, the landlord inspects the rented unit. If there is no reason for forfeiture, the landlord refunds the deposit within 30 days.

**SECURITY INTEREST** an interest in **real estate** in which the real estate serves as **collateral.**
**Example:** A **mortgage** lender holds a *security interest* in real estate. He doesn't own the real estate, but does have a **lien** against it.

**SEED MONEY** amounts needed to begin a real estate development, prior to being able to borrow under a **mortgage** loan. Required

costs include those for a **feasibility study, loan application** and **loan commitment** fees, attorney and accountant fees, land **option** costs, and others. See **front money.**
**Example:** To begin a $2,000,000 **condominium** development, about 2% of the total cost is needed as *seed money.*

**SEISIN** the **possession** of **realty** by one who claims to own a **fee simple** estate or a **life estate** or other salable **interest.** See also **ownership rights to realty, title.**
**Example:** *Seisin* is used to describe the **possession** of real estate by one who claims a **freehold** interest.

**SELF-AMORTIZING MORTGAGE** one that will **retire** itself through regular **principal and interest payments.** Contrast with **balloon mortgage, interest-only loan.**
**Example:** Collins borrowed $100,000 with a *self-amortizing mortgage* at 12% **interest** with a 30-year **term. Principal and interest payments** are $1,029 each month for the 30 years, at the end of which her loan will be amortized fully.

**SELF-HELP** the efforts of a landlord to cure a **default** on the **lease** without aid of legal proceedings. In most states, self-help remedies are not considered a legitimate substitute for a legal **eviction.**
**Example:** When Simmons' tenant fell 3 months behind in rent, Simmons changed the locks on the apartment and cut off the heat. The tenant took Simmons to court and forced him to follow eviction procedures in lieu of these *self-help* activities.

**SELLER'S MARKET** economic conditions that favor sellers, reflecting rising prices and market activity. Contrast with **buyer's market.**
**Example:** *Seller's markets* in real estate are often caused by:
• population influx
• lower interest rates
• lack of building activity

**SELLING BROKER (AGENT)** the licensed real estate **broker (agent)** that brings forth the buyer. Contrast with **listing broker (agent).**
**Example:** Abel was the *selling broker* under a **multiple listing** agreement. He showed the property to Collins, the buyer. Abel will share the **commission** with the listing broker.

**SEMIANNUAL** twice a year; same as **biannual.**

**SENSITIVITY ANALYSIS** a technique of investment analysis whereby different values of certain key variables are tested to see how sensitive investment results are to possible change in assumptions. It is a method of evaluating the riskiness of an investment.

**Example:** *Sensitivity analysis* was applied to a certain income property investment. It was found that forecasting a 15% vacancy rate produced a rate of return on investment of 16% versus an 18% rate of return for a 5% vacancy factor. On the other hand, varying the property's appreciation rate from 10% per year to 5% reduced the return from 20% to 4%.

**SEPARATE PROPERTY** property acquired by either spouse prior to marriage or by gift or **devise** after marriage, as distinct from **community property.**
**Example:** At a divorce trial, each party tries to show that property owned prior to marriage or acquired in his or her own right is *separate property.*

**SERVICING** the act of billing, collecting payment, and filing reports for a **mortgage** loan; may also include loan analysis, **default** follow-up, and management of tax and insurance **escrow** accounts. Often performed for a fee by **mortgage bankers** after loans are sold to investors.
**Example:** Gray, a mortgage banker, originates loans and markets them in groups to large investors. On each loan originated, Gray receives a monthly fee for *servicing,* thereby freeing the investors of loan management burdens. The fee is ⅜ of 1% of the loan balance.

**SERVIENT TENANT** contrast with **dominant tenant.**

**SETBACK** the distance from the curb or other established line within which no buildings may be erected. See also **building line.**
**Example:** A 50-ft setback is shown in Figure 160.

50 ft

Setback

FIGURE 160

**SETTLEMENT** same as **closing.**

**SETTLEMENT STATEMENT** same as **closing statement.**

**SEVERALTY** the ownership of **real property** by an individual as an individual. See **tenancy in severalty.**
**Example:** The owner in *severalty* enjoys working the land without partners in its ownership.

**SEVERANCE DAMAGES** an element of **value** arising out of a **condemnation** to which a **tract** was a part.
**Example:** The state highway department needed a strip of land 100 feet wide from the middle of Dooley's farm. They awarded $1,000 per **acre** for the land taken, plus $15,000 *severance damages* for Dooley's inconvenience in getting from one side of the highway to the other.

**SEWER** a system of pipes, containments, and treatment facilities for the disposal of plumbing wastes.
**Example:** A sanitary *sewer* collects waste water from individual buildings and homes, for treatment and disposal at a public facility.
**Example:** To prevent flooding, a storm *sewer* collects water drainage from streets and other surfaces.

**SHARED APPRECIATION MORTGAGE** a residential loan with a fixed **interest rate** set below **market rates,** with the lender entitled to a specified share of **appreciation** in property **value** over a specified time interval. Loan payments are set to **amortize** the loan over a long-term **maturity,** but repayment is generally required after a much shorter term. The amount of appreciation is established by sale of the home or by **appraisal** if no sale is made.
**Example:** Hogan obtains a *shared appreciation mortgage.* The interest rate on the loan is 10%, with the lender receiving ⅓ of any appreciation after 10 years. At the end of 10 years, Hogan does not wish to sell the home. An appraisal is made to establish the appreciation amount. Hogan must **retire** the loan by **refinancing** with a new loan the amount of the unpaid balance plus the appreciation share.

**SHARED EQUITY MORTGAGE** a home **loan** in which the lender is granted a share of the **equity,** thereby allowing the lender to participate in the proceeds from resale. After satisfying the unpaid balance of the loan, the borrower splits the residue of the proceeds with the lender. Shared equity plans often require the lender to buy a portion of the equity by providing a portion of the **down payment.**
**Example:** Ingram obtains a *shared equity mortgage* from a **mortgage banker.** The lender provides one half of the necessary down

payment. Ingram makes loan payments on a fixed-rate, level payment basis. At resale, Ingram and the lender split the proceeds after repayment of the balance of the loan.

**SHED ROOF** one having a single, sloped side.
**Example:** Figure 161.

Shed

FIGURE 161

**SHOPPING CENTER** a collection of retail stores with a common parking area and generally one or more large department, discount, or food stores; sometimes including an enclosed **mall** or walkway. See also **anchor tenant.**
**Example:** *Shopping centers* developed after World War II as population shifted to the suburbs. Providing a variety of stores with easy access and ample parking, the centers became a strong alternative to downtown retail centers. Types of shopping centers are shown in Table 38.

**SHORT-FORM** an **instrument,** seldom more than 2 pages, that refers to another document. The short form is often recorded in lieu of a cumbersome longer document.
**Example:** The Giant Development Company leased part of a shopping center to Malee's Department Store. The **lease** required 150 printed pages. A *short-form* lease was recorded.

**SHORT-TERM CAPITAL GAIN** gain on the sale of a **capital asset** that was held, generally, for less than 6 months. A taxpayer's *short-term capital gains* and losses are merged, the net is then merged with net long-term capital gains.
**Example** :An investor sold land that was owned for 4 months at a $10,000 profit The sale was the investor's only capital transaction that year, so the $10,000 *short-term capital gain* is added to ordinary income.
   The difference in tax treatment of various kinds of income has been diminished by the Tax Reform Act of 1986 which generally taxes all income at the same rate. Consequently, short- and long-term capital gains are, in general, taxed at the same rate after 1987.

**TABLE 38**

|              | Building area, sq ft | Anchor tenant |
|--------------|----------------------|---------------|
| Neighborhood | 30,000–100,000       | supermarket or drugstore |
| Community    | 100,000–500,000      | junior department store and supermarket |
| Regional     | 500,000–1,000,000    | at least one major department store |
| Superregional| over 1,000,000       | several major department stores |

**SIMPLE INTEREST** a method of calculating the future value of a sum assuming that interest paid is not compounded, i.e., that interest is paid only on the **principal.** See also **compound interest.**

**Example:** An account is established paying *simple interest* of 10% on a principal of $1,000. Table 39 shows the current value of the account for the next 5 years.

**TABLE 39**

| Year | Value |
|------|-------|
| 1    | $1100 |
| 2    | 1200  |
| 3    | 1300  |
| 4    | 1400  |
| 5    | 1500  |

**SINGLE-FAMILY HOUSING** a type of residential structure designed to include one **dwelling.** Adjacent units may share walls and other structural components but generally have separate access to the outside and do not share plumbing and heating equipment.

**Example:** *Single-family housing* includes:
• **detached housing** units
• **town houses**
• **zero lot line** homes

**SINKING FUND** an account that, when compounded, will equal a specified sum after a specified time period. See **compound interest.**

**Example:** The Johnsons wish to buy a home 3 years from now. They estimate the **down payment** will equal $5,000. To accumulate the necessary money, they set up a *sinking fund* at the local bank. At 5% interest, the fund requires monthly deposits of $129. After 36 payments, the account will contain $5,000.

**SITE** a plot of land prepared for or underlying a structure or development. The location of a property.
**Example:** The Smith Building is located on a half-**acre** *site* in downtown Smithville. Several new buildings are being constructed on *sites* nearby.

**SITE PLAN** a document which describes how a parcel of land is to be improved. It includes the outlines of all structures and site improvements, such as driveways, parking lots, landscaping and utility connections.
**Example:** The *site plan* indicates that the office tower will be set back 100 feet from the street and be surrounded by surface parking for 2,000 cars.

**SITUS** the economic attributes of location, including the relationship between the property and surrounding properties, as well as distant points of interest and the linkages to those points. *Situs* is considered to be the aspect of location that contributes to the market value of a real property.
**Example:** The *situs* of a commercial property includes surrounding commercial establishments, the location of suppliers' warehouses, competing establishments, and the homes of employees and customers.

**SMALL BUSINESS ADMINISTRATION (SBA)** a federal government agency in Washington, D.C. that encourages small business.
**Example:** The *SBA* offers low-interest rate loans to qualified businessmen and businesswomen.
**Address:**
Small Business Administration
1441 L Street, N.W.
Washington, D.C. 20416

**SOCIETY OF INDUSTRIAL REALTORS® (SIR)** an organization, affiliated with the **National Association of Realtors®**, whose members are mainly concerned with the sale of warehouses, factories, and other **industrial property.** Confers SIR designation. Publishes *SIR Market Letter* (bimonthly) and *SIR Newsletter* (monthly).
**Address:**
Society of Industrial Realtors®
925 Fifteenth Street, N.W.
Washington, D.C. 20005

**SOCIETY OF REAL ESTATE APPRAISERS (SREA)** an organization in Chicago, Illinois dedicated to professionalism in real estate **appraisal.** They award designations, **SRA, SRPA, SREA.**
Address:
Society of Real Estate Appraisers
645 N. Michigan Avenue
Chicago, Illinois 60611

**SOFT MONEY** 1. in a development or an investment, money contributed that is **tax-deductible.**
**Example: Equity** required for a development is $100,000, of which 50% is promised to be tax-deductible and therefore is *soft money.*
2. sometimes used to describe costs that do not physically go into construction, such as interest during construction, architect's fees, legal fees, etc.

**SOIL BANK** land held out of agricultural production in an effort to stabilize commodity prices and promote soil conservation. Subsidies to farmers participating in the soil bank program are provided by the U.S. Department of Agriculture.
**Example:** A farmer normally plants her land in corn. To avoid a surplus of corn production, the federal government pays the farmer to hold the land out of production for a year. The farmer is participating in the *soil bank* program.

**SOLAR HEATING, HOT WATER** see **active solar heating, passive solar heating.**

**SOLE PROPRIETORSHIP** ownership of a business, with no formal entity as a vehicle or structure. Contrast **corporation, limited partnership, partnership.**
**Example:** Jessica goes into the real estate appraising business with all business activities in her own name and no partners. She is a *sole proprietor.*

**SOUTHERN COLONIAL** a large, early American style, 2 or 3-story frame house with a characteristic colonnade extending across the front. The roof extends over the colonnade.
**Example:** Figure 162.

**SPANISH VILLA** a Latin style, asymmetrical, 1- to 3-story house with painted stucco exterior walls and red tile roof.
**Example:** Figure 163.

**SPEC HOUSE** a **single-family** dwelling constructed in anticipation of finding a buyer.
**Example:** Keene, a **developer,** is convinced there is local demand for 3-bedroom houses priced in the $80,000 range. Keene therefore

constructs a number of *spec houses* and mounts a marketing campaign.

FIGURE 162

FIGURE 163

**SPECIAL AGENT** one who is engaged to act for another, with limited authority.
   **Example:** A real estate **broker,** engaged by an owner to find a buyer, is considered a *special agent* of the owner.

**SPECIAL ASSESSMENT** an **assessment** made against a property to pay for a public **improvement** by which the assessed property is supposed to be especially benefited.
**Example:** The Lawsons own a house in a developing section of the city. When the city constructs curbs and gutters along their street, the Lawsons are levied a *special assessment*, in the form of a one-time tax, to pay for the construction.

**SPECIALIST IN REAL ESTATE SECURITIES (SRS)** a professional designation awarded by the **Real Estate Securities and Syndication Institute (RESSI).** Qualification is based on experience, education, examination, and demonstration of expertise in preparing a **syndication** report.

**SPECIAL USE PERMIT** a right granted by a local **zoning** authority to conduct certain activities within a zoning district. Such activities are considered conditional uses, which are permitted within the zone only upon special approval of the zoning authority. Also termed a "conditional use permit."
**Example:** A local government allows, as a conditional use, the operation of parking lots within its high-**density** residential zoning districts. A landowner wishing to operate a parking lot must obtain a *special use permit* following review of the plans of the development.

**SPECIAL WARRANTY DEED** a **deed** in which the **grantor** limits the title **warranty** given to the **grantee** to anyone claiming by, from, through, or under him, the grantor. The grantor does not warrant against **title** defects arising from conditions that existed before he owned the property. See **warranty deed.**
**Example:** Because of **bankruptcy** of its owner, a property goes under trusteeship. When the property is sold to satisfy creditor claims, the **trustee** conveys a *special warranty deed* to the buyer. This provides the buyer with warranty against claims incurred only during the time the property was held by the trustee.

**SPECIFICATIONS** detailed instructions provided in conjunction with plans and blueprints for construction. Specifications may stipulate the type of materials to be used, special construction techniques, dimensions, and colors.
**Example:** The building *specifications* state that:
• number 3 lumber shall be used for all framing
• studs are to be on 16-inch centers
• all exterior surfaces shall be painted white

**SPECIFIC PERFORMANCE** a legal action in which the court requires a party to a **contract** to perform the **terms** of the contract when he has refused to fulfill his obligations. Used in real estate, since each **parcel** of land is unique.

**Example:** Baker agrees in writing to sell his house to Abel. Baker changes his mind when his adult daughter decides to buy the house. Baker offers to refund Abel's **earnest money** and pay living expenses for one month, but Abel insists on buying the house as agreed and sues for *specific performance.*

**SPECULATOR** one who invests with the anticipation that an event or series of events wil occur to increase the value of the investment.
**Example:** The value of **single-family houses** has been appreciating rapidly for several months. Munson, a *speculator,* purchases several houses in anticipation that this rapid rate of **appreciation** will continue.

**SPENDABLE INCOME** same as **after-tax cash flow.**

**SPOT ZONING** the act of rezoning a **parcel** of land where all surrounding parcels are zoned for a different use, in particular where the rezoning creates a use which is incompatible with surrounding land uses. Spot **zoning** is generally disallowed in the courts.
**Example:** Figure 164 may be construed as *spot zoning.*

FIGURE 164

**SPREAD** 1. the difference between the **bid** price and **asking price.**
**Example:** The buyer offers to pay $1,000 per **acre,** but the seller asks $1,300. The *spread* is $300.
2. the difference between the cost of money and the earnings rate.
**Example:** Good Money Savings and Loan pays an average interest rate of 10% to its depositors. It earns an average of 12% on its investments. The 2 point *spread* is adequate to pay **operating expenses** and leave some profit.

**SPREADING AGREEMENT** an agreement that extends the **collateral** of a loan to include several properties.
**Example:** Abel owns 7 shopping centers; all have **first mortgages.** He wants to borrow $5 million from a lender. The lender insists he

sign a *spreading agreement* that gives a second **lien** on all 7 shopping centers.

**SQUARE FOOTAGE** the area, measured in square feet, of a piece of **real estate.** Generally measured from outside the exterior walls in the case of structures.
**Example:** The outside dimension of a rectangular home is 40 × 50 feet. Its *square footage* is 2,000.

**SQUATTER'S RIGHTS** the legal allowance to use the property of another in absence of an attempt by the owner to force **eviction;** this right may eventually be converted to **title** to the property over time by **adverse possession,** if recognized by state law.
**Example:** Various poor families take up residence in a vacant building, acquiring *squatter's rights.* Since ownership of the property is uncertain, no one attempts to evict the families.

**SRA** a person who is a Senior Residential Appraiser, a designation awarded by the **Society of Real Estate Appraisers** for residential **appraisers.**
**Example:** To assure that the appraiser was ethical and qualified, Good Money Savings Association engaged one with the *SRA* designation.

**SREA** Senior Real Estate Analyst, the highest designation awarded by the **Society of Real Estate Appraisers.**
**Example:** A complicated **condemnation** of multiuse properties required the services of an *SREA.*

**SRPA** Senior Real Property Appraiser. Awarded by the **Society of Real Estate Appraisers** to those qualified to appraise **residential** and income-producing **property.**
**Example:** The *SRPA* is careful in estimating the **market value** of the subject office building. She considers all **appraisal** approaches before arriving at a value estimate.

**STANDARD METROPOLITAN STATISTICAL AREA (SMSA)** a designation of the U.S. Census Bureau for **metropolitan areas** with a central city having a specified minimum population (50,000 in the 1970 census) and including all counties that are economically linked to the central city. Statistics compiled for the SMSA are considered more descriptive of the importance of a city than those for the political jurisdiction of the city only.
**Example:** In 1980, the city of Houston had a population of 1.5 million. The Houston *standard metropolitan statistical area,* which included 6 counties, had a population of almost 3 million.

**STANDBY FEE** the sum required by a lender to provide a standby **commitment.** See **standby loan.** The fee is **forfeited** should the loan not be closed within a specified time.

**Example:** A **developer** obtains a **standby loan** on a project to be developed. The developer hopes **interest rates** will decline during the construction period so that permanent **financing** may be arranged with **terms** better than those on the standby loan. However, a permanent loan commitment is required to obtain a **construction loan.** The developer pays a *standby fee* to compensate the lender for making the standby loan commitment. At the completion of construction, the developer has the **option** of exercising the standby commitment or forfeiting the fee.

**STANDBY LOAN** a **commitment** by a lender to make available a sum of money at specified terms for a specified period. A **standby fee** is charged for this commitment. The borrower retains the **option** of closing the loan or allowing the commitment to lapse.
**Example:** See **standby fee.**

**STATUTE** a law established by an act of legislature.
**Example:** When a bill is passed by the legislature and signed by the governor, it becomes a state *statute.* Similarly, when a bill is passed by Congress and signed by the President, it becomes a federal *statute.*

**STATUTE OF FRAUDS** a state law that provides that certain **contracts** must be in writing in order to be enforceable. Applied to **deeds, mortgages,** and other **real estate** contracts, with the exception of **leases** for periods shorter than one year.
**Example:** An oral contract for the sale of land is considered unenforceable under the *statute of frauds.*

**STATUTE OF LIMITATIONS** a specified statutory period after which a claimant is barred from enforcing his claim by suit.
**Example:** Abel bought a **limited partnership** interest in a real estate transaction. The **syndicator** failed to mention in the **prospectus** that the land is in a flood-prone area. Abel discovers the fact and sues 4 years later but is barred from collecting under the *statute of limitations.*

**STEERING** an illegal practice of limiting the housing shown to a certain ethnic group.
**Example:** Though the minority couple wanted to be shown all available rental housing that they could afford, the unlicensed person *steered* them from certain neighborhoods.

**STEPPED-UP BASIS** an income tax term used to describe a change in the **adjusted tax basis** of property, allowed for certain transactions. The old basis is increased to **market value** upon inheritance, as opposed to a **carry-over basis** in the event of a

tax-free exchange.
**Example:** Dooley dies, leaving land worth $100,000. The land was purchased for $20,000, but the heirs receive a *stepped-up basis* to the **fair market value** at death. The $80,000 **unrealized gain** to Dooley escapes **capital gains** tax.

**STEP-UP LEASE** see **graduated lease.**

**STICK STYLE OR CARPENTER GOTHIC** a nineteenth century style house with exposed framing members, high steep roofs, complex silhouettes, diagonal braces, and a large amount of gingerbread trim.
**Example:** Figure 165.

Exposed framing members
High steep roof
Lots of "Gingerbread"
Ornate windows and doors
Complex silhouette

FIGURE 165

**STIPULATIONS** the **terms** within a written **contract.**
**Example:** A sales contract contains *stipulations* concerning the type of **financing** the buyer must be able to obtain, the price, proration of **closing** cost between buyer and seller, and the date and location of the closing.

**STOP CLAUSE** in a **lease,** stipulates an amount of **operating expense** above which the tenant must bear. Often the base amount is the amount of expense for the first full year of operation under the lease.

**Example:** The *stop clause* requires the tenant to pay all **utilities in** excess of $2,500 per year. If utilities are less than that amount, the landlord pays them.

**STRAIGHT LEASE** see **flat lease.**

**STRAIGHT-LINE DEPRECIATION** equal annual reductions in the **book value** of property. It is used in accounting for replacement and tax purposes. See **depreciation (accounting).**

**Example:** A property has a **depreciable basis** of $275,000. For tax purposes, a **useful life** of 27½ years is used with no **salvage value.** Using *straight-line depreciation,* the book value of the property is decreased by $10,000 ($275,000/27.5) per year. The tax deduction for depreciation is $10,000 per year.

**STRAIGHT-LINE RECAPTURE RATE** the part of a **capitalization rate** that accounts for the annual erosion of a **wasting asset** by assuming an equal amount of loss in value each year of the **useful life** of the asset.

**Example:** A retail building's **useful life** is estimated at 50 years. The *straight-line recapture rate* is 2% per year, which will recover the asset cost over its estimated useful life. The 2% should be added to the **discount rate** to derive the **capitalization rate.**

**STRAW MAN** one who purchases property that is, in turn, **conveyed** to another for the purpose of concealing the identity of the eventual purchaser.

**Example:** A **developer** is assembling land, for a **subdivision,** from a large number of individually owned plots. To avoid the possibility that a few landowners will hold out for high prices, the developer uses *straw men* to purchase the **parcels. Agents** of the developer purchase plots in their own names and later convey the land to the developer.

**STRIP DEVELOPMENT** a form of commercial land use in which each establishment is afforded direct access to a major thoroughfare; generally associated with intensive use of signs to attract passersby.

**Example:** Map of *strip development* (Figure 166).

**STRUCTURE** any constructed improvement to a **site.**

**Examples:** *Structures* include:
- buildings
- fencing and enclosures
- garages

• gazebos, greenhouses, and kiosks
• sheds and utility buildings

| Auto parts store | Fast food | Tire store | Car wash | Service station |
|---|---|---|---|---|

| Fast food | Shoe store | Hardware store | Fast food |
|---|---|---|---|

FIGURE 166

**SUBCHAPTER S CORPORATION** a **corporation** with a limited number of stockholders (35 or fewer) that elects not to be taxed as a regular corporation, and meets certain other requirements. Shareholders include, in their personal tax return, their pro-rata share of **capital gains, ordinary income, tax preference** items, and so on. See **passive income.**
**Example:** To avoid **double taxation,** the ABC Real Estate Corporation elects *Subchapter S* status. Its shareholders will include corporate income in their own tax return, whether or not they receive a dividend. The corporation itself will not pay an income tax, but will file a tax return.

**SUBCONTRACTOR** one who performs services under **contract** to a **general contractor.**
**Example:** A general contractor agrees to construct a building for a **developer.** The contractor arranges with individual *subcontractors* who are specifically responsible to the contractor for performance of carpentry, plumbing, electrical, and masonry work.

**SUBDIVIDER** one who partitions a **tract** of land for the purpose of selling the individual plots. If the land is improved in any way, the subdivider becomes a **developer.**
**Example:** Olsen, a *subdivider,* purchases a 100-acre tract of land. The tract is subdivided into 5-acre plots that are marketed to investors and developers.

**SUBDIVIDING** dividing a **tract** of land into smaller tracts.
**Example:** See **subdivider.**

**SUBDIVISION a tract** of land divided into lots suitable for home-
building purposes. Some states and localities require that a subdivision **plat** be recorded.
**Example:** A residential *subdivision* (Figure 167).

Access
road

FIGURE 167

**SUBJECT PROPERTY** in appraisal, the property being appraised.
**Example:** The *subject property* compares favorably with other
homes in the neighborhood.

**SUBJECT TO** acquiring property with an existing mortgage, but not
becoming **personally liable** for the debt. Contrast with **assumption
of mortgage.**
**Example:** Abel bought **land** for $1,000 cash, *subject to* a $99,000
mortgage. If Abel defaults on the **mortgage** he will lose the cash
**down payment** but is not responsible for the $99,000 **debt.**

**SUBJECT TO MORTGAGE** circumstance in which a buyer takes
**title** to mortgaged **real property** but is not personally liable for the
payment of the amount due. The buyer must make payments in
order to keep the property; however, with default, only the buyer's **equity** in that property is lost. Contrast **assumption of mortgage.**
**Example:** Queen purchases a house from Parsons *subject to* the
existing *mortgage*. Parson's mortgage has an outstanding balance
of $40,000 and the sales price is $60,000. Queen pays Parsons
$20,000 in cash and takes over the payments on the mortgage.
Should Queen **default,** Parsons is liable under the **promissory note**
given to the lender.

**SUBLEASE** a lease from a lessee to another lessee. The new lessee is a sublessee or subtenant. See **sandwich lease.**
**Example:** Acme, Inc., leases office space under a 10-year lease. Acme wishes to relocate but cannot break the lease. With the landlord's permission, Acme finds a subtenant, Medcorp, to sign a *sublease* for the space. Medcorp pays rent to Acme, which, in turn, continues to pay rent to the landlord.

**SUBLET** see **sublease.**

**SUBORDINATION** moving to a lower **priority,** as a **lien** would if it changes from a **first mortgage** to a **second mortgage.**
**Example:** The land seller who held a first mortgage allowed *subordination* so the **development loan** could be arranged. In return, the seller is promised mortgage **retirement** in 2 years.

**SUBORDINATION CLAUSE** a clause or document that permits a **mortgage** recorded at a later date to take **priority** over an existing mortgage.
**Example:** Even though the **first mortgage** was recently **retired, the second mortgage** remained a second mortgage. The *subordination clause* in the second mortgage provided that a mortgage that replaces the existing first mortgage will become a first mortgage; the second mortgage will not move up in priority.

**SUBSTITUTION** in appraisal, the principle that market value is indicated by the value of another property with similar utility. A typical buyer is assumed to be indifferent to substituting one property for the other.
**Example:** By the principle of *substitution,* the market value of a property can be estimated by analyzing sales prices of comparable properties.

**SUBSURFACE RIGHTS** same as **mineral rights.**

**SUBURB** a town or unincorporated developed area in close proximity to a city. Suburbs, largely residential, are often dependent on the city for employment and support services; generally characterized by low-**density** development relative to the city.
**Example:** Figure 168.

**SUMMARY POSSESSION** same as **eviction, actual.**

**SUM-OF-YEARS-DIGITS DEPRECIATION** in tax and accounting, a method of allocating the cost of an **asset** over its **useful life.** It requires a fraction to be computed each year, which is applied against the depreciable amount. The numerator is the number of years left to be depreciated. The denominator is the sum of the years digits of the depreciable life. The formula for the denominator is:

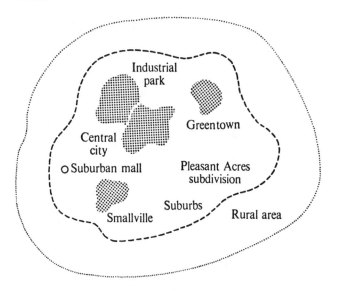

FIGURE 168

$$\frac{N(N + 1)}{2}$$

where N = the depreciable life. See **accelerated depreciation.**
**Example:** An automobile used in business cost $10,000 and has a
4-year depreciable life. *Sum-of-the-years-digits depreciation*
results in the deductions shown in Table 40.

TABLE 40

| Year | Fraction | Asset | Depreciation deduction |
|------|----------|-------|------------------------|
| 1 | 4/10 | $10,000 | $4,000 |
| 2 | 3/10 | 10,000 | 3,000 |
| 3 | 2/10 | 10,000 | 2,000 |
| 4 | 1/10 | 10,000 | 1,000 |

**SUMP** as part of a drainage system, a pit in the basement to collect
excess moisture and liquids. To avoid flooding, a *sump* pump may
be installed to remove accumulated water in the sump pit.
**Example:** Figure 169

FIGURE 169

**SUNSPACE** a room, generally with glass walls and roof, designed to collect solar heat.
**Example:** By adding a *sunspace* to the south side of their home, the Sols were able to save money on their winter heating bills.

**SURETY** one who guarantees the performance of another.
**Example:** Ridley employs a **contractor** to construct a house. Under the **contract,** the contractor is required to obtain a **performance bond** against failure to perform the work. Ace Bonding Co. provides the bond, thereby acting as a *surety*. Should the contractor fail to perform, Ace compensates Ridley for damages.

**SURRENDER** the cancellation of a **lease** by mutual consent of the **lessor** and the **lessee.**
**Example:** Simmons rents a house under a 2-year lease. Simmons is forced to move due to a job transfer. The landlord agrees to allow Simmons to *surrender* the **premises** if Simmons finds an acceptable new tenant.

**SURVEY** 1. the process by which a **parcel** of land is measured and its area ascertained. 2. the plan showing the measurements, boundaries, area, and contours.
**Example:** A simplified *survey* (Figure 170).

**SURVEYOR** one who prepares **surveys.**
**Example:** Prior to selling her property, Collins had to hire a *surveyor* to prepare a survey of the land.

**SURVIVORSHIP** the right of a joint tenant or tenants to maintain ownership rights following the death of another joint tenant. Survivorship prevents heirs of the deceased from making claims against the property. See **joint tenancy.**
**Example:** Travers and Vance Mead are brothers who own an

apartment building, with the right of survivorship. When Travers Mead dies, Vance Mead, through *survivorship,* becomes sole owner of the building.

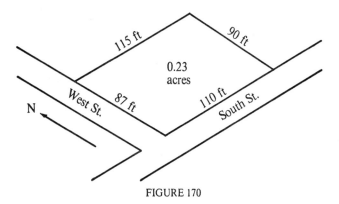

FIGURE 170

**SWEAT EQUITY** value added to a property due to **improvements** as a result of work performed personally by the owner.
**Example:** The Watsons purchase an old house for $20,000. Working in their spare time, the Watsons repair and repaint the structure to the point that the property is valued at $30,000. The $10,000 increment is *sweat equity.*

**SWISS CHALET** a Swiss style 1½- to 2½-story, gable roof house with extensive natural decorative woodwork on the exterior.
**Example:** Figure 171.

**SYNDICATION** a method of selling property whereby a sponsor (or **syndicator**) sells interests to investors. May take the form of a **partnership, limited partnership, tenancy in common, corporation,** or **subchapter S Corporation.**
**Example:** A *syndication* was formed whereby limited partnership interests were sold to investors. The partnership bought land with the **equity** raised.

**SYNDICATOR** a person in business who sells an investment in shares or units.
**Example:** Collins, licensed as both a real estate **broker** and a **securities** salesperson, is a *syndicator.* She contracts with investors to buy shopping centers, then sells **partnership** interests conveying ownership in the centers to 30 different investors.

Natural wood look

Gable roof

1½ to 2½ stories

Decorative wood work

Large glass windows

Open porches

Curved cornice

FIGURE 171

# T

**TACKING** adding on to a time period.
  **Example:** A squatter was on property for 10 years, moved away for one year, then returned for 10 years. If he were allowed to *tack* both 10-year periods, his claim to **squatter's rights** to the land would be a strong one.

**TAKEOUT FINANCING** a **commitment** to provide permanent **financing** following construction of a planned project. The takeout commitment is generally predicated upon specific conditions, such as a certain percentage of unit sales or leases, for the permanent loan to "takeout" the **construction loan.** Most construction lenders require takeout financing.
  **Example:** Young, a developer, applied for a construction loan on a small office building. The construction lender requires Young to obtain *takeout financing* in the form of a commitment from a permanent lender. The takeout loan will be granted following con-

struction and leasing of at least 65% of **net rentable area** to credit-worthy tenants.

**TAKING** 1. acquisition of a **parcel** of land through **condemnation.**
**Example:** The Highway Department acquires much of its **right-of-way** for new roads through *takings*. These are usually parcels whose owners are unwilling to settle on a price through negotiation.
2. in land use law, application of **police power** restrictions to a parcel of land that are so restrictive as to preclude any reasonable use.
**Example:** A local community zones a parcel of land for agricultural use. The owner argues the land is unsuitable for growing crops but could be used for building homes. The owner's argument is the **zoning** is a *taking* of the property without just compensation, which is contrary to the Fourteenth Amendment to the U.S. Constitution.

**TANDEM PLAN** a program of the **Government National Mortgage Association (GNMA)** working together with the **Federal National Mortgage Association (FNMA)** to provide low interest rate home loans.
**Example:** Under the *tandem* plan, FNMA purchases qualified low-interest rate mortgages at a discount from GNMA. GNMA absorbs the loss as a subsidy to the qualified low-income home buyer.

**TANGIBLE PROPERTY** real estate and other valuables which can be seen and touched.
**Example:** A home, farm, furniture and fixtures are types of *tangible properties*. In contrast, a deed, mortgage, or stock certificate are intangibles in that they represent ownership in something but are not the thing itself.

**TAX** a charge levied upon persons or things by a government.
**Example:**
• ad valorem *tax*
• county *tax*
• excise *tax*
• income *tax*
• property *tax*
• sales *tax*
• school *tax*
• use *tax*

**TAXABLE VALUE** see **assessed value.**

**TAX AND INSURANCE ESCROW** an account required by a mortgage lender to fund annual property tax assessments and hazard

insurance premiums for the mortgaged property. Funded through monthly contributions by the mortgagor. See **PITI.**
**Example:** When the mortgage loan was originated, a *tax and insurance escrow* was set up by the lender to pay tax and insurance expenses. The borrower's monthly mortgage payment was increased by an amount necessary to accumulate a balance in the account sufficient to cover these expenses.

**TAX ASSESSOR** see **assessor.**

**TAX BASE** the collective value of property, income or other taxable activity or assets subject to a tax. Tax revenues are computed as the tax base times the tax rate. For property taxation, the tax base is the total assessed value of all taxable property less exemptions.
**Example:** American Widgetworks plans to build a new plant in Centerville. The plant will add $15 million to the property *tax base* of the city.

**TAX BASIS** same as **basis (tax);** see **adjusted tax basis.**

**TAX BRACKET** marginal rate for income taxes; the percentage of each additional dollar in income required to be paid as income taxes.
**Example:** Abel is considering an investment that will produce $1,000 in taxable income for the next year. Abel's taxable income is currently $20,000, which places Abel in the 28% *tax bracket.* Thus, should Abel make the investment, $280 of the $1,000 will be paid in taxes.

**TAX CREDIT** a reduction against income tax payments that would otherwise be due. Contrast with **tax deductions** that reduce taxable income.
**Example:** *Tax credits* that are available to real estate owners include:
• rehabilitation tax credits for older properties and **historic structures**
• low income housing .

**TAX DEDUCTIBLE** a type of expense that can be used to reduce taxable income. See **tax deduction.**
**Example:** Interest and ad valorem taxes are generally *tax deductible* for all types of property. **Depreciation,** repairs, **maintenance, utilities,** and other ordinary and necessary expenses are *tax deductible* for **income property.**

**TAX DEDUCTION** one that can be used to reduce taxable income. See **tax deductible.** Contrast with **tax credit.**
**Example:** Abel has a $75,000 annual salary and $25,000 worth of *tax deductions.* Taxes for the year are figured on taxable income of $50,000.

**TAX DEED** the type of instrument given to a **grantee** by a government that had claimed the **property** for unpaid taxes.

**Example:** The city acquired a **parcel** of land because the former owner failed to pay **ad valorem** taxes. The city then auctioned it. Baker, the highest bidder, received a *tax deed* as evidence of ownership.

**TAX-EXEMPT PROPERTY** real **property** that is not subject, in whole or in part, to **ad valorem** property taxes.
**Examples:** In many local communities, the following types of property are *tax-exempt property:*
• churches
• government land and buildings
• **homesteads** (in part)
• solar-powered heating systems

**TAX FORECLOSURE** the process of enforcing a lien against property for nonpayment of delinquent property taxes. Taxing authorities hold a superior lien against all taxable property to enforce the payment of their taxes. See **foreclosure.**
**Example:** The owner of the old apartment house had failed to pay property taxes on the building for the past 2 years. The county was forced to pursue a *tax foreclosure* against the property and have it sold at auction.

**TAX-FREE EXCHANGE** same as tax-deferred exchange.

**TAX LIEN** a **debt** attached against **property** for failing to pay taxes.
**Example:** A *tax lien* may be imposed for failing to pay the following taxes:
• city
• county
• estate
• income
• payroll
• sales
• school

**TAX MAP** a document showing the location, dimensions, and other information pertaining to a **parcel** of land subject to **property taxes.** Maps are generally bound into books and kept as public records at the local tax office.
**Example:** A *tax map* showing parcel 65 in district A5-300 (Figure 172).

**TAX PREFERENCE ITEMS** certain types of **income** or deductions that are added to adjusted **gross income** to calculate the **alternative minimum tax.**
**Examples:** *Tax preference items* in 1987 and thereafter include:
• **depreciation** on **real estate** to the extent it exceeds 40-year **straight-line depreciation**

- **accelerated depreciation** on leased **personal property** to the extent it exceeds **straight-line depreciation**
- bargain element of an incentive stock option
- certain rapid write-offs
- losses from passive activity investment
- certain itemized deductions (state and local income taxes, real estate taxes, medical expenses not greater than 10% of adjusted gross income)
- miscellaneous deductions in excess of 2% of adjusted gross income
- all interest expense, except home mortgage interest and investment interest, to the extent of net investment income
- interest on certain tax exempt bonds issued after August 7, 1986
- the excess of value deducted over the cost of property given to charitable organizations.

FIGURE 172

**TAX RATE** the ratio of a tax **assessment** to the amount being taxed.

**Example:** In a certain community, the *tax rate* for **property taxes** is $0.35 per $100 of **assessed value**. A home is valued at $20,000. A **homestead exemption** of $2,000 is allowed for this type of property. The tax collected is

$$\$0.35 \times \frac{(\$20,000 - \$2,000)}{\$100} = \$63.00$$

**TAX ROLL** the list of all properties subject to a tax in a county or other property taxing jurisdiction. It identifies all properties and indicates their assessed values.

**Example:** A *tax roll* was prepared by the county tax assessor's office, showing $100 million worth of assessed value in the jurisdiction. The county commissioners needed to collect $1 million of taxes to run the government this year, so they applied a 10 mill tax rate to the tax roll.

**TAX SALE** the sale of property after a period of nonpayment of taxes. The **grantee** receives a **tax deed.** In most states the **defaulting** party has a **redemption period** during which he may pay the unpaid taxes, interest, court costs, and the purchase price to redeem the property.
**Example:** The failure to pay property **ad valorem** taxes resulted in a *tax sale* of Abel's land. Since the property was worth more than the back taxes, Abel erred by failing to pay.

**TAX SHELTER** an investment that produces after-tax income that is greater than before-tax income. The investment may produce **before-tax cash flow** while generating losses to shield, from taxation, income from sources outside the investment.
**Example:** Dunn purchases an income-producing property which provides *tax shelter*. In the first year, the property produces a **net operating income** of $100,000. **Debt service** is $80,000, of which $75,000 is **interest.** Dunn's **before-tax cash flow** is $20,000. First-year **depreciation** is $50,000, so that a tax loss is generated as shown in Table 41.

**TABLE 41**

| | |
|---|---|
| $100,000 | Net operating income |
| 75,000 | Interest deduction |
| 50,000 | Depreciation deduction |
| (25,000) | Taxable income (loss) |

Dunn not only pays no tax on the $20,000 cash flow but might be allowed to shelter $25,000 of income from other sources. The Tax Reform Act of 1986 places limits and restrictions on the deductibility of passive losses. See **passive income, active participation, material participation.**

**TAX STOP** a clause in a **lease** that stops a **lessor** from paying **property taxes** above a certain amount. See **escalator clause, stop clause.**
**Example:** The *tax stop* in the lease required the tenant to pay all property taxes in excess of $1,200.

**TEASER RATE** a contract interest rate charged on an adjustable rate mortgage for the initial adjustment interval that is significantly lower than the fully indexed rate at the time. It is an incentive to encourage borrowers to accept adjustable rate mortgage loans. In general, the interest rate reverts to the fully indexed rate at the first adjustment date. See **fully indexed rate.**

**Example:** An adjustable rate mortgage is indexed to the average contract rate for mortgage loans made by all lenders. Although the current average rate is 10%, the loan is offered at a *teaser rate* of 8%.

**TENANCY** the right of possession of real property. See **tenancy in common, joint tenancy.**

**TENANCY AT SUFFERANCE** tenancy established when a person who had been a lawful tenant wrongfully remains in **possession** of property after expiration of a **lease.**

**Example:** A *tenant at sufferance* may be ejected from the property anytime the landlord decides to do so.

**TENANCY AT WILL** a **license** to use or occupy lands and buildings at the will of the owner. The tenant may decide to leave the property at any time or must leave at the landlord's will. Agreement may be oral or written. See also **emblements.**

**Example:** Under an oral agreement, Abel is using Baker's property. Baker may ask Abel to leave at any time; Abel may leave at any time.

**TENANCY BY THE ENTIRETY** an **estate** that exists only between husband and wife with equal right of **possession** and enjoyment during their joint lives and with the **right of survivorship,** i.e., when one dies, the property goes to the surviving tenant. Recognized in some states.

**Example:** A married couple owns property as *tenants by the entirety.* Neither can convey his or her part of the property during their lives unless the other consents. Divorced spouses become tenants in common. See **tenancy in common.**

**TENANCY FOR YEARS** created by a **lease** for a fixed term, such as 2 months, 3 years, 10 years, and so on.

**Example:** Big Buy Groceries leased a building for 10 years, beginning April 1, 1984 and ending March 31, 1994, 10 years later. The company has a *tenancy for years.*

**TENANCY IN COMMON** an ownership of **realty** by 2 or more persons, each of whom has an **undivided interest,** without the right of **survivorship.** Upon the death of one of the owners, the ownership share of the decedent is inherited by the party or parties designated in the decedent's **will.** Compare **partition.** See **syndication.**

**Example:** A syndicate is formed using a *tenancy in common.* Under this arrangement all of the investors have to sign the **deed** for the entire property to be conveyed. Each tenant may convey his or her share independently.

**TENANCY IN SEVERALTY** ownership of property by one person or one legal entity (corporate ownership).
**Example:** Abel owns land as a *tenant in severalty*. He enjoys the absence of partners or cotenants.

**TENANT** one who is given possession of real estate for a fixed period or at will. See **lessee, tenancy at will.**
**Example:** Enwright signs a lease to rent office space. Enwright is a *tenant* of the office building.

**TENDER** 1. an offer to perform an obligation, together with actual performance or evidence of present ability to perform. 2. to perform under a contract 3. to pay or deliver.
**Example:** Abel thought Baker would default under the sales contract but did not know for certain until Baker *tendered* the deed.

**TENEMENTS** 1. possessions that are permanent and fixed; structures attached to land.
**Example:** Real property consists of *tenements* and hereditaments: tenements are the physical and legal property that may be enjoyed by the owner; hereditaments are property one can pass on to one's heirs.
2. older apartment units.
**Example:** In the inner city, many people live in *tenements*.

**TENURE** the nature of an occupant's ownership rights; an indication of whether one is an owner or a tenant.
**Example:** For economic analysis, one may differentiate the occupied housing stock by *tenure:* one portion may be owner-occupied; the other portion may be renter-occupied.

**TENURE IN LAND** the mode in which a person holds an estate in lands.
**Example:** If one purchases all rights to real estate, *tenure in land* is fee simple ownership. A tenant's *tenure in land* is a leasehold.

**TERM** the period of time during which something is in effect.
**Example:** Fowler leases an apartment for a *term* of one year. At the end of the year, Fowler moves from the apartment and buys a house. To finance the purchase, Fowler gets a mortgage loan with a *term* of 30 years. At the end of 30 years, the loan will be paid off.

**TERM, AMORTIZATION** for a loan, the period of time during which principal and interest payments must be made; generally the time needed to amortize the loan fully.
**Example:** *Amortization terms* of 25 and 30 years are commonly

used on real estate mortgage loans. Monthly principal and interest payments are set to fully liquidate loans over the **term.**

**TERMITE INSPECTION** an examination of a structure by qualified personnel to determine the existence of infestation by **termites.** Often required by the **terms** of a **sales contract.** See **wood-destroying insect.**
**Example:** Gross sells a house to Handy. As protection for Handy, the sales contract stipulates that a *termite inspection* will be performed at Gross' expense and the sale is contingent on a finding of no termite infestation.

**TERMITE CLAUSE** a provision in a sales contract that allows the buyer to have the property inspected for termite infestation. In general, if termites are discovered, the buyer may require the seller to treat the property or the buyer may cancel the contract. Most clauses now use the term **wood-destroying insects** to protect against other types of insects that harm structures, such as the powder post beetle and old house borer.
**Example:** Under the *termite clause* in the sales contract, the buyer may get the home inspected before the closing. The seller will pay to exterminate any termites found. The buyer pays for the inspection.

**TERMITES** insects that bore into wood and destroy it.
**Example:** *Termites* are a threat to any wooden structure or members of a structure. *Termites* generally act to weaken support members in proximity to the ground or in contact with it. *Termites* are often confused with winged adult ants. The differences are shown in Figure 173.

**TERM LOAN** one with a set maturity date, typically without **amortization.**
**Example:** Terry purchased a tract of land for $15,000, and borrowed $10,000 from a lender with a 5-year *term loan.* The interest rate is 10% annually; the entire principal is due at the end of the 5-year term.

**TERMS** conditions and arrangements specified in a **contract.**
**Example:** A **sales contract** will generally include *terms* relating to the price, **financing** available to the buyer, contingencies based on the condition of the property, **how to prorate closing costs,** and items of personal property included in the sale. See also **as is, cancellation clause, contingency clause.**

**TESTAMENT** a **will.** Generally to dispose of **personal property.** Common usage employs the words **will,** *testament,* and *last will and testament* as synonyms.
**Example:** Ewen wrote her *testament* that directed the disposition of her property upon her death.

**TESTATE** having made a valid **will.** Contrast **intestate.**

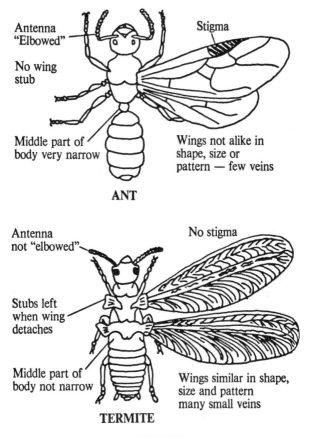

Antenna "Elbowed"

Stigma

No wing stub

Middle part of body very narrow

Wings not alike in shape, size or pattern — few veins

**ANT**

Antenna not "elbowed"

No stigma

Stubs left when wing detaches

Middle part of body not narrow

Wings similar in shape, size and pattern many small veins

**TERMITE**

FIGURE 173

**Example:** A person who dies *testate* has left a will disposing of property.

**TESTATOR** a person who makes a **will**.
  **Example:** By will the *testator* left his property to his wife.

**TESTATRIX** a woman who makes a **will**.
  **Example:** By will the *testatrix* left her property to her husband.

**TESTIMONIUM** a clause that cites the act and date in a **deed** or other **conveyance.** Before signing a deed, the grantor should make sure that everything is in order, e.g., the spelling of names and legal descriptions. This is the *testimonium* clause.

**Example:** *Testimonium* clause: "In witness whereof, the parties to these presents have hereunto set their hands and seals this day and year written above."

**THIRD PARTY** one who is not directly involved in a transaction or **contract** but may be involved or affected by it.

**Example:** An apartment owner sells the property to a **condominium** converter. The **tenants,** as *third parties,* may be forced to move or buy their units at the expiration of their **lease.**

**Example:** A trusted *third party* was designated as **escrow** agent by the **principals.**

**TIME IS OF THE ESSENCE** a phrase that, when inserted in a **contract,** requires that all references to specific dates and times of day noted in the contract be interpreted exactly. In its absence extreme delays might be acceptable.

**Example:** A **sales contract** contains the clause: *time is of the essence.* This statement reinforces the content of other clauses, such as the time provided to the buyer to arrange **financing** and the date of **closing.**

**TIME-SHARING** a form of property ownership under which a **property** is held by a number of people, each with the right of **possession** for a specified time interval. Time-sharing is most commonly applied to resort and vacation properties.

**Example:** Ingram is an owner in a *time-sharing* arrangement for a lakefront cottage. Ingram is entitled to use the cottage each year from July 1 to July 15. Use of the property during the remainder of the year is divided among other owners. All property expenses are paid by an owner's association to which Ingram pays an annual fee.

**TITLE** evidence that the owner of land is in lawful **possession** thereof; evidence of ownership. See also **adverse possession,** certificate of title, **clear title, color of title, cloud on the title, marketable title.**

**Example:** *Title* to land does not merely imply that a person has the right of **possession,** because one may have the right to possession and have no title. Title does ordinarily signify rights to possession in addition to evidence of ownership.

**Example:** Abel sold land to Baker. *Title* to the **property** was transferred at closing by the deed Baker received.

**TITLE ABSTRACT** see abstract of title.

**TITLE COMPANY** one in the business of examining **title** to real

estate and/or issuing **title insurance.**
**Example:** The Chicago Lawyer Title Company searched courthouse records to be sure that Whitman would get **marketable title** on a house she planned to buy. They charged a $500 one-time **premium.** The bank wouldn't issue a loan without the policy.

**TITLE DEFECT** an unresolved claim against the ownership of property which prevents presentation of a marketable title. Such claims may arise from failure of the owner's spouse, or former part owner, to sign a deed, current liens against the property, or an interruption in the title records to a property. See **cloud on the title.**
**Example:** Prior to the closing, the attorney for the title insurance company discovered a *title defect* which delayed the transaction. It seems the property had once been owned by the seller's parents and a deed had never been signed over to the seller.

**TITLE INSURANCE** an insurance policy that protects the holder from loss sustained by **defects in the title.**
**Example:** When property is purchased, most **mortgage** lenders require the buyer to obtain *title insurance*. After a satisfactory **title search** and in exchange for a one-time **premium**, the title company insures the buyer against most claims to the title of the property.

**TITLE REPORT** a document indicating the current state of the **title**, such as **easements, covenants, liens** and any **defects.** The title report does not describe the **chain of title.** See **abstract of title.**
**Example:** A buyer wishes to assure receipt of **clear title** to a property. The buyer authorizes a *title search* by an experienced attorney. The attorney examines the public records for all recorded encumbrances and past claims. The attorney renders to the buyer an **abstract of the title.**

**TITLE SEARCH** an examination of the public records to determine the ownership and **encumbrances** affecting **real property.**
**Example:** A buyer wishes to assure receiving **clear title** to a property. The buyer authorizes a *title search* by an experienced attorney. The attorney examines the public records for all recorded encumbrances and past claims. The attorney renders to the buyer an **abstract of the title.**

**TITLE THEORY STATES** states in which the law splits the **title** of mortgaged property into legal title, held by the lender, and **equitable title,** held by the borrower. The borrower gains full title to the property upon **retiring** the mortgage debt. The lender is granted more immediate cure to a **default** than in **lien theory states.** Contrast **lien theory states.**
**Example:** In *title theory states,* mortgage lenders may possess the

property upon default of the borrower. In **lien theory states,** lenders must go through the process of **foreclosure.**

**TOPOGRAPHY** the state of the surface of the land; may be rolling, rough, flat, etc.
**Example:** The *topography* in Oklahoma is mostly flat; in West Virginia, mountainous; in Ohio, rolling.

**TORRENS SYSTEM** a **title** registration system used in some states; the condition of the **title** can easily be discovered without resorting to a **title search.**
**Example:** A property owner in Chicago wishes to register the property under the *Torrens System.* An application is made with the appropriate court. Following a title examination and **notice to** all who wish to make a claim, the court issues a **certificate of title** setting forth the nature of the applicant's title. When the owner sells the property, a new certificate is issued to the buyer. Anyone establishing a claim to the property following registration is compensated from a special fund for any losses suffered.

**TORT** a wrongful act that is neither a crime nor a **breach of contract,** but that renders the perpetrator **liable** to the victim for damages.
**Examples:**
• **nuisance**
• **trespass**
• negligence
An example of negligence is a landlord's failure to fix reported defective wiring. The law provides remedy for damages from resulting fire.

**TOWN HOUSE** a **dwelling** unit, generally having 2 or more floors and attached to other similar units via **party walls.** Town houses are often used in **planned unit developments** and **condominium** developments, which provide for clustered or attached housing and common open space. See **cluster housing, row house, brownstone.**
**Example:** Figure 174.

**TOWNSHIP** a 6-mile square **tract** delineated by **government rectangular survey.**
**Example:** 16 *townships* (Figure 175).

**TRACT** a **parcel** of land, generally held for **subdividing;** a **subdivision.**
**Example:** Reynolds, a **subdivider** purchases a *tract* of land. For marketing purposes, she subdivides the *tract* into lots (Figure 176).

FIGURE 174

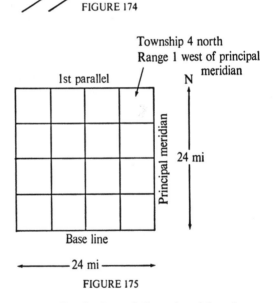

Township 4 north
Range 1 west of principal meridian

1st parallel

N

Principal meridian

24 mi

Base line

— 24 mi —

FIGURE 175

**TRACT HOUSE** a dwelling that has a similar style and **floor plan** to those of all other houses in a development. Contrast **custom builder.**
**Example:** Pleasant Acres is a **subdivision** of *tract houses*. Each home is a 3-bedroom ranch style house with the same basic floor plan.

**TRADE FIXTURE** articles placed in rented buildings by the tenant to help carry out trade or business. The tenant can remove the

**fixtures** before the expiration of the **lease,** but if the tenant fails to do so shortly after the lease expires, the fixtures become the landlord's property.
**Examples:** *Trade fixtures* include:
• bar stools
• neon signs
• decorative or functional light fixtures
• stoves and refrigerators

FIGURE 176

**TRAILER PARK** same as **mobile home park.**

**TRANSACTION COSTS** the costs associated with buying and selling **real estate.**
**Examples:** The following are *transaction costs:*
• **appraisal** fees
• **brokerage** commission
• legal fees
• mortgage **discount points**
• mortgage **origination fees**
• **recording** fees
• **survey** fees
• **title search**

**TRANSFER DEVELOPMENT RIGHTS** a type of **zoning ordinance** that allows owners of property zoned for low-density development or conservation use to sell development rights to other property owners. The development rights purchased permit the landowners to develop their **parcels** at higher **densities** than otherwise. The system is designed to provide for low-density uses, such as historic preservation, without unduly penalizing some landowners.
**Example:** Under a *transfer development rights* system, a land-

owner whose property is restricted to open space is assigned development rights in proportion to some overall desirable density for the jurisdiction. The landowner cannot utilize the rights but may sell them on the open market to landowners in other locations who are allowed to develop their properties. The rights may be used to develop additional structures on the unrestricted properties. In this way, restricted areas may be maintained as open space without completely destroying the development value of the properties.

**TRANSFER TAX** one paid upon the passing of **title** to property or to a valuable **interest.**
**Example:** In a state that imposes a high *transfer tax* on the sale of **real estate,** the seller formed a **corporation** as the owner of a valuable building and sold stock that was subject to a lower transfer tax. The state is claiming that it was a sale of real estate.

**TRESPASS** unlawful entry or **possession** of property.
**Example:** Thompson rents an apartment from Turner. When Thompson is away, Turner enters with a passkey and checks on the apartment's condition. Even though Turner owns the property, he is guilty of *trespass,* since the right to possession has been granted to Thompson exclusively. It is possible for Turner to reserve the right to enter the property periodically.
**Example:** Smith fenced in his farm and posted signs to prevent *trespass* by hunters.

**TRIPLE-NET LEASE** one in which the tenant is to pay all **operating expenses** of the property; the landlord receives a net rent.
**Example:** Big Buy Supermarkets enters into a *triple-net lease.* They are to pay for all the taxes, **utilities,** insurance, repairs, janitorial services, and license fees; any **debt service** and the landlord's income taxes are the responsibility of the landlord.

**TRUST** an arrangement whereby property is transferred to a trusted **third party** (trustee) by a **grantor** (trustor). The **trustee** holds the property for the benefit of another (**beneficiary).**
**Example:** An inter vivos *trust* was established by a living person who gave her warehouse to a trustee for the benefit of her children.
**Example:** A testamentary *trust* was established upon the death of a trustor, according to his **will.**

**TRUST ACCOUNT** a separate bank account segregated from a broker's own funds, in which the **broker** is required by state law to deposit all monies collected for clients. In some states called an **escrow** account.
**Example:** A broker who fails to deposit **earnest money** into a sep-

arate *trust account* may be held **liable** for penalties under the state's real estate **license** laws.

**TRUST DEED** a **conveyance** of real estate to a **third party** to be held for the benefit of another. Commonly used in some states in place of **mortgages** that conditionally convey **title** to the lender.
**Example:** Same as **deed of trust.**

**TRUSTEE** one who holds property in **trust** for another to secure performance of an obligation; the neutral party in a **trust deed** transaction.
**Example:** Johnson purchases property and finances it with a **deed of trust** from a lender. The **title company** is the *trustee,* holding legal title to the property pending Johnson's satisfaction of the debt. Should Johnson **default** on the loan, the trustee may sell the property to satisfy the debt.

**TRUTH IN LENDING** see **Regulation Z.**

**TUDOR** an English style imposing looking house with fortress-lines. Siding is chiefly stone and brick with some stucco and half timbers. Windows and doors have moulded cement or stone trim around them.
**Example:** Figure 177.

FIGURE 177

**TURNKEY PROJECT** a development in which a **developer** completes the entire project on behalf of a buyer; the developer turns over the keys to the buyer at completion.
**Example:** Many government-owned public housing projects are *turnkey projects*. A private developer undertakes all activities necessary to producing the project, including land purchases, **permits,** plans, and construction, and sells the project to the housing authority.

# U

**UNDERIMPROVEMENT** a structure or development of lower cost than the **highest and best use** of the site. Compare **overimprovement.**
**Example:** Construction of a $40,000 bungalow on a vacant lot in a **neighborhood** of $100,000 homes would represent an *underimprovement* of the **site.**

**UNDERLYING MORTGAGE** refers to the first mortgage when there is a **wraparound mortgage.**
**Example:** A wraparound for $100,000 includes a $60,000 *underlying mortgage* in its balance, so the additional funds provided by the wrap are $40,000.

**UNDERWRITER** one who insures another or takes certain **risks.** In **mortgage** lending, the one who approves or denies a loan based on the property and the applicant. In securities, it is the **broker** that sells the issue and, unless sold on a "best efforts" basis, agrees to purchase the shares not bought by the public.
**Example:** The *underwriter* analyzed the loan submission package carefully, because she didn't want her firm to accept excessive risk.

**UNDIVIDED INTEREST** an ownership right to use and possession of a property that is shared among co-owners, with no one co-owner having exclusive rights to any portion of the property. Compare **partition.**
**Example:** Ten investors form a **tenancy in common** and purchase a 100-**acre** tract of land. Each cotenant obtains an *undivided interest* in the property. All decisions as to the use and disposition of the land are made collectively by all cotenants. No one cotenant may unilaterally mortgage, develop, or sell a portion of the **tract.**

**UNEARNED INCREMENT** an increase in the **value** of real estate unrelated to effort on the part of the owner; often due to an increase in population.
**Example:** Murphy buys a **tract** of land in the county for $2,000 per

acre. As the city grows, the surrounding county begins to develop, with paved highways eventually extended to Murphy's land. Murphy sells the land for $5,000 per acre, realizing an *unearned increment* in value of $3,000 per acre.

**UNENCUMBERED PROPERTY** real estate with **free and clear title.**
**Example:** Nash owns an *unencumbered property*. Nash's **interest** is **fee simple,** there are no **mortgage, vendor, mechanic's** or **tax liens** on the property, no **restrictive covenants** exist, and no **easements** have been granted.

**UNIFORM COMMERCIAL CODE (UCC)** a group of laws to standardize the state laws that are applicable to commercial transactions. Few of the laws have relevance to **real estate.**
**Example:** The *Uniform Commercial Code* applies to **chattel mortgages, promises, commercial paper, securities, etc.**

**UNILATERAL CONTRACT** an obligation given by one party contingent on the performance of another party, but without obligating the second party to perform. Compare **bilateral contract.**
**Example:** A **broker** makes a *unilateral contract* with her associates. She offers a trip to Hawaii to any salesman who sells one million dollars of property during the month. None of the salesmen is obligated to meet the goal, but the broker is obligated to provide the trip should any salesman perform the feat.

**UNIMPROVED PROPERTY** land that has received no development, construction, or **site** preparation. See **raw land.**
**Example:** O'Brien is **subdividing** a **tract** of land and selling lots to investors. In all marketing materials, O'Brien must disclose the fact that the land is *unimproved property* that must receive extensive development before being suitable for urban uses.

**UNINCORPORATED ASSOCIATION** an organization formed by a group of people. If the organization has too many characteristics of a **corporation** it may be treated like one for income tax purposes.
**Example:** Many **condominium** associations, **limited partnerships,** and real estate investment **trusts** are examples of *unincorporated associations*.

**UNIT** in multi-family residential property, a suite of rooms making up a residence for 1 tenant. It is generally characterized by a private entrance and some method of individuality from other units in the building or complex.
**Example:** The apartment building has 45 dwelling *units*. Each *unit* has a private bath and kitchen. Some are 2 bedroom *units* and others have 3 bedrooms.

**UNIT-IN-PLACE METHOD** a technique used by **appraisers** to estimate the **reproduction cost** (new) of a structure. The method
involves estimating the cost of producing and installing individual
components, such as the foundation, exterior walls, and plumbing. Similar methods include the trade-breakdown method and
segregated-costs method. See **cost approach.**
**Example:** A simplified cost estimate using the *unit-in-place method* is shown in Table 42.

TABLE 42

| Item | Cost per unit ($/ft²) | Cost |
|------|:---:|---:|
| Foundation 1500 ft² | 2 | $3,000 |
| Walls 1600 ft² | 4 | 6,400 |
| Roof 1500 ft² | 3 | 4,500 |
| Flooring 1500 ft² | 2 | 3,000 |
| Plumbing | | 2,500 |
| Heating | | 1,500 |
| Electrical | | 2,000 |
| Total | | $22,900 |
| Fees, interest and overhead (10%) | | 2,290 |
| Reproduction cost (new) | | $25,190 |

**UNREALIZED GAIN** the excess of current **market value** over cost
for an asset that is unsold.
**Example:** Collins bought land for $10,000; she had an offer to sell
it for $15,000, but decided to keep the land. Her *unrealized gain* is
$5,000.

**UNRECORDED DEED** an **instrument** that transfers **title** from one
party (**grantor**) to another party (**grantee**) without providing public
**notice** of change in ownership. **Recording** is essential to protect
one's **interest** in **real estate.**
**Example:** Uncas purchases a lakefront lot from Upson. At **closing,**
Uncas receives a **deed** but fails to record it at the county courthouse. In the meantime, Upson fradulently sells the lot to Ustinov. Ustinov's attorney does a **title search** but, because of the
*unrecorded deed,* does not turn up the sale to Uncas. When Uncas
discovers what has occurred, he is forced to pursue legal proceedings against Upson for recovery. Ustinov, who purchased in **good
faith,** owns the land.

**UPSET PRICE** the minimum acceptable price for property being
auctioned. See also **asking price, bid.**
**Example:** If the bidding at **auction** fails to reach the *upset price,*
the property will not be sold.

**URBAN LAND INSTITUTE (ULI)** a nonprofit organization providing research and information on land use and development. Among the many publications of the ULI are the periodicals, *Urban Land* and *Environmental Comment,* and several development guides for specific types of land use.
Address:
Urban Land Institute
1200 18th St. N.W.
Washington, D.C. 20036

**URBAN PROPERTY real estate** located in an urban area, generally characterized by relatively high-**density** development and extensive availability of city water and sewer services.
**Example:** Typical development of 3 types of property is shown in Table 43.

**TABLE 43**

| Urban | Suburban | Rural |
|---|---|---|
| High-rise office | Office parks | Farms |
| High-rise apartment | Industrial parks | Low-density housing |
| Department stores | Shopping centers | Recreational lands |
| Public buildings | Garden apartments | Summer camps |
| Moderate density single-family housing | Low-density housing | |

**URBAN RENEWAL** the process of redeveloping deteriorated sections of the city, often through **demolition** and new construction. Although urban renewal may be privately funded, it is most often associated with government renewal programs.
**Example:** Most large cities have experienced some *urban renewal* in the last 20 years. The typical program attempts to demolish concentrations of dilapidated housing and attract **developers** of middle-income or mixed housing. Often, however, urban renewal areas become **sites** for new public buildings, such as civic auditoriums, sports arenas, and universities.

**USEFUL LIFE** the period of time over which a building is expected to provide a competitive return. *Useful life* provides the basis for allowable **depreciation** deductions on properties acquired prior to 1981. For tax purposes, this was replaced in 1981 by the **accelerated cost recovery system.**

**Example:** A property acquired in 1980 has a depreciable basis of $100,000 and a *useful life* of 25 years. Using **straight-line depreciation,** the owner may deduct $4,000 per year for tax reporting.

**USUFRUCTUARY RIGHTS** interests that provide for the use of property that belongs to another. Compare **emblement.**

**Example:** The owner of land that bounds or contains a natural water channel has a *usufructory right* to use of the water. The water itself is considered to be held by the public with all **adjacent** property owners holding rights to its use. **Restrictions** on that use vary under state law.

**USURY** charging a rate of interest greater than that permitted by state law. In most states, usury limits vary according to the type of lender and type of loan. Federal laws have passed to preempt certain usury limits under certain conditions.

**Example:** The **interest rate** that must comply with *usury* limitation is defined differently in the various states. The stated maximum rate may apply to the **face interest rate, effective rate** to the borrower, or the actual **yield** to the lender. If a loan is found to be usurious, severe penalties may be imposed, including loss of the **principal,** interest, a multiple of the interest, and/or damages.

**UTILITIES** 1. services, such as water, sewer, gas, electricity, and telephones, that are generally required to operate a building.
2. the periodic charges for such services.

**Example:** The building will be ready for occupancy as soon as the *utilities* are connected. When available, the *utility* bill is expected to average $100 per month. All *utilities* are paid for by the **landlord.**

**UTILITY EASEMENT** use of another's property for the purpose of laying gas, electric, water, and sewer lines.

**Example:** A property owner grants a *utility easement* to the electric power company to extend power lines to the owner's home.

# V

**VACANCY RATE** the percentage of all units or space that is unoccupied or not rented. On a **pro-forma** income **statement** a projected vacancy rate is used to estimate the vacancy allowance, which is deducted from potential **gross income** to derive effective gross income.

**Example:** The *vacancy rate* for apartment units in Boom City is currently 4.5%. For the Hightower Building, the *vacancy rate* is 9.5% (of 100,000 square feet of **net leasable area,** 9,500 square feet are not rented). If this 9.5% *vacancy rate* is expected to be the average through next year, a vacancy allowance of $95,000 (at $10 per square foot) should be deducted from potential rent when projecting income.

**VACANT LAND** land not currently being used. May have **utilities** and **off-site improvements.** Contrast with **raw land.**
**Example:** *Vacant land* was cleared and graded for future use as a **shopping center.**

**VACATE** to move out.
**Example:** A tenant *vacates* an apartment by terminating occupancy and removing all possessions. The tenant is responsible for **rent** to the end of the **lease** term.

**VACATION HOME** a dwelling used by the owner occasionally for recreational or resort purposes. It may be rented to others for a portion of the year. Income tax deductions pertaining to *vacation homes* depend on the frequency of use by the owner. Generally, a business loss cannot be claimed on a vacation home. See **second home.**
**Example:** The Travers have a *vacation home* in the mountains that they use on weekends during the summer. At other times it is rented to strangers on a weekly basis. If business deductions including depreciation exceed income, the loss cannot be deducted.

**VALID** having legally binding force; legally sufficient and authorized by law.
**Examples:** A *valid* **deed, will, lease, mortgage,** or other **contract.**

**VA LOAN** home loan **guaranteed** by the U.S. **Veterans Administration (VA)** under the Servicemen's Readjustment Act of 1944 and later. The VA **guarantees** restitution to the lender in the event of **default.** The guaranty is 60% of the loan, but not more than $27,500. Home must be a principal residence.
**Example:** Abel, a veteran of the U.S. Army, wishes to purchase a home. Abel may apply for a *VA loan* with the Veterans Administration and, if qualified, may obtain a **mortgage** loan from a lending institution with no **down payment.**

**VALUABLE CONSIDERATION** a type of promised payment upon which a promisee can enforce a claim against an unwilling promisor. Includes money, extension of time, and other equivalents for the grant. Distinguished from good **consideration,** which may be love and affection toward a relative, generosity, and the like.
**Example:** A man promised to give certain land to a suitor of his daughter, provided they marry. This was not considered *valuable consideration,* so the suitor could not enforce it and he did not marry the daughter.

**VALUATION** 1. estimated worth or price.

**Example:** The *valuation* of the land is $100,000.
2. the act of estimating the worth of a thing. See **appraisal.**
**Example:** The *valuation* was prepared in accordance with instructions provided by the tax **assessor.**

**VALUE** the worth of all the rights arising from ownership; the quantity of one thing that will be given in exchange for another.
**Example:** A property may have a certain *value* to its owner (value in use) equal to the amount of other property (typically cash) that the owner would be willing to accept in exchange for the property without loss in wealth or well-being. The same property may have a different **market value** (value in exchange) equal to the amount of other property exchanged for the property when many typically motivated buyers and sellers are allowed to interact.

**VARIABLE INTEREST RATE** an amount of compensation to a lender that is allowed to vary over the **maturity** of a loan. The amount of variation is generally governed by an appropriate index. See **variable rate mortgage, renegotiated rate mortgage.**
**Example:** A 20-year loan is made with a *variable interest rate*. The initial rate is 14% but may be changed each year in relation to changes in a published index of average loan rates. If, at the end of the first year, the index has risen one percentage **point,** the rate on the loan may be raised to 15%. Similarly, a fall in the index at one point would allow a decrease in the loan rate to 13%.

**VARIABLE MATURITY MORTGAGE** a long-term **mortgage** loan, under which the **interest rate** may be adjusted periodically. Payment levels remain the same but the loan **maturity** is lengthened or shortened to achieve the adjustment.
**Example:** Abel obtains a *variable maturity mortgage* originated at 12% with a **term** of 25 years. At the end of one year, the interest rate is increased to 12¼%. Abel's monthly payment of $527 remains the same after the adjustment; however, the remaining term is no longer 24 years, but is increased to 27 years.

**VARIABLE PAYMENT PLAN** any **mortgage** repayment schedule that provides for periodic change in the amount of monthly payments. Changes may occur as a result of: the expiration of an interest-only period (**flexible payment mortgage**), a planned step-up in payments (**graduated payment mortgage**), or a change in the **interest rate** due to fluctuation in an index (**variable rate mortgage**).
**Example:** A loan is made with a *variable payment plan*. The interest rate on the loan may be adjusted once a year according to a published index. As the interest rate is changed, the monthly payment is adjusted to provide for full **amortization** of the outstanding **principal** over the remaining life of the loan.

**VARIABLE RATE MORTGAGE (VRM)** a long-term **mortgage** loan applied to residences, under which the **interest rate** may be adjusted on a 6-month basis over the **term** of the loan. Rate increases are restricted to no more than ½ **point** per year and 2½ points over the term.
**Example:** Abel obtains a *variable rate mortgage* originated at a 12% interest rate. In 6 months, the index upon which the rate is based increases by one percentage point. Abel's rate is adjusted to 12½% and cannot be further increased during the year because of the ½% annual cap.

**VARIANCE** permission granted by a **zoning** authority to a property owner to allow for a specified violation of the zoning requirements. Variances are generally granted when compliance is impossible without rendering the property virtually unusable.
**Example:** Sherman owns a lot that is zoned for low-**density** housing. Because of the peculiar shape and **topography** of the lot, Sherman cannot build a home with the required minimum floor area without violating the **setback** requirements for the area. Sherman may be granted a *variance* to either construct a smaller dwelling or encroach on the setback line.

**VENDEE** a buyer. Generally used for **real estate;** one who purchases **personal property** is usually called the buyer.
**Example:** The *vendee* is the party that pays for the real estate bought.

**VENDEE'S LIEN** a **lien** against property under a **contract of sale,** to secure the **deposit** paid by a purchaser.
**Example:** Moore, the vendee (buyer), gave a substantial deposit. Since Moore did not trust the seller, she secured a *vendee's lien* against the property. The lien provides the vendee with a claim against the property should the seller attempt to sell to another party prior to closing.

**VENDOR** a seller, usually of **real estate.** The term *seller* is commonly used for **personal property.**
**Example:** The *vendor* receives cash, **notes,** and **mortgage relief** from the **vendor.**

**VENDOR'S LIEN** see **purchase money mortgage.**

**VENEER** wood or brick exterior that covers a less attractive and less expensive surface.
**Example:** Beneath the sturdy-looking oak *veneer* was low-grade hollow board (Figure 178).

**VENTURE CAPITAL** money raised for high-risk investments.
**Example:** Money raised for oil exploration, theatrical produc-

tions, and the like is considered *venture capital.*

**VERIFICATION** sworn statements before a duly qualified officer that the contents of an **instrument** are correct.
**Example:** A tenant takes a landlord to court to recover a **security** deposit. The tenant files a claim describing the **conditions** under which the **deposit** is to be refunded and the manner in which the tenant complied with the conditions. The tenant then supplies *verification* of this description by a sworn statement.

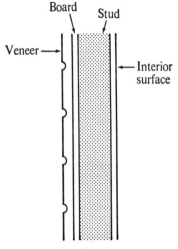

FIGURE 178

**VEST** to create an entitlement to a privilege or right.
**Example:** By crossing Baker's property regularly for 20 years, Abel's right to an easement became *vested.* Baker can no longer prevent Abel from crossing.
**Example:** If she stays employed by the same **brokerage** firm for 10 years, Collins' right to a pension will *vest.*

**VETERANS ADMINISTRATION (VA)** an agency of the federal government that provides services for eligible veterans. Generally, a veteran who has served (beyond basic training) more than 120 days active duty in the armed forces is eligible for a **home loan** with no **down payment.**
**Address:**
Veterans Administration
810 Vermont Avenue
Washington, D.C. 20420

**VIOLATION** an act or a condition contrary to law or to permissible use of **real property.**
**Example:** According to most **zoning ordinances,** operating a business from one's home is a *violation* of the restriction for a residential zone. In many cities, owning an occupied **apartment building** with nonfunctioning plumbing is a *violation* of the **housing code.**

**VOID** having no legal force or effect; unenforceable. See **null and void.**
**Example:** In a **listing** contract with a **broker,** Smith stipulates that the property be sold only to a person of a certain race. Since the stipulation is contrary to antidiscrimination laws, it is *void* and thereby unenforceable.

**VOIDABLE** capable of being voided, but not **void** unless action is taken to void it. A **contract** to **real estate** entered into by a **minor** is voidable only by the minor.
**Example:** A **landlord** leases an apartment to a minor. The minor may honor the **lease** and rent the apartment. However, should the minor decide not to rent the apartment, he may void the lease without **liability** for performance. The lease is a *voidable* contract.

**VOLUNTARY LIEN** a **debt** that the property owner agrees to have recorded. Typically a **mortgage.** Contrast **involuntary lien.**
**Example:** The **mortgage** was a *voluntary lien,* since the real estate owner agreed to pledge the property as **security.**

---

# W

---

**WAIVER** the voluntary renunciation, **abandonment,** or surrender of some claim, right, or privilege.
**Example:** A **violation** of a contract causes the need for a *waiver* from the other party who does not feel injured.

**WAREHOUSING (LOAN)** the packaging of a number of **mortgage** loans for sale in the **secondary mortgage market** by a financial institution or **mortgage banker** who has originated the loans.
**Example:** Willard, a mortgage banker, is regularly engaged in loan *warehousing.* He would originate a number of FHA-insured mortgages and sell the package to **FNMA** at **auction.** After origination but before the sale to FNMA, the loans are considered to be in Willard's *warehouse.*

**WARRANTY** a promise contained in a **contract.**

**Example:** The **vendee** received a one-year *warranty* from the builder as to the structural soundness of the property.

**WARRANTY DEED** one that contains a **covenant** that the **grantor** will protect the **grantee** against any and all claims. Usually contains covenants assuring good **title**, freedom from **encumbrances**, and **quiet enjoyment.** See also **general warranty deed** and **special warranty deed.**
**Example:** The grantor was willing to give a *warranty deed* because she was confident that she had good title to the property.

**WARRANTY OF HABITABILITY** an implied assurance given by a **landlord** that an apartment offered for rent is free from safety and health hazards.
**Example:** Todd signed a one-year **lease** to rent an apartment from Landon. Todd later discovered that the apartment's heating system was not functioning. Todd sought to break the lease, claiming the apartment was deficient under Landon's implied *warranty of habitability*.

**WASTE** unauthorized use or neglect of property by a party with the right to **possession** when another party owns an **interest** in the property. The party may be a **tenant, a mortgagor,** or a **life tenant.**
**Example:** A tenant neglecting to heat an apartment in the winter with the result of damage to the plumbing.
**Example:** A mortgagor failing to pay property taxes, thereby risking a tax **foreclosure.**
**Example:** A life tenant converting a residential property into a production center for some specialized product.

**WASTING ASSET** something of value that deteriorates over time.
**Example: Improvements** to land will not last forever, so they are *wasting assets;* in contrast **land** is not wasting because it will last forever.

**WATER RIGHTS** see **riparian rights, usufructory** rights.

**WATER TABLE** the upper level at which underground water is normally encountered in a particular area.
**Example:** Cross section showing the *water table* (Figure 179).

FIGURE 179

**WEAR AND TEAR** physical deterioration of property as the result of use, weathering, and age.
**Example:** A carpet is expected to last only 8 years because of *wear and tear*, or deterioration resulting from foot traffic and cleaning.

**WESTERN ROW HOUSE OR WESTERN TOWNHOUSE** a nineteenth century style house usually built to cover an entire street or block. It has common side walls with the house on either side.
**Example:** Figure 180.

2 or 3 stories   Common side walls
Bay windows   Pitched roof   Heavily decorated, painted

FIGURE 180

**WETLANDS** land, such as a marsh or swamp, normally saturated with water.
**Example:** A typical coastal *wetlands* (Figure 181).

**WILL** the disposition of one's property, to take effect after one's death. Same as **testament.**
**Example:** If one does not prepare a *will,* state law will govern the disposition of one's property after death.

**WILLIAMSBURG GEORGIAN OR EARLY GEORGIAN** an English style house built in Williamsburg and representative of the early Georgian houses built in America throughout the early 1700s. They had simple exterior lines and generally fewer of the

FIGURE 181

decorative devices characteristic of the later Georgian houses. Most were 2- or 3-story rectangular houses with two large chimneys rising high above the roof at each end.
**Example:** Figure 182.

FIGURE 182

**WINDOW** an opening in the wall of a building to let in light and air. Most are made of transparent material and have the ability to **be** opened and closed.
**Example:** Figure 183.

Fixed

Sliding

Double or single-hung

Casement

Awning

Hopper

Center pivot

Jalousie

FIGURE 183

**WITHOUT RECOURSE** words used in endorsing a **note** or bill to denote that the holder is not to look to the debtor personally in the event of nonpayment: the creditor has **recourse** only to the property. A form of exculpation. Same as **nonrecourse**. See **endorsement, exculpatory clause**.
**Example:** Abel insisted that the **mortgage** to the seller be *without recourse*. In the event that the value of the property declines, Abel may lose the property but he loses nothing else.

**WOMEN'S COUNCIL OF REALTORS® (WCR)** an organization, affiliated with the **National Association of Realtors®**, devoted to preparing women in **real estate** for their emerging roles in society, to encouraging members to a productive career in real estate, and to developing leadership potential. Publishes *The Real Estate Scene* (monthly) and the *WCR Communiqué* (quarterly).
**Address:**
Women's Council of Realtors®
430 N. Michigan Avenue
Chicago, Illinois 60611

**WOOD-DESTROYING INSECT** a term used in certain home **inspection** forms; as a condition for purchase, the property must be free of these insects.
**Examples:**
• subterranean termites
• dry wood termites
• powder post beetles

**WORKING CAPITAL** the difference between current **assets** and current **liabilities**.
**Example:** The *working capital* is $2,500 ($4,000 minus $1,500) according to the balance sheet in Table 44.

**WORKOUT** a mutual effort by a property owner and lender to avoid **foreclosure** or **bankruptcy** following a **default**; generally involves substantial reduction in the **debt service** burden during an economic depression. See **distressed property**.
**Example:** Because of an economic slowdown, the hotel suffered high **vacancy rates** and failed to generate enough income to meet **mortgage** payments. The owner approached the lender about a *workout*. It was agreed to reduce the outstanding loan **principal** and extend the **maturity** date to reduce the debt service. In turn the lender would participate in the income when the economy recovered and hotel income exceeded a specified amount. See **participation mortgage**.

**TABLE 44**

| Assets | | Liabilities & equity | |
|---|---|---|---|
| Current | | Current | |
| cash | $1,000 | | |
| acc'ts receivable | 1,000 | accounts payable | $ 500 |
| inventory | 2,000 | 3-month note | 1,000 |
| Current assets | $4,000 | Current liabilities | $1,500 |
| Fixed | | Long-term | |
| Land | 6,000 | Mortgage | $10,000 |
| Buildings | 10,000 | Equity | 8,500 |
| Total assets | $20,000 | Total liabilities and equity | $20,000 |

**WRITE-DOWN** to diminish in amount on the records, generally to reflect a **market value** loss.
**Example:** Bank auditors, upon discovering that a certain **mortgage** was worthless, insisted on a *write-down*. The bank recorded the value decline as a bad debt expense.

**WRAPAROUND MORTGAGE** a loan arrangement in which an existing loan is retained and an additional loan, larger than the existing loan, is made. The new lender accepts the obligation to make payments on the old loan. The existing loan generally carries an **interest rate** below the rate available on new loans. Consequently, the **yield** to the wraparound lender is higher than the rate charged on the new loan. Sellers are the most common wraparound lenders.
**Example:** Figure 184 and Table 45.

**WRIT OF EJECTMENT** see **ejectment.**

# Y

**YIELD** 1. a measurement of the rate of earnings from an investment. See **current yield, yield to maturity.**
**Example:** A loan is arranged to *yield* 15% a year to the lender.
2. the productivity of agricultural land.
**Example:** A farm produces a *yield* of 5,000 bushels of corn per acre.

**YIELD TO MATURITY** the **internal rate of return** on an investment.

**TABLE 45**

Wraparound mortgage

Seller gets $10,000 from buyer
and $20,000 from wraparound
lender.
Wraparound lender makes
payments on existing
mortgage.
Buyer makes payments on
wraparound mortgage.
Lender gets payment of
$632
$-336$

$296 per month on $20,000
outlay for a yield over 25
years of 17.5%.

Home sale price: $70,000

Wraparound loan:
$60,000    12%
25 years   $632 payments

Existing loan:
$40,000 principal
25 years left
9%
$336 payments

FIGURE 184

Considers all inflows and outflows of investment returns and their timing.

**Example:** An income-producing property requires a $10,000 investment. It promises a $1,000 annual return for 5 years, then resale proceeds of $15,000. The *yield to maturity* is 17.1%. See **internal rate of return** for formulas.

---

# Z

---

**ZERO LOT LINE** a form of **cluster housing** development in which individual dwelling units are placed on separately platted lots but are attached to one another. See **planned unit development, plat, row house, town-house.**

**Example:** A representative *zero lot line* development (Figure 185).

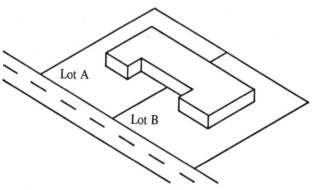

FIGURE 185

**ZONE** an area set off by local **ordinance** for specific use, subject to certain **restrictions** or conditions. See **zoning.**

**Example:** A zoning map designates various *zones* with associated land use restrictions (Figure 186).

C-1: commercial (service station, convenience store, etc.)

R-2: low-**density** residential (**single-family** housing)

R-4: high-density residential (apartments)

**ZONING** a legal mechanism for local governments to regulate the use of privately owned **real property** by specific application of **police power** to prevent conflicting land uses and promote orderly development. All privately owned land within the jurisdiction is

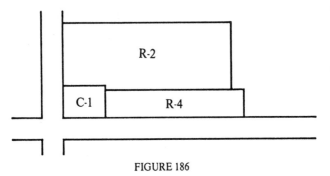

FIGURE 186

placed within designated zones that limit the type and intensity of development permitted. See **zone.**

**Example:** Before a **tract** of land may be developed, the intended use must be permitted under the existing *zoning* classification. If the proposed use is not permitted, the developer must apply for an amendment to the **zoning ordinance,** or for rezoning. Such amendments are granted by the local governing body, generally following a public hearing and recommendation from the **planning commission.**

**ZONING MAP** a map of the local jurisdiction that indicates current **zoning** designations.
**Example:** A typical *zoning* map (Figure 187).

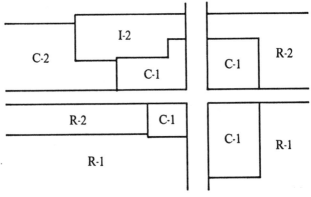

FIGURE 187

**ZONING ORDINANCE** act of city or county or other authorities
   specifying the type of use to which property may be put in specific
   areas. See **zone, zoning.**
   **Example:** A typical *zoning ordinance* defines:
   • the purpose for which the ordinance is adopted
   • the various zoning classifications and permitted uses within
     each
   • **restrictions,** such as height limitations
   • the procedure for handling nonconforming uses
   • the procedure for granting amendments, **variances,** and hearing
     appeals
   • penalties for **violation** of the ordinance

# APPENDIX

## House Cross Section

## Description of Number Parts in House

1—Collar beam
2—Ceiling joist
3—Chimney cap
4—Chimney pots
5—Chimney flashing
6—Rafters
7—Roof boards
8—Stud
9—Eave trough or gutter
10—Downspout or leader gooseneck
11—Frieze
12—Door jamb
13—Basement stair riser
14—Stair stringer
15—Girder post
16—Chair rail
17—Furring strips
18—Girder
19—Footing for foundation wall
20—Foundation drain tile
21—Diagonal subflooring
22—Foundation wall
23—Termite shield
24—Wall studs
25—Pilaster
26—Window casing
27—Wainscoting
28—Baseboard
29—Floor joists
30—Fire brick
31—Newel cap
32—Window sash
33—Mantel
34—Newel

FIGURE 188

From Boyce's *Real Estate Appraisal Terminology*, Copyright 1975, The American Institute of Real Estate Appraisers and The Society of Real Estate Appraisers. Reprinted with permission from Ballinger Publishing Company.

## ABBREVIATIONS

**A/C**  air conditioning

**ACRS**  accelerated cost recovery system

**ADR**  asset depreciation range

**AIREA**  American Institute of Real Estate Appraisers

**ALTA**  American Land Title Association

**AMI**  alternative mortgage instrument

**AML**  adjustable mortgage loan

**APA**  American Planning Association

**app**  appreciation (in appraisal terminology)

**APR**  annual percentage rate

**AREUEA**  American Real Estate and Urban Economics Association

**ARM**  adjustable rate mortgage

**ASA**  American Society of Appraisers

**ASREC**  American Society of Real Estate Counselors

**BOMA**  Building Owners and Managers Association

**CAI**  Community Associations Institute

**CBD**  central business district

**CCIM**  Certified Commercial-Investment Member (RNMI)

**CD**  certificate of deposit

**CPI**  consumer price index (see cost of living index)

**CPM**  Certified Property Manager (IREM)

**CRB**  Certified Real Estate Brokerage Manager (RNMI)

**CRE**  Counselor in Real Estate (ASREC)

**CRS**  Certified Residential Specialist (RNMI)

**DCR**  debt coverage ratio

**dep**  depreciation (in appraisal terminology)

**EIS**  environmental impact statement

**EPA**  Environmental Protection Agency

**FAR**  floor-area ratio

**FDIC**  Federal Deposit Insurance Corporation

**FHA**  Federal Housing Administration

**FHLB**  Federal Home Loan Bank

**FHLMC**  Federal Home Loan Mortgage Corporation (Freddie Mac)

**FmHA**  Farmers Home Administration

**FMRR**  financial management rate of return

**FMV**  fair market value

**FNMA**  Federal National Mortgage Association (Fannie Mae)

**FPM**  flexible payment mortgage

**FSLIC**  Federal Savings and Loan Insurance Corporation

**FTC**  Federal Trade Commission

**FY**  fiscal year

**GEM**  growing equity mortgage

**GIM**  gross income multiplier

**GNMA**  Government National Mortgage Association (Ginnie Mae)

**GPM**  graduated payment mortgage

**GRI**  Graduate, Realtors® Institute

**GRM**  gross rent multiplier

**HOW** homeowners warranty

**HUD** Department of Housing and Urban Development

**HVAC** heating, ventilation, and air conditioning

**IAAO** International Association of Assessing Officers

**IRA** individual retirement account

**IREM** Institute of Real Estate Management

**IRR** internal rate of return

**IRS** Internal Revenue Service

**IRWA** International Right-of-Way Association

**L/V** loan-to-value ratio

**MAI** Member, Appraisal Institute (AIREA)

**MBA** Mortgage Bankers Association of America

**MGIC** Mortgage Guaranty Insurance Corporation

**MLS** multiple listing service

**MMC** money market certificate of deposit

**NAA** National Apartment Association

**NACORE** National Association of Corporate Real Estate Executives

**NAHB** National Association of Home Builders

**NAR** National Association of Realtors®

**NAREB** National Association of Real Estate Brokers

**NARELLO** National Association of Real Estate Licensing Law Officials

**NOI** net operating income

**NOW** negotiable order of withdrawal (account)

**NPV** net present value

**OAR** overall rate of capitalization

**OILSR** Office of Interstate Land Sales Registration

**PAM** pledged account mortgage

**P & I** principal and interest (payment)

**PITI** principal, interest, taxes and insurance (payment)

**PMI** private mortgage insurance

**PUD** planned unit development

**RAM** reverse annuity mortgage

**REIT** real estate investment trust

**RESPA** Real Estate Settlement Procedures Act

**RESSI** Real Estate Securities and Syndication Institute

**RM** Residential Member (AIREA)

**RNMI** Realtors® National Marketing Institute

**RRM** renegotiated rate mortgage

**R/W** right-of-way

**SAM** shared appreciation mortgage

**SBA** Small Business Administration

**SEC** Securities and Exchange Commission

**SIR** Society of Industrial Realtors®

**S&L** savings and loan association

**SMSA** standard metropolitan statistical area

**SRA** Senior Residential Appraiser (SREA)

**SREA**  Senior Real Estate Analyst (SREA)

**SREA**  Society of Real Estate Appraisers

**SRPA**  Senior Real Property Appraiser (SREA)

**SYD**  sum-of-the-years-digits (method of depreciation)

**TDR**  transferable development rights

**TIL**  truth-in-lending law

**UCC**  Uniform Commercial Code

**ULI**  Urban Land Institute

**VA**  Veterans Administration

**VRM**  variable rate mortgage

**WCR**  Women's Council of Realtors

**YTM**  yield to maturity

**MORTGAGE TABLE**

Monthly Principal and Interest Payments
Per $10,000 Initial Principal

| Interest Rate | TERM OF MORTGAGE IN YEARS | | | | | |
|---|---|---|---|---|---|---|
| | 5 | 10 | 15 | 20 | 25 | 30 |
| 6.00 % | 193.33 | 111.02 | 84.39 | 71.64 | 64.43 | 59.96 |
| 6.25 % | 194.50 | 112.28 | 85.74 | 73.09 | 65.97 | 61.57 |
| 6.50 % | 195.66 | 113.55 | 87.11 | 74.56 | 67.52 | 63.21 |
| 6.75 % | 196.84 | 114.82 | 88.49 | 76.04 | 69.09 | 64.86 |
| 7.00 % | 198.01 | 116.11 | 89.88 | 77.53 | 70.68 | 66.53 |
| 7.25 % | 199.19 | 117.40 | 91.29 | 79.04 | 72.28 | 68.22 |
| 7.50 % | 200.38 | 118.70 | 92.70 | 80.56 | 73.90 | 69.92 |
| 7.75 % | 201.57 | 120.01 | 94.13 | 82.09 | 75.53 | 71.64 |
| 8.00 % | 202.76 | 121.33 | 95.57 | 83.64 | 77.18 | 73.38 |
| 8.25 % | 203.96 | 122.65 | 97.01 | 85.21 | 78.84 | 75.13 |
| 8.50 % | 205.17 | 123.99 | 98.47 | 86.78 | 80.52 | 76.89 |
| 8.75 % | 206.37 | 125.33 | 99.94 | 88.37 | 82.21 | 78.67 |
| 9.00 % | 207.58 | 126.68 | 101.43 | 89.97 | 83.92 | 80.46 |
| 9.25 % | 208.80 | 128.03 | 102.92 | 91.59 | 85.64 | 82.27 |
| 9.50 % | 210.02 | 129.40 | 104.42 | 93.21 | 87.37 | 84.09 |
| 9.75 % | 211.24 | 130.77 | 105.94 | 94.85 | 89.11 | 85.92 |
| 10.00 % | 212.47 | 132.15 | 107.46 | 96.50 | 90.87 | 87.76 |
| 10.25 % | 213.70 | 133.54 | 108.99 | 98.16 | 92.64 | 89.61 |
| 10.50 % | 214.94 | 134.94 | 110.54 | 99.84 | 94.42 | 91.47 |
| 10.75 % | 216.18 | 136.34 | 112.09 | 101.52 | 96.21 | 93.35 |
| 11.00 % | 217.42 | 137.75 | 113.66 | 103.22 | 98.01 | 95.23 |
| 11.25 % | 218.67 | 139.17 | 115.23 | 104.93 | 99.82 | 97.13 |
| 11.50 % | 219.93 | 140.60 | 116.82 | 106.64 | 101.65 | 99.03 |
| 11.75 % | 221.18 | 142.03 | 118.41 | 108.37 | 103.48 | 100.94 |
| 12.00 % | 222.44 | 143.47 | 120.02 | 110.11 | 105.32 | 102.86 |
| 12.25 % | 223.71 | 144.92 | 121.63 | 111.86 | 107.17 | 104.79 |
| 12.50 % | 224.98 | 146.38 | 123.25 | 113.61 | 109.04 | 106.73 |
| 12.75 % | 226.25 | 147.84 | 124.88 | 115.38 | 110.91 | 108.67 |

**MORTGAGE TABLE**

Monthly Principal and Interest Payments
Per $10,000 Initial Principal

| Interest Rate | TERM OF MORTGAGE IN YEARS | | | | | |
|---|---|---|---|---|---|---|
| | 5 | 10 | 15 | 20 | 25 | 30 |
| 13.00 % | 227.53 | 149.31 | 126.52 | 117.16 | 112.78 | 110.62 |
| 13.25 % | 228.81 | 150.79 | 128.17 | 118.94 | 114.67 | 112.58 |
| 13.50 % | 230.10 | 152.27 | 129.83 | 120.74 | 116.56 | 114.54 |
| 13.75 % | 231.39 | 153.77 | 131.50 | 122.54 | 118.47 | 116.51 |
| 14.00 % | 232.68 | 155.27 | 133.17 | 124.35 | 120.38 | 118.49 |
| 14.25 % | 233.98 | 156.77 | 134.86 | 126.17 | 122.29 | 120.47 |
| 14.50 % | 235.28 | 158.29 | 136.55 | 128.00 | 124.22 | 122.46 |
| 14.75 % | 236.59 | 159.81 | 138.25 | 129.84 | 126.15 | 124.45 |
| 15.00 % | 237.90 | 161.33 | 139.96 | 131.68 | 128.08 | 126.44 |
| 15.25 % | 239.21 | 162.87 | 141.68 | 133.53 | 130.03 | 128.45 |
| 15.50 % | 240.53 | 164.41 | 143.40 | 135.39 | 131.97 | 130.45 |
| 15.75 % | 241.86 | 165.96 | 145.13 | 137.25 | 133.93 | 132.46 |
| 16.00 % | 243.18 | 167.51 | 146.87 | 139.13 | 135.89 | 134.48 |
| 16.25 % | 244.51 | 169.07 | 148.62 | 141.00 | 137.85 | 136.49 |
| 16.50 % | 245.85 | 170.64 | 150.37 | 142.89 | 139.82 | 138.51 |
| 16.75 % | 247.18 | 172.22 | 152.13 | 144.78 | 141.80 | 140.54 |
| 17.00 % | 248.52 | 173.80 | 153.90 | 146.68 | 143.78 | 142.57 |
| 17.25 % | 249.87 | 175.39 | 155.68 | 148.58 | 145.76 | 144.60 |
| 17.50 % | 251.22 | 176.98 | 157.46 | 150.49 | 147.75 | 146.63 |
| 17.75 % | 252.58 | 178.58 | 159.25 | 152.41 | 149.75 | 148.67 |
| 18.00 % | 253.93 | 180.19 | 161.04 | 154.33 | 151.74 | 150.71 |
| 18.25 % | 255.30 | 181.80 | 162.84 | 156.26 | 153.74 | 152.75 |
| 18.50 % | 256.66 | 183.42 | 164.65 | 158.19 | 155.75 | 154.79 |
| 18.75 % | 258.03 | 185.04 | 166.47 | 160.13 | 157.76 | 156.84 |
| 19.00 % | 259.41 | 186.67 | 168.29 | 162.07 | 159.77 | 158.89 |
| 19.25 % | 260.78 | 188.31 | 170.11 | 164.02 | 161.78 | 160.94 |
| 19.50 % | 262.16 | 189.95 | 171.95 | 165.97 | 163.80 | 162.99 |
| 19.75 % | 263.55 | 191.60 | 173.79 | 167.92 | 165.82 | 165.05 |
| 20.00 % | 264.94 | 193.26 | 175.63 | 169.88 | 167.85 | 167.10 |

## MEASUREMENT TABLES

### ENGLISH SYSTEM

#### Linear Measure

| | |
|---|---|
| 12 inches (in or ") | = 1 foot (ft or ') |
| 3 feet | = 1 yard (yd) |
| 5½ yards | = 1 rod (rd), pole, or perch (16½ feet) |
| 40 rods | = 1 furlong (fur) |
| | = 220 yards |
| | = 660 feet |
| 6076.11549 feet | = 1 international nautical mile |

#### Gunter's or Surveyor's Chain Measure

| | |
|---|---|
| 7.92 inches (in) | = 1 link |
| 100 links | = 1 chain (ch) |
| | = 4 rods |
| | = 66 feet |
| 80 chains | = 1 statute mile (mi) |
| | = 320 rods |
| | = 5,280 feet |

#### Area Measure

Squares and cubes of units are sometimes abbreviated by using "superior" figures. For example, ft$^2$ means square foot, and ft$^3$ means cubic foot.

| | |
|---|---|
| 144 square inches | = 1 square foot (ft$^2$) |
| 9 square feet | = 1 square yard (yd$^2$) |
| | = 1,296 square inches |
| 30¼ square yards | = 1 square rod (rd$^2$) |
| | = 272¼ square feet |
| 160 square rods | = 1 acre |
| | = 4,840 square yards |
| | = 43,560 square feet |
| 640 acres | = 1 square mile (mi$^2$) |
| 1 mile square | = 1 section (of land) |
| 6 miles square | = 1 township |
| | = 36 sections |
| | = 36 square miles |

## METRIC SYSTEM

### Linear Measure

| | |
|---|---|
| 10 millimeters (mm) | = 1 centimeter (cm) |
| 10 centimeters | = 1 decimeter (dm) |
| | = 100 millimeters |
| 10 decimeters | = 1 meter (m) |
| | = 1,000 millimeters |
| 10 meters | = 1 dekameter (dam) |
| 10 dekameters | = 1 hectometer (hm) |
| | = 100 meters |
| 10 hectometers | = 1 kilometer (km) |
| | = 1,000 meters |

### Area Measure

| | |
|---|---|
| 100 square millimeters (mm$^2$) | = 1 square centimeter (cm$^2$) |
| 10,000 square centimeters | = 1 square meter (m$^2$) |
| | = 1,000,000 square millimeters |
| 100 square meters | = 1 are (a) |
| 100 ares | = 1 hectare (ha) |
| | = 10,000 square meters |
| 100 hectares | = 1 square kilometer (km$^2$) |
| | = 1,000,000 square meters |

## EQUIVALENTS BETWEEN ENGLISH AND METRIC SYSTEMS

### Lengths

| | |
|---|---|
| angstrom | = 0.1 nanometer (exactly) |
| | = 0.000 1 micron (exactly) |
| | = 0.000 000 1 millimeter (exactly) |
| | = 0.000 000 004 inch |
| 1 cable's length | = 120 fathoms |
| | = 720 feet |
| | = 219.456 meters (exactly) |
| 1 centimeter (cm) | = 0.3937 inch |
| 1 chain (ch), (Gunter's or surveyor's) | = 66 feet |
| | = 20.1168 meters (exactly) |
| 1 chain (engineer's) | = 100 feet |
| | = 30.48 meters (exactly) |
| 1 decimeter (dm) | = 3.937 inches |
| 1 dekameter (dam) | = 32.808 feet |
| 1 fathom | = 6 feet |
| | = 1.8288 meters (exactly) |

| | |
|---|---|
| 1 foot (ft) | = 0.3048 meters (exactly) |
| 1 inch (in) | = 2.54 centimeters (exactly) |
| 1 kilometer (km) | = 0.621 mile |
| | = 3,280.8 feet |
| 1 league (land) | = 3 statute miles |
| | = 4.828 kilometers |
| 1 link (Gunter's or surveyor's) | = 7.92 inches |
| | = 0.201 meter |
| 1 link (engineer's) | = 1 foot |
| | = 0.305 meter |
| 1 meter (m) | = 39.37 inches |
| | = 1.094 yards |
| 1 mile (mi) (statute or land) | = 5,280 feet |
| | = 1.609 kilometers |
| 1 international nautical mile (INM) | = 1,852 kilometers (exactly) |
| | = 1.150779 statute miles |
| | = 6,076.11549 feet |
| 1 rod (rd), pole, or perch | = 16½ feet |
| | = 5½ yards |
| | = 5.029 meters |
| 1 yard (yd) | = 0.9144 meter (exactly) |

## Areas or Surfaces

| | |
|---|---|
| 1 acre | = 43,560 square feet |
| | = 4,840 square yards |
| | = 0.405 hectare |
| 1 are (a) (100 square meters) | = 119.599 square yards |
| | = 0.025 acre |
| 1 hectare (ha) (10,000 square meters) | = 2.471 acres |
| [1 square (building)] | = 100 square feet |
| 1 square centimeter (cm$^2$) | = 0.155 square inch |
| 1 square decimeter (dm$^2$) | = 15.500 square inches |
| 1 square foot (ft$^2$) | = 929.030 square centimeters |
| 1 square inch (in$^2$) | = 6.452 square centimeters |
| 1 square kilometer (km$^2$) | = 247.105 acres |
| | = 0.386 square mile |
| | = 1,196 square yards |
| 1 square meter (m$^2$) | = 10.764 square feet |
| 1 square mile (mi$^2$) | = 640 acres 258.999 hectares |
| 1 square millimeter (mm$^2$) | = 0.002 square inch |
| 1 square rod (rd$^2$), sq. pole, or sq. perch | = 25.293 square meters |
| 1 square yard (yd$^2$) | = 0.836 square meter |

## MATHEMATICAL FORMULAS

To find the **CIRCUMFERENCE** of a:

**Circle**—Multiply the diameter by 3.14159265 (usually 3.1416).

To find the **AREA** of a:

**Circle**—Multiply the square of the diameter by .785398 (usually .7854).

**Rectangle**—Multiply the length of the base by the height.

**Sphere (surface)**—Multiply the square of the radius by 3.1416 and multiply by 4.

**Square**—Square the length of one side.

**Trapezoid**—Add the length of the 2 parallel sides, multiply by the height and divide by 2.

**Triangle**—Multiply the length of the base by the height and divide by 2.

# More selected BARRON'S titles:

DICTIONARY OF COMPUTER TERMS
*Douglas Downing and Michael Covington*
Nearly 1,000 computer terms are clearly explained, and sample
programs included. Paperback, $8.95, Canada $11.95/ISBN 4152-6

DICTIONARY OF FINANCE AND INVESTMENT TERMS
*John Downes and Jordan Goodman*
Defines and explains over 2500 Wall Street terms for professionals,
business students, and average investors.
Paperback $9.95, Canada $13.95/ISBN 2522-9, 495 pages

DICTIONARY OF INSURANCE TERMS, *by Harvey W. Rubin*
Approximately 2500 insurance terms are defined as they relate to
property, casualty, life, health, and other types of insurance.
Paperback, $8.95, Canada $11.95/ISBN 3772-3, 448 pages

DICTIONARY OF REAL ESTATE TERMS
*Jack P. Friedman, Jack C. Harris, and Bruce Lindeman*
Defines over 1200 terms, with examples and illustrations. A key
reference for everyone in real estate. Comprehensive and current.
Paperback $9.95, Canada $13.95/ISBN 3898-3, 224 pages

REAL ESTATE HANDBOOK
*Jack P. Friedman, Jack C. Harris, and Bruce Lindeman*
A dictionary/reference for everyone in real estate. Defines over 1500
legal, financial, and architectural terms.
Cloth $21.95, Canada $29.95/ISBN 5758-9, 700 pages

HOW TO PREPARE FOR REAL ESTATE LICENSING
EXAMINATIONS-SALESPERSON AND BROKER, 3rd EDITION
*Jack P. Friedman and Bruce Lindeman*
Reviews current exam topics and features updated model exams and
supplemental exams, all with explained answers.
Paperback, $9.95, Canada $13.95/ISBN 2996-8, 340 pages

BARRON'S FINANCE AND INVESTMENT HANDBOOK
*John Downes and Jordan Goodman*
This hard-working handbook of essential information defines more
than 2500 key terms, and explores 30 basic investment opportunities.
The investment information is thoroughly up to date. Cloth $21.95,
Canada $29.95/ISBN 5729-5, 864 pages

FINANCIAL TABLES FOR BETTER MONEY MANAGEMENT
*Stephen S. Solomon, Dr. Clifford Marshall, and Martin Pepper*
Pocket-sized handbooks of interest and investment rates tables used
easily by average investors and mortgage holders. Paperback
Savings and Loans, $6.95, Canada $9.95/ISBN 2745-0, 272 pages
Real Estate Loans, $6.95, Canada $9.95/ISBN 2744-2, 336 pages
Mortgage Payments, $5.50, Canada $7.95/ISBN 2728-0, 304 pages
Stocks and Bonds, $5.50, Canada $7.95/ISBN 2727-2, 256 pages
Comprehensive Annuities, $5.50, Canada $7.95/ISBN 2726-4, 160 pages
Canadian Mortgage Payments, Canada $8.95/ISBN 3939-4, 336 pages
Adjustable Rate Mortgages, *Jack P. Friedman and Jack C . Harris*
$5.95, Canada $8.50/ISBN 3764-2, 288 pages

All prices are in U.S. and Canadian dollars and subject to change without notice.
At your bookseller, or order direct adding 10% postage (minimum charge
$1.50, Canada $2.00), N.Y. residents add sales tax.

Barron's Educational Series, Inc.
250 Wireless Boulevard, Hauppauge, NY 11788
Call toll-free: 1-800-645-3476, in NY 1-800-257-5729
In Canada: Georgetown Book Warehouse
34 Armstrong Ave., Georgetown, Ontario L7G 4R9